Reproducible Research Repository

https://reproducibility.worldbank.org

A reproducibility package is available for this
book in the Reproducible Research Repository at
https://reproducibility.worldbank.org/index.php/catalog/187.

BUSINESS
READY

WORLD BANK GROUP

2024

CONTENTS

Tables

FOREWORD

Whenever the odds seem stacked against human aspirations—when economic growth looks set to remain feeble as far as the eye can see, when too many countries seem destined to grow old before they become rich, when climate change seems to have crossed the tipping point—it is worth remembering the distinctive virtue of our species. Predictions of global doom have proliferated throughout history. Yet the sky hasn't fallen, for one reason: human ingenuity.

It was ingenuity that disarmed the so-called "population bomb"—the idea that "hundreds of millions of people" would starve to death in the 1970s as rapid population growth exhausted finite supplies of food. In fact, agricultural innovations—such as the development of high-yield, pest-resistant crops—caused global food production to grow faster than the population in nearly every part of the world. It was human ingenuity that defeated deadly diseases including once-dreaded HIV/AIDS and, most recently, COVID-19. If climate change is somehow tamed by the middle of this century, the main propellant of that success will be human ingenuity.

But this progress is seldom the fruit of a big eureka moment. Human ingenuity works instead through the miracles that occur when governments, private enterprises, and individuals act in ways that benefit entire societies. That depends on conducive conditions, cultivated by a measured blend of rules and practices. The World Bank Group has been inclined to call this "the business climate" or "the business-enabling environment"—because sustained economic development usually reflects systemwide business success.

For too long, though, the focus has been too much on what governments can do for the good of business—and not enough on what businesses can do for the good of all. This report marks a crucial first step to correct that imbalance. The *Business Ready* (B-READY) project aims to build a comprehensive instrument panel that by 2026 will enable about 180 economies to dial in the precise settings needed for a vibrant private sector development—the combination of conditions that will reduce poverty, advance shared prosperity, and speed up the transition to a low-carbon economy. Its goal is to accelerate smart development by encouraging healthy competition among businesses—and countries. It is designed expressly to discourage "a race to the bottom" or simplistic solutions that were the unintended by-product of *Doing Business*, our previous effort to help countries establish the right conditions for private sector development.

Business Ready's analytical framework recognizes that there is more to a healthy business environment than the "ease of doing business." It accounts for the possibility that reducing the "cost of doing business" can unintentionally mean raising the costs for society at large. Accordingly, *Business Ready* assesses not only the regulatory burden on enterprises—how long it takes to start a business, for example—but also the quality of regulations: Do labor laws, for example, protect workers from being arbitrarily fired? Do they inadvertently make women workers less competitive than men and discourage them from seeking work?

Beyond assessing the rules and regulations that govern business, *Business Ready* delves into the public services needed to transform intentions into reality. Do public utilities provide reliable water and electricity for businesses? Do governments make it easy for businesses to fulfill their tax obligations and comply with environmental and social safeguards? Do they set up systems to enable government agencies to share business-related information with one another? Do they provide public databases that support transparency and the free flow of information necessary for a healthy business climate?

The result is a data set of breathtaking detail that encompasses nearly 2,000 data points per economy. It is possible to zero in, for example, on the frequency of power outages suffered by firms, how long it takes to file and pay taxes, or the average cost to settle a commercial dispute in different economies. Comparable data of this quality simply are not available anywhere else. That makes *Business Ready* an essential public good. The trove of insights it offers will enable businesses to make better decisions about where and how they operate. It will spur governments to adopt better policies by learning from one another. And it will permit researchers everywhere to join the effort to get global private sector development right.

This first edition of *Business Ready* covers only 50 economies. That is a reflection of the care and deliberation we are putting into getting the analysis right. Next year, the project will include more than 100 economies, and in 2026 the coverage will expand to about 180 economies. With each iteration, the report's design and methods will be refined to reflect the lessons learned from the rollout. So why not wait for the methods to be perfected before publishing the data? Because the world does not enjoy the luxury of time—development delayed is development denied—and because it speeds the process of getting feedback from the intended beneficiaries of an assessment, a big part of getting the assessment right. In any case, in a dynamic global economy, accuracy will always be a moving target.

The data and methods used here are both more rigorous and more transparent than those of *Doing Business*. They consolidate the judgments of more than 2,500 experts in the business climate and the survey responses of more than 29,000 businesses. They are more exhaustive, in short, than anything that has been attempted so far by an international institution—and they are of immediate value to the 50 economies covered here. Moreover, every piece of data collected for this report is now publicly available on the B-READY website—so it can be checked and verified by anyone who so chooses.

Analysis of this year's data leads to two general observations. First, economies tend to perform better at enacting regulations to improve the national business climate than they do in providing the public services needed to secure actual progress. In short, there is a sizeable implementation gap. But the good news is that the gap shrinks when the quality of regulations improves. Second, richer economies tend to be more business-ready, but a country need not be wealthy to create a good business environment. Among the 50 economies assessed this year, several developing economies rank among the top 10 in several categories: Rwanda for public services and operational efficiency, Colombia for its regulatory framework and public services, and Georgia for its regulatory framework and operational efficiency.

This suggests progress is possible for most countries. Governments should step up efforts to become business-ready—but not for the fleeting satisfaction of national bragging rights, or the uncertain promise of a big surge in foreign investment. The rewards are far more encompassing: When correctly chosen and carefully sequenced, business reforms can accelerate economic growth, boost productivity, and help reduce carbon emissions at the same time. It creates the conditions for human ingenuity to flourish— exactly what the world needs at a time of slowing growth, rising debt, and climate change. *Business Ready* illuminates the path forward.

Indermit Singh Gill
Chief Economist and Senior Vice President
for Development Economics
World Bank Group

ACKNOWLEDGMENTS

Business Ready (B-READY) is a product of the World Bank Development Economics Vice-Presidency (DECVP), led by Indermit Gill, Senior Vice President and Chief Economist of the World Bank Group. B-READY is housed in the Global Indicators Group, Development Economics (DECIG), and is supervised by Norman Loayza, DECIG Director. The B-READY report was prepared by a team led by Valeria Perotti, Manager, *Business Ready*, in collaboration with other DECIG units: Enterprise Analysis, led by Jorge Rodriguez Meza, and *Subnational Business Ready*, managed by Madalina Papahagi, and since April 1, 2024, managed by Valentina Saltane.

The project was managed with support from Santiago Croci Downes, Kirsten Hommann, Charlotte Nan Jiang, Trimor Mici, Valentina Saltane, and Julien Vilquin.

The B-READY team is composed of Nourhan Mohamed Hashem Abdellatif, Nurana Ahmadova, Youmna Al Hourani, Ritula Anand, Vitor Argella da Silveira, Todor Arsovski, Leoni Ayoub, Elodie Mathilde Raymonde Bataille, Tersit Berhane Ghiday, Ravneek Kaur Bhullar, Taylor Boyce, Liliya F. Bulgakova, Jung Ryun Byun, Maria Magdalena Chiquier, Victoria Chiseliov, Kamal Clark-Chakaroun, Cyriane Marie Coste, Santiago Croci Downes, Marie-Lily Delion, Milagros Deza Delgado, Nadine DiMonte, Trang Le Thi Huyen Doan, Selda Dudu, Luisa Daniela Dyer Melhado, Varun Eknath, Viktoriya Ereshchenko, Miren Escos Lerga, Marcial Falconi, Subika Farazi, Israel Fierro, Rose Wairimu Gachina, Manuel Galilea Izquierdo, Dorina Peteva Georgieva, Ziad Ghandour, Diana Maria Guevara Duque, Kirsten Hommann, Charlotte Nan Jiang, Consuelo Jurado Tan, Tommy Kairuz Harb, Mikhail Kan, Rinat Kapev, Natallia Karkanitsa, Marina Kayumova, Seo Yeon Kim, Klaus Koch-Saldarriaga, Maimouna Konate, Sarah Kouhlani Nolla, Irina Koval, Iryna Lagodna, Nghia Piotr Le Trong, Selina Tabea Lehmann, Julia Liniado, Camilla Shuang Liu, Ricardo Martins Maia, Dagmara Maj-Swistak, Ramiro Maldonado, Leslie Malher, Valerie Erica Marechal, Raman Maroz, Melanie Silvia Martinz, Tamar Matiashvili, Nuno Mendes Dos Santos, Liying Meng, Trimor Mici, Nabintu Olivia Mutambo Mpatswe, Marie Ndiaye Lixi, Antoni Albert Nogués i Comas, Nadia Novik, Enrique Orellana Tamez, Debasmita Padhi, Madalina Papahagi, Monique Pelloux Patron, Valeria Perotti, Elena Popic, Oleksandra Popova, Juicy Zareen Qureishi-Huq, Mahban Noemie Razaghi, Thomas Philip Romano, Harshita Sakhamuri, Valentina Saltane, Pierre Yvon Yann Ahui Seka, Xiaoqiao Shen, Yundi Shi, Syuzanna Simonyan, Ben Omar Heli Solis Sosa, Ines Sosa, Jayashree Srinivasan, Lynn Talouzian, Kerenny Torres Negron, Judit Trasancos

Rodríguez, Attique Ur Rehman, Yulia Valerio, Julien Vilquin, Yue Wu, Tiffany Rongpeng Yang, Ray Yazbek, Inés Zabalbeitia Múgica, Caline Zakher, and Gustavo Alonso Zanabria Gainza.

The B-READY interns team is composed of Rami Rajih Alkhafaji, Lorena Beatriz Cuenca Cardozo, Raka De, Edouard De Castellan, Sebastiano Paul Dell'Acqua, Yixiu Dong, Elizabeth English Duncan, Lorena Akouvi Edah, Mohamed El Guindi, Runjia Gao, Alessa Garrido Sosa, Yuwen Guo, My Ha Vuong, Francisca Halpern Pereira Faden Da Silva, Muhammad Fahd Iqbal Khan, Vasudha Jalan, Taicheng Jin, Monika Dora Kollar, Revathi Krishnan, Zhongyang Li, Qian Liu, Shitong Liu, Jimena Madrigal Brenes, Martina Mancini, Carlo Milani, Alessio Cesaro Milo, Mattia Moretta, Andi Mujollari, Biru Nitis Anjanie, Diana Noelly Rivas Garcia, Santiago Satizabal Acosta, Emilia Stazi, Lucie Nathalie Marie Taieb, Sara Teixeira Bacelos Ascenso Gaspar, Unnati Tolani, Jonato Lucio Xavier Natu, Haipeng Yan, Runfei Yan, Jingxi Yang, Nguessan Sharon Lys Yapi, Hermine Marie Yikyinboula Durand, Minha Yoon, and Shirui Zhou.

The Enterprise Analysis team collected all the B-READY firm-level data via the expanded World Bank Enterprise Surveys and provided invaluable advice on questionnaire design and indicator development. This team is led by Jorge Rodríguez Meza (manager), and consists of Gemechu Ayana Aga, Nesma Ali, Mohammad Amin, David C. Francis, Caroline Gomes Nogueira, Norma Janeth Gomez Caceres, Arvind Jain, Filip Jolevski, Nona Karalashvili, Hibret Belete Maemir, Davide Salvatore Mare, Eugenia Aurora Rodríguez Cuniolo, William Soh, M. Nazim Tamkoç, Kohei Ueda, Domenico Viganola, Rose Wairimu Gachina, and Joshua Wimpey.

The B-READY 2024 outreach strategy is managed by Cyriane Marie Coste, Camilla Shuang Liu, and Joseph Rebello, and supported by Tommy Kairuz Harb, Mariana Lozzi Teixeira, Ramiro Maldonado Zuleta, Kristen Milhollin, Karolina Ordon, Mahban Razaghi, and Shane Romig, along with World Bank Group communications colleagues around the world. The Information and Technology External Clients Solutions (ITSES) team is led by Flora Rezaei and consists of Huda Bazyan, Botyo Dimitrov Botev, Shahroze Hussan Khan, Akash Pradhan, and Geoffrey Alan Shot. The B-READY website was developed in collaboration with Todor Arsovski, Cyriane Marie Coste, Nadia Novik, Camilla Shuang Liu, and Tiffany Rongpeng Yang. Dorsey Kaufmann designed the website data visualizations.

The Development Data Group, Development Economics (DECDG), supervised by Haishan Fu, provided helpful consultations and support on the setup and operation of the Survey Solutions software that facilitates the implementation of *Business Ready* surveys for data collection. In particular, the team is thankful to Vitalii Balabanov, Volodymyr Fedosieiev, Sergiy Radyakin, and Pavlo Stovpivskyi for their support.

The Information and Technology Solutions Data Management office (ITSDM) team, led by Arvind Srinivasan and consisting of Ying Chi, Varun V. Doiphode, Anna Maria Kojzar, Parisa Nazarijam, Yuliyan Nikolaev Bogdanov, Tsvetelina Nikolova Stefanova, and Kunal H. Patel, provided valuable support by developing and maintaining the technology platforms required for core operations, offering technical support essential to the project's success. The team also gained from insights of Leonard Orens Newmark and Marianne Deborah Rossert from the Ethics and Business Conduct Department (EBC).

The team would also like to acknowledge the valuable feedback received from the B-READY Advisory Group on Indicator Scoring: Gianfilippo Carboni, Aart Kraay, Nikolaus Nebe, and Sylvia Solf (Business Entry); Somik Lall (Business Location); Vivien Foster and Maria Vagliasindi (Utility Services); Raian Divanbeigi and Maho Hatayama (Labor); Ana Fiorella Carvajal and Sephooko Motelle (Financial Services); Alina Monica Antoci and William John Gain (International Trade); Chiara Bronchi, Ruud De Mooij, Jan Loeprick, Tuan Minh Le, and Claudia Vargas Pastor (Taxation); David S. Bernstein (Dispute Resolution); Tania Begazo Gomez, Alexandre Borges de Oliveira, Martha Martinez Licetti, and Graciela Miralles Murcielagoa (Market Competition); and Sergio Muro (Business Insolvency).

The team is grateful for the valuable comments provided by colleagues both within and outside the World Bank Group, and for the guidance provided by World Bank Group Executive Directors. The team would especially like to acknowledge the comments and guidance of Oya Pinar Ardic Alper, Francisco Avendano, Lucero Burga, Kuntay Celick, Joyce Antone Ibrahim, Roberto N. Fattal Jaef, Elaine MacEachern, Collen Masunda, Harish Natarajan, Quyen Thuc Nguyen, Tristan Reed, Martijn Gert Jan Regelink, Bob Rijkers, Luz Maria Salamina, Umar Serajuddin, Khondoker Tanveer Haider, and John Wilson. The team also benefited from extensive and valuable external consultation during the Concept Note stage.

The report was edited by Nancy Morrison and Sabra Ledent and proofread by Ann O'Malley and Gwenda Larsen. Dania Kibbi and Debra Naylor designed the report. Stephen Pazdan coordinated and oversaw the formal production of the report. Jewel McFadden managed the overall publication process.

B-READY 2024 would not be possible without the expertise and generous input of a network of more than 2,750 local partners, including legal experts, business consultants, accountants, freight forwarders, and other professionals routinely administering to or advising the team on the relevant legal and regulatory requirements in the 50 economies covered. The team is also very grateful to the 29,000 firms that responded to the Enterprise Surveys.

EXECUTIVE SUMMARY

Introduction

A vibrant private sector is central to efforts to end extreme poverty and boost shared prosperity on a livable planet.[1] When it functions well, the private sector sparks innovation and entrepreneurship. It can unlock economic opportunities for people who need them the most. It can drive more efficient and sustainable use of natural resources.[2,3]

Today, the private sector generates about 90 percent of jobs,[4] 75 percent of investment,[5] more than 70 percent of output,[6] and more than 80 percent of government revenues in developing economies.[7] But it has been stalled since the global financial crisis of 2008–09. Private investment in these economies has slowed substantially. Per capita investment growth between 2023 and 2024 is expected to average only 3.7 percent, barely half the rate of the previous two decades.[8]

The private sector must become more dynamic and resilient to meet formidable development challenges. In the coming decade alone, the world must create jobs for 44 million young people each year, 30 percent of them in Africa.[9] To end extreme poverty within a decade, most low-income economies will need to achieve a gross domestic product (GDP) per capita growth of about 9 percent each and every year.[10] To escape the "middle-income trap," developing economies will need a GDP per capita growth of more than 5 percent per year over extended periods.[11] To tackle climate change and achieve other key global development goals by 2030, they need to secure a hefty increase in investment—about US$2.4 trillion per year.[12]

These challenges are far beyond the capacity of governments to tackle alone. Any viable plan for overcoming them will depend on a particular type of private sector development—one that mobilizes private capital and maximizes the benefits for businesses, entrepreneurs, workers, and society as a whole. That requires answering some critical questions. What exactly are the elements of a business climate that can deliver such benefits? Which economies have done best at creating that climate, and how can others learn from them? Which policies must be introduced or ramped up? Which should be phased out?

A reproducibility package is available for this book in the Reproducible Research Repository at https://reproducibility.worldbank.org/index.php/catalog/187.

This report is designed to help economies answer those questions. It is the first of an annual series that will assess the business climate of a successively larger number of economies over the next three years, reaching worldwide coverage by 2026. Until then, its design and methodology will evolve in accordance with lessons learned from each rollout year.

What is *Business Ready*?

Business Ready (B-READY) (https://www.worldbank.org/en/businessready) is a new data collection and analysis project of the World Bank Group to assess the business and investment climate worldwide, accompanied by an annual corporate flagship report. It is a key instrument of the World Bank Group's new strategy to facilitate private investment, generate employment, and improve productivity to help economies accelerate development in inclusive and sustainable ways. It replaces and improves upon the World Bank Group's earlier *Doing Business* project (refer to box ES.1). It reflects a more balanced and transparent approach toward evaluating an economy's business and investment climate, building on recommendations from hundreds of experts from within and outside the World Bank Group, including from governments, the private sector, and civil society organizations. B-READY will provide a quantitative assessment of the business environment with an annual frequency and worldwide coverage. The project aims to balance de jure and de facto measures, ensuring that the data produced are both comparable across economies and representative within each economy.

BOX ES.1

Comparison of the key features of *Doing Business* and B-READY

On September 16, 2021, the senior management of the World Bank Group decided to discontinue the *Doing Business* report and data collection. It also announced the development of a new approach for assessing the business and investment climate: the *Business Ready* (B-READY) project. This new project draws on advice from experts in the

World Bank Group and recommendations from qualified academics and practitioners outside the institution, including the External Panel Review on *Doing Business* methodology (World Bank 2021), as well as feedback from an extensive consultation process with potential users in government, the private sector, and civil society.

(Continued)

BOX ES.1

Comparison of the key features of *Doing Business* and B-READY *(Continued)*

While the focus of the *Doing Business* project was on assessing the business environment for small and medium enterprises, the B-READY project targets private sector development as a whole. *Doing Business* centered on the regulatory burden for firms, with some attention to public services. In contrast, B-READY evaluates the regulatory burden as well as the quality of regulations and provision of related public services, along with the ease of compliance with the regulatory framework and the effective use of public services directly relevant to firms. All topics examined by B-READY are structured under three pillars: (I) Regulatory Framework, (II) Public Services, and (III) Operational Efficiency. Furthermore, the new project assesses not only the ability to conduct business for individual firms (firm flexibility), but also the inclusive and sustainable aspects of private sector development (social benefits). To gather data, B-READY uses 21 questionnaires, compared with 11 questionnaires used by *Doing Business*. In its first year, it collected data on almost 1,200 indicators (from about 2,000 data points) per economy. It also covers all major topics related to a firm's life cycle, whereas *Doing Business* sometimes omitted critical areas such as labor.

Doing Business collected data through expert consultations and extensive case studies with strict assumptions, covering either de jure or de facto regulations, but not both uniformly. In contrast, B-READY combines expert consultations and firm surveys to capture a balanced view of de jure and de facto aspects. This allows B-READY to achieve a better balance between data comparability across economies.

Doing Business assessed economies' performance based on rankings and scores, focusing on aggregate rankings to drive public interest and motivate reforms. B-READY uses quantifiable disaggregated indicators, aggregating points into scores by topic and pillar. This approach identifies specific areas for reform and encourages reforms without overhyping economywide rankings.

While *Doing Business* covered the main business city in 191 economies and the second-largest business city in 11 economies, B-READY aims for wide coverage within and across economies, with coverage for different topics based on whether regulations are national or local.

Like *Doing Business*, B-READY updates data each year for indicators based on expert consultations. For data derived from firm-level surveys, it updates data for different sets of economies each year, resulting in stable data for each economy over a three-year cycle.

B-READY assessments aim to improve the private sector, not only by advancing the interests of individual firms but also by elevating the interests of workers, consumers, potential new enterprises, and the natural environment. B-READY aims to achieve this objective by focusing on three main areas:

1. *Reform advocacy:* B-READY advocates for policy reform through the effective communication of international benchmarking, opening the door for knowledge sharing and policy dialogue for governments, the private sector, the World Bank Group, and other development institutions.

2. *Policy guidance:* B-READY guides specific policy change through comprehensive and relevant data and information, showing how and by how much each economy lags in international good practice.

3. *Analysis and research:* B-READY provides granular data for research and analysis, shedding light on the drivers and mechanisms of private sector development.

As a new project, B-READY is in a three-year rollout phase, spanning 2024 to 2026. During this period, the project will grow in geographic coverage and refine its process and methodology. This 2024 report is the first of three during the rollout. It covers 50 economies that span all income levels and geographic regions around the world. Due to the limited number of economies included in this first report, the regional and income trends are suggestive, not definitive. Likewise, the methodology remains open to refinement and may evolve through subsequent iterations. The second report, expected to be released in September 2025, will cover more than 100 economies. The third report, expected to be released in September 2026, will assess about 180 economies, bringing the rollout phase to conclusion and providing a full global benchmark for future business readiness assessments. There is no straightforward advantage or disadvantage of economies being in one round versus another. In fact, there are pros and cons of participating either earlier or later in the project. Earlier participation will bring data faster for potential attention and action, while later participation will bring a more refined methodology and a broader economy coverage for enhanced benchmarking.[13]

B-READY's analytical framework: Ten topics, three pillars, three cross-cutting themes

Ten topics. B-READY is organized according to topics essential for private sector development that correspond to various stages of the life cycle of a firm and its participation in the market while opening, operating (or expanding), and closing (or reorganizing) a business (refer to figure ES.1). The 10 topics are *Business Entry, Business Location, Utility Services, Labor, Financial Services, International Trade, Taxation, Dispute Resolution, Market Competition,* and *Business Insolvency.*

FIGURE ES.1 **B-READY topics correspond to various stages of the life cycle of a firm and examine three cross-cutting themes**

Source: B-READY project.

Note: Although Business Entry and Business Insolvency are the clear beginning and end stages of a firm's life cycle, the remaining eight topics can occur in varying sequences during a firm's operating and expanding stages. The topics are interconnected. This figure is not intended to represent a linear progression in a firm's life cycle or to suggest strictly that these ought to be the exact phases, but to give an overall assessment of the business environment of the typical stages of the life cycle of a firm.

Three pillars. For each topic, B-READY considers three pillars: *Pillar I, Regulatory Framework; Pillar II, Public Services;* and *Pillar III, Operational Efficiency.*

1. *Pillar I:* The Regulatory Framework consists of the rules and regulations that firms must follow as they open, operate (or expand), and close (or reorganize) a business. Indicators under this pillar distinguish between rules and regulations that promote clarity, fairness, and the sustainability of the business environment and those that unnecessarily inhibit entrepreneurial activity.

2. *Pillar II:* Public Services spans the facilities that governments provide to support compliance with regulations and the institutions and infrastructure that enable business activities. Indicators under this pillar are limited to the scope of the business environment in areas related to the life cycle of the firm. They emphasize such aspects as digitalization, interoperability of government services, and transparency.

3. *Pillar III:* Operational Efficiency captures the ease of compliance with the regulatory framework and the effective use of public services directly relevant to firms.

To differentiate the B-READY benchmarking exercise from other well-established international measures, B-READY concentrates on the regulatory framework and public service provision at the microeconomic level: that is, as enacted and implemented to directly affect the behavior and performance of active and potential enterprises (refer to figure ES.2).

FIGURE ES.2 B-READY pillars define the scope of the project

Pillar I

Regulatory Framework

Rules and regulations that firms must follow as they open, operate, and close a business

Pillar II

Public Services

Facilities to support regulatory compliance and institutions and infrastructure to enable business activities

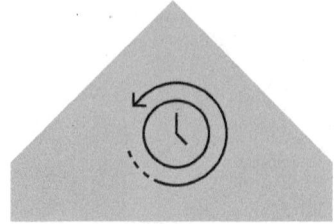

Pillar III

Operational Efficiency

Ease of regulatory compliance and effective use of public services directly relevant to firms

Source: B-READY project.

Within these pillars, common features inform the grouping into a particular *category*. Each category contains a number of *subcategories*.

Indicators: Each subcategory has a number of indicators. Across all topics and pillars, B-READY analyzes nearly 1,200 indicators. The B-READY project focuses on issues where established good practices exist and utilizes quantifiable measures that highlight actionable areas subject to change through policy reform. The data, derived from primary sources specifically collected for the B-READY project, encompass the most relevant aspects of each topic (refer to box ES.2).

BOX ES.2

Assessing business climate conditions: Insights from examples of B-READY indicators

The B-READY indicators measure the detailed conditions that determine the business environment. These conditions vary greatly among the 50 economies assessed this year. For each economy, the B-READY website (https://www.worldbank.org/en/businessready) presents data for all the indicators (nearly 1,200) and the granular data points on which they are built (about 2,000 data points). This box illustrates some of this granular information (refer to chapter 4 for more details about indicators collected for each B-READY topic).

Pillar I, Regulatory Framework. Consider, for example, how the performance of the 50 economies varies on the following indicators

(Continued)

BOX ES.2

Assessing business climate conditions: Insights from examples of B-READY indicators *(Continued)*

collected on the Regulatory Framework. Verification of the identify of beneficial owners is required by law in 68 percent of economies, strengthening business accountability and anti-money laundering efforts (Business Entry topic). Paid annual leave and paid sick leave are legally mandated in 72 percent and 88 percent of economies, respectively, allowing workers time for recovery without risking their income (Labor). In 90 percent of economies, the regulatory frameworks prohibit anticompetitive agreements between firms, fostering higher productivity and product quality (Market Competition). Laws and regulations enabling foreign transactions are a policy concern, as evidenced by the recognition of foreign-issued electronic contracts (77 percent of economies), foreign electronic signatures (75 percent of economies), and the absence of limits to cross-border electronic payments (71 percent of economies) (International Trade). Enabling speedy resolution of commercial disputes is also an area of regulatory concern, with only 8 percent of economies legally providing a time standard for all four procedures measured by B-READY and 66 percent of economies mandating the recognition and enforcement of foreign court judgments (Dispute Resolution).

Pillar II, Public Services. Consider a few examples of indicators collected on Public Services. While 92 percent of economies have taxpayer online tax portals, only 4 percent offer all three electronic self-service tools measured by B-READY—chatbots, e-forums, and e-learning—on their website (Taxation). Similarly, while 92 percent of economies have operational credit bureaus and registries, data

from institutions such as retailers, merchants, and utility companies are collected and distributed in only 20 percent of economies (Financial Services). Only 21 percent of economies implement all seven coordinated border management features measured by B-READY (International Trade). Innovation remains a challenge in some countries, with 26 percent of economies having either only innovation incubators or accelerators, or lacking both (Market Competition). Lastly, only 44 percent of economies have operational courts with specialized expertise in insolvency (Business Insolvency).

Pillar III, Operational Efficiency. Finally consider a selection of indicators on Operational Efficiency. The registration process for a domestic firm ranges between 3 and 80 days in the sampled economies, while foreign firms may wait up to 106 days (Business Entry). Obtaining a construction-related permit takes 30 days on average across economies, but this can extend up to 120 days in some. Securing an environmental permit generally requires even more time, averaging 218 days, and, in some cases, exceeding two years (Business Location). Firms face an average of four electrical outages per month, although the number can be as high as 22 in some economies (Utility Services). The time to obtain a loan varies significantly, ranging from 7 days in the best-performing economy to 45 days in the worst (Financial Services). Resolving a business dispute in court takes, on average across economies, just over 2 years, but the duration can vary widely, from as little as 105 days to as long as 5 years (Dispute Resolution).

Three cross-cutting themes. Across the 10 topics, the assessment includes data on three cross-cutting areas increasingly important in modern economies: digital adoption, environmental sustainability, and gender. B-READY looks at digital adoption, either by governments or businesses, anchored in specific areas of the business environment. For environmental sustainability, B-READY assesses relevant indicators that reflect environmental regulatory provisions affecting business operations. For gender, the report focuses on the collection and availability of anonymized data disaggregated by sex, as well as measuring the implementation and targeting of programs and gender-sensitive regulations affecting businesses in economies around the world.

Scoring

For each economy, B-READY produces two sets of scores: one consisting of 10 topic scores and another comprising three pillar scores. Topic and pillar scores can range from a minimum of 0 to a maximum of 100.

For topic scores, every score is generated by averaging the scores assigned to each of the three pillars (Regulatory Framework, Public Services, Operational Efficiency) for that topic. Within these pillars, common features inform the grouping into a particular *category*. Each category contains a number of *subcategories*. In turn, each subcategory contains a number of *indicators*.

Points are allocated to each indicator according to its contribution to firm flexibility (that is, ease of business from a firm's perspective) and/or social benefits (that is, the impact to the broader private sector). Indicator points are then compiled to determine the total points for the subcategory, category, and ultimately, the pillar. Categories and subcategories are weighted to reflect their significance and relevance to that pillar. Each pillar score in a topic is standardized to potentially range from 0 to 100.

For pillar scores, each score is generated by averaging the scores assigned to that pillar (Regulatory Framework, Public Services, or Operational Efficiency) across 10 topics.

Data collection and governance

B-READY combines primary data collected from thousands of specialists— each an expert in the private sector of a specific economy—with data collected directly from businesses operating in that economy. To accomplish this, B-READY uses expert questionnaires tailored to collect data for the Regulatory Framework and Public Services pillars from specialists in each topic.[14] The questionnaires are administered to three to five experts per questionnaire and economy. Additionally, the World Bank Enterprise Surveys directly collect data from businesses for indicators within the Operational Efficiency pillar.[15] The project also uses expert questionnaires to collect data on Operational Efficiency indicators not routinely faced by firms themselves, in topics such as Business Entry and Business Insolvency, because ad hoc surveys would be prohibitively expensive.

The complementary use of expert questionnaires and firm-level surveys is an important innovation that capitalizes on the advantages of both data collection modes and represents a significant increase in the data available to policy makers, development practitioners, and researchers. For each economy, expert questionnaire data will be updated every year, while Enterprise Surveys data will be updated every three years (refer to figure ES.3). The World Bank Enterprise Surveys program has been expanded from 15 to about 60 surveys per year to accommodate the data collection effort.

B-READY attempts to achieve a balance between data comparability across economies and data representativeness within each economy. Expert questionnaires address this balance by using broad parameters, instead of narrow case studies, to measure the business environment that most firms face, while retaining comparability across economies. Firm-level surveys address the balance by using representative samples of registered firms, allowing for the comparison of the average or typical experience of actual firms. B-READY, therefore, covers information relevant to firms of different sizes and locations, various economic sectors, and foreign and domestic ownership.

B-READY is governed by the highest data integrity standards, including sound data-gathering processes, robust data safeguards, and clear approval protocols (refer to box ES.3). The two B-READY foundational documents are publicly available on the project website: the *B-READY Manual and Guide*,[16] specifying the protocols and safeguards to ensure the integrity of the assessments, and the *B-READY Methodology Handbook*,[17] detailing the project's topics, indicators, and scoring approach. These documents will be updated and improved as the three-year rollout phase of the project progresses.[18]

Transparency and replicability are the cornerstones of B-READY governance. All the granular data used for scoring are made publicly available on the B-READY website (https://www.worldbank.org/en /businessready), and all results presented in B-READY reports are replicable using straightforward toolkits made available on the same website.

FIGURE ES.3 **B-READY relies on data obtained directly from experts and enterprises**

Expert questionnaires	World Bank Enterprise Surveys
• Data from experts, all in the private sector except for credit registries, who regularly deal with business regulations and related public services and institutions. • Provide de jure information (Pillar I) and de facto information (Pillars II–III). • Data collection through 21 questionnaires, filled in by three to five experts per questionnaire and economy. • Updated annually for each economy.	• Data from the owners or managers of a representative sample of registered firms. • Provide de facto information (Pillar III). • Data collection embedded in the World Bank Enterprise Surveys program (expanded from 15 to about 60 surveys per year). • Updated every three years for each economy.

Source: B-READY project.

BOX ES.3
Data validation and quality assurance

Data collected through both expert consultations and Enterprise Surveys are subject to rigorous validation and quality assurance processes. When discrepancies arise in questionnaire responses in data collected through expert consultations—such as divergence in private sector responses, divergence between private sector responses and government inputs, or misalignment in the unit of measurement for numerical variables—questionnaires are returned to relevant experts through the survey software, providing them an opportunity to review and change the response if needed.

The Enterprise Surveys also follow a robust quality control process, which includes several aspects to monitor the order for contacting firms, weekly progress reports, and data quality checks (refer to the *Enterprise Surveys Manual and Guide*).[a]

Following data validation and quality assurance processes, the individual data are aggregated to economy-level variables, applying standard aggregation methods of taking the median, mean, or mode, depending on the question type (refer to the *B-READY Methodology Handbook*).[b] This step is critical for transforming individual expert and firm insights into a coherent, economywide perspective.

a. https://www.worldbank.org/content/dam/enterprisesurveys/documents/methodology/Enterprise%20Surveys_Manual%20and%20Guide.pdf.
b. https://thedocs.worldbank.org/en/doc/357a611e3406288528cb1e05b3c7dfda-0540012023/original/B-READY-Methodology-Handbook.pdf.

B-READY 2024 data and summary results

B-READY granular data provide a wealth of information that can be used to guide specific policy reform. These data are presented in the main body of the report and, in more detail, on the B-READY website (https://www .worldbank.org/en/businessready) through accessible facilities and tools, including economy profiles.

Performance by pillar

The data for the 50 economies featured in the first report are summarized in table ES.1. Economies are divided into five equal groupings (quintiles), from highest to lowest performers, based on their scores within each pillar. This classification system allows policy makers to readily identify the areas for improvement in their economy: regulations, public services, and operational efficiency.

TABLE ES.1 B-READY 2024 performance, by pillar

Pillar I Regulatory Framework		Pillar II Public Services		Pillar III Operational Efficiency	
Hungary	78.23	Estonia	73.31	Singapore	87.33
Portugal	78.11	Singapore	70.40	Georgia	84.75
Georgia	77.67	Croatia	70.24	Rwanda	81.31
Slovak Republic	77.29	Portugal	69.53	Estonia	80.28
Colombia	76.50	Hungary	69.50	Hong Kong SAR, China	78.52
Bulgaria	76.33	New Zealand	68.91	New Zealand	76.39
Romania	76.19	Slovak Republic	68.17	North Macedonia	75.81
Greece	75.60	Rwanda	67.37	Bulgaria	74.82
Mexico	75.07	Colombia	66.28	Kyrgyz Republic	74.71
Croatia	73.48	Greece	64.51	Viet Nam	72.78
Estonia	72.84	Bulgaria	64.03	Nepal	72.21
Montenegro	72.48	Costa Rica	63.58	Slovak Republic	71.14
Hong Kong SAR, China	72.40	Indonesia	63.44	Montenegro	71.03
Singapore	72.37	Georgia	63.33	Hungary	70.68
Costa Rica	71.41	Romania	63.19	Portugal	70.53
Philippines	70.68	Hong Kong SAR, China	62.64	Bangladesh	70.49
Rwanda	70.35	Peru	59.76	Bosnia and Herzegovina	70.05
North Macedonia	69.95	Morocco	58.66	Mauritius	69.79
Peru	69.51	Mexico	57.25	Samoa	68.32
Togo	69.03	Mauritius	56.28	Croatia	68.31

Quintile: ■ Top ■ Second ▦ Third ▢ Fourth   Bottom

(Continued)

TABLE ES.1 B-READY 2024 performance, by pillar *(Continued)*

Pillar I Regulatory Framework		Pillar II Public Services		Pillar III Operational Efficiency	
Morocco	68.92	North Macedonia	53.56	Botswana	67.73
Côte d'Ivoire	68.16	Viet Nam	53.41	Barbados	66.55
Bosnia and Herzegovina	67.45	Tanzania	51.56	Colombia	66.38
New Zealand	67.45	Philippines	50.80	Lesotho	66.06
Ghana	66.91	Paraguay	50.68	Pakistan	65.90
Viet Nam	66.81	Togo	49.58	Romania	65.74
Botswana	66.01	Nepal	49.29	Togo	64.36
Kyrgyz Republic	65.22	Montenegro	48.92	Seychelles	63.57
Tanzania	65.00	Botswana	48.52	Tanzania	62.15
Mauritius	64.55	Ghana	47.67	Mexico	61.73
Indonesia	63.98	Barbados	46.40	Indonesia	61.31
Cambodia	62.94	El Salvador	45.36	Cambodia	60.66
Chad	61.22	Pakistan	44.97	Paraguay	60.60
Central African Republic	61.11	Bangladesh	41.64	Morocco	59.66
Paraguay	60.90	Kyrgyz Republic	41.23	Greece	58.98
El Salvador	60.38	Côte d'Ivoire	40.34	Philippines	57.95
Nepal	59.34	Samoa	40.04	Peru	56.20
Pakistan	59.10	Cambodia	39.14	El Salvador	54.53
Seychelles	58.85	Lesotho	37.89	Ghana	54.42
Barbados	58.81	Bosnia and Herzegovina	37.81	Costa Rica	53.66
Madagascar	57.38	Seychelles	37.21	West Bank and Gaza	52.75
Samoa	57.13	Vanuatu	32.06	Sierra Leone	52.51
Bangladesh	56.99	Madagascar	31.64	Madagascar	52.29
Lesotho	54.94	Sierra Leone	30.73	Côte d'Ivoire	50.31
Sierra Leone	54.09	West Bank and Gaza	28.42	Gambia, The	48.44
Gambia, The	53.37	Timor-Leste	23.80	Chad	48.05
Vanuatu	50.44	Chad	23.51	Iraq	46.79
Iraq	49.39	Iraq	21.45	Timor-Leste	44.83
West Bank and Gaza	47.54	Gambia, The	20.11	Vanuatu	43.94
Timor-Leste	46.21	Central African Republic	18.35	Central African Republic	40.36

Quintile: ■ Top ■ Second ■ Third ☐ Fourth   Bottom

Source: B-READY 2024 data.
Note: The economies are ordered according to their scores in each of the three pillars: Pillar I, Regulatory Framework; Pillar II, Public Services; and Pillar III, Operational Efficiency. They are further grouped in quintiles, which are marked with varying shades of blue (with darker shades representing better performance).

Top quintile. Economies in the top quintile (indicated by the darkest shade of blue in table ES.1) represent the highest performers, encompassing the top 20 percent of the data, from the 80th percentile to the maximum values. In the Regulatory Framework pillar, Hungary leads with a score of 78.23 points; the average score is 76.45 points. This pillar has the narrowest range among all three pillars (4.75 points). This narrow range shows that economies within this quintile maintain similar high standards, demonstrating a widespread adoption of internationally recognized good practices in the Regulatory Framework pillar.

In the Public Services pillar, Estonia emerges as the top performer, with a score of 73.31 points. This pillar has the lowest average score across all pillars (68.82 points), with a range of 8.80 points. The moderate range suggests variability in the quality of public services, although most economies still offer superior support for businesses through enhanced transparency, digitalization, and interoperability of government services.

In the Operational Efficiency pillar, Singapore stands out as the top performer, with a score of 87.33 points. The average score in this pillar is 78.67 points, the highest among pillars. However, scores also have the most significant variation among all pillars, with a range of 14.55 points. This relatively wide range indicates uneven performance levels among top-performing economies.

Overall, economies in the top quintile perform well across multiple pillars, often ranking highly across various topics. For instance, Estonia scores in the top quintile of economies in 7 of the 10 topics, and Rwanda scores in the first quintile in 6 of the 10 topics. This strong performance across pillars showcases the broad strengths of these economies, although it also reveals specific areas where further improvements could enhance their overall competitiveness.

Second quintile. This quintile includes the economies ranked between the 60th and 80th percentiles. These economies exhibit strong performance but also show potential for improvement. In this quintile, the Regulatory Framework pillar has the highest average score (71.10 points) among the three pillars, coupled with the narrowest range (3.81 points), indicating a relatively consistent performance across these economies and adherence to regulatory good practices. Estonia leads this pillar with a score of 72.84 points.

In the Public Services pillar, Bulgaria achieves the highest score of 64.03 points. Pillar II has the lowest average score (61.22 points) with the widest range (7.75 points) among the three pillars. This broader range suggests disparities in public services that could be addressed to further elevate these economies.

The Operational Efficiency pillar shows a relatively higher average score of 70.26 points compared to Pillar II, with a lower range of 3.90 points. Nepal leads this pillar with a score of 72.21 points. While most economies in this quintile demonstrate relatively strong operational efficiency, slight disparities suggest that targeted reforms could enhance efficiency further.

Third quintile. This quintile covers the middle 20 percent of economies, ranging from the 40th to the 60th percentile. These economies exhibit a mix of strengths and weaknesses in their business environment. In the Regulatory Framework pillar, the average score of the third quintile is 66.65 points, with Morocco achieving the highest score of 68.92 points. The Operational Efficiency pillar follows closely, with an average score of 65.02 points, led by Botswana at 67.73 points. The Public Services pillar has the lowest average score among the three (50.40 points), with North Macedonia scoring the highest at 53.56 points.

In the third quintile, the ranges between the highest and lowest scores across all pillars are relatively similar, indicating consistent levels of performance within each pillar among these economies. However, while these economies may have established laws and regulations, deficiencies in public services appear to be hindering them from developing a robust private sector. To improve their overall business environment, these economies should address weaknesses in the topics and pillars where they currently underperform.

Fourth quintile. This quintile encompasses the economies ranked from the 20th to the 40th percentile. These economies grapple with a challenging business environment characterized by relatively weak regulatory frameworks and public services, which constrains the operational efficiency of their businesses. Among the pillars, the Public Services pillar has the lowest average score (41.48 points), reflecting the relatively low level of support available to businesses. The Operational Efficiency pillar comes next with an average of 57.80 points, while the Regulatory Framework pillar has the highest average score, at 60.66 points. Indonesia achieves the highest score in this quintile for the Regulatory Framework pillar with 63.98 points, while Barbados scores the lowest with 58.81 points. In the same quintile for the Public Services pillar, Barbados attains the highest score of 46.40 points, while Bosnia and Herzegovina records the lowest with 37.81 points. These relatively low scores underscore the pressing need for improvement in these economies to foster a more conducive business environment.

Bottom quintile. Economies in the bottom quintile (lightest shade of blue in table ES.1) represent the lowest performance in each pillar. These economies particularly struggle in the Public Services pillar, with an average score of 26.73 points. In contrast, they show relatively higher average scores in the Regulatory Framework pillar (52.75 points) and Operational Efficiency pillar (48.03 points). Notably, the range between the highest and lowest scores within these pillars is the widest in this quintile, highlighting the significant disparities in performance. For example, Madagascar achieves the highest score in this group for the Regulatory Framework pillar, with 57.38 points, while Timor-Leste scores the lowest, with 46.21 points. Similarly, the Seychelles records the highest score in the Public Services pillar, with 37.21 points, while the Central African Republic records the lowest, with 18.35 points. These wide ranges indicate that while some economies in this quintile manage to maintain moderately stable regulatory and operational frameworks, others fall severely behind, especially in public service delivery. Entrepreneurs in these economies, some of which are fragile and conflict-affected, need to show remarkable resilience in conducting their operations. The pronounced disparity in pillar performance underscores the uneven development within these economies and points to critical areas that require urgent attention and reform.

There is significant diversity in the distribution of economies by income level across the three pillars. Figure ES.4 shows how economies in each of the quintiles are distributed by income across the three pillars. These patterns yield several important insights.

Economies of varying income levels can adopt strong regulatory frameworks (refer to figure ES.4, panel a). The top quintile in the Regulatory Framework pillar consists mostly of high-income economies, but 40 percent are upper-middle-income economies (Bulgaria, Colombia, Georgia, Mexico). The second quintile features all income levels: 3 high-income economies (Estonia; Hong Kong SAR, China; Singapore); 4 upper-middle-income economies (Costa Rica, Montenegro, North Macedonia, Peru); 1 lower-middle-income economy (the Philippines); and 2 low-income economies (Rwanda, Togo). Such regional and income-level diversity emphasizes the potential for any economy to establish a robust legal and regulatory framework that can boost its business climate. Additionally, it presents an opportunity for mutual learning among peers. The third quintile mainly consists of lower-middle-income economies, with 1 high-income economy (New Zealand) and 3 upper-middle-income economies (Bosnia and Herzegovina, Botswana, Mauritius). The fourth quintile is diverse, spanning all income levels, while the bottom quintile consists mostly of lower-middle-income economies, with 2 upper-middle-income economies (Iraq, West Bank and Gaza) and 3 low-income economies (The Gambia, Madagascar, Sierra Leone).

FIGURE ES.4 **The distribution of economies by income level varies considerably across pillars and by performance**

a. Pillar I, Regulatory Framework

Number of economies

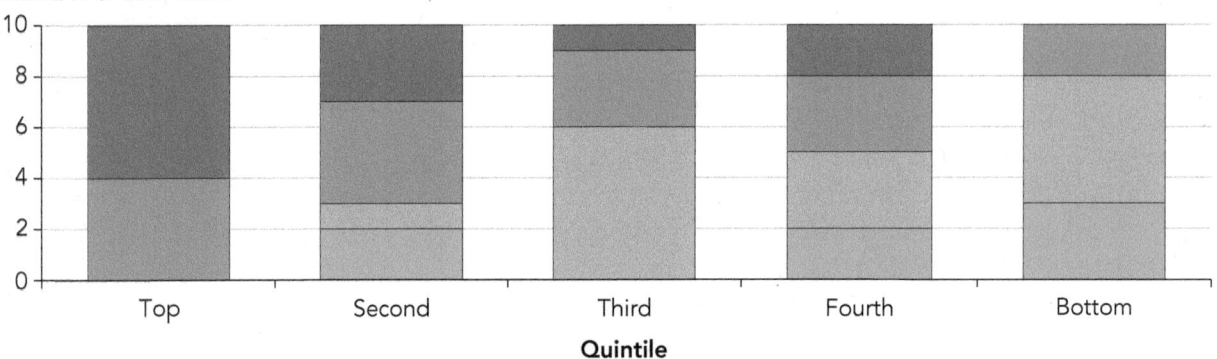

b. Pillar II, Public Services

Number of economies

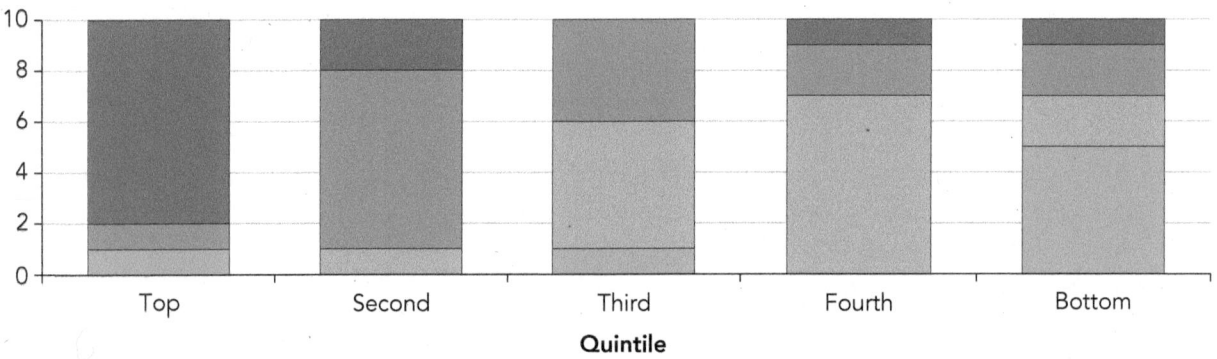

c. Pillar III, Operational Efficiency

Number of economies

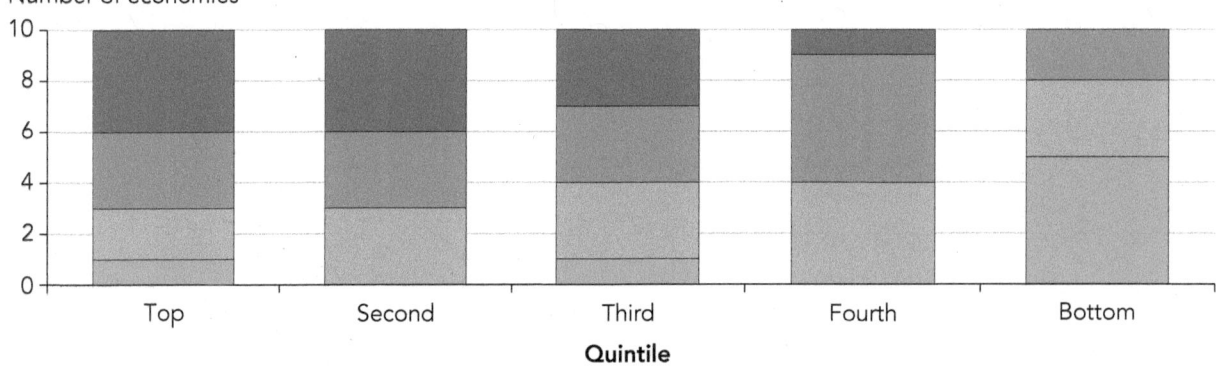

■ High income ■ Upper middle income ■ Lower middle income ■ Low income

Source: B-READY 2024 data.

Note: The income classification data are as of June 2024 to ensure alignment with the latest data collection period.

High-income economies tend to provide higher quality public services to support businesses, but all income levels are represented across top quintiles (refer to figure ES.4, panel b). The Public Services pillar shows higher diversity of income levels across the quintiles. High-income economies make up 80 percent of the top quintile; however, the group also contains 1 upper-middle-income economy (Colombia) and 1 low-income economy (Rwanda). The second quintile includes 2 high-income economies (Hong Kong SAR, China; Romania), 7 upper-middle-income economies, and 1 lower-middle-income economy (Morocco). The third quintile also shows diversity, with 4 upper-middle-income economies (Botswana, Montenegro, North Macedonia, Paraguay), 5 lower-middle-income economies (Ghana, Nepal, the Philippines, Tanzania, Viet Nam), and 1 low-income economy (Togo). The fourth quintile follows suit and consists of 1 high-income economy (Barbados), 2 upper-middle-income economies (Bosnia and Herzegovina, El Salvador), and 7 lower-middle-income economies. The bottom quintile is evenly split between low-income economies (the Central African Republic, Chad, The Gambia, Madagascar, Sierra Leone) and economies in other income levels (Iraq, the Seychelles, Timor-Leste, Vanuatu, West Bank and Gaza).

Economies across all income levels can facilitate the operational efficiency of firms (refer to figure ES.4, panel c). High-income economies comprise 40 percent of the top quintile in the Operational Efficiency pillar (Estonia; Hong Kong SAR, China; New Zealand; Singapore), while economies from other income levels make up the remaining 60 percent. This distribution demonstrates the potential for any economy to achieve relatively high levels of operational efficiency across its business environment. In the second quintile, 40 percent of economies are high-income (Croatia, Hungary, Portugal, the Slovak Republic), with the rest split equally between upper-middle-income (Bosnia and Herzegovina, Mauritius, Montenegro) and lower-middle-income economies (Bangladesh, Nepal, Samoa). The third quintile has equal representation from high-income (Barbados, Romania, the Seychelles), upper-middle-income (Botswana, Colombia, Mexico), and lower-middle-income economies (Lesotho, Pakistan, Tanzania), with 1 low-income economy (Togo). The fourth quintile consists of 1 high-income economy (Greece), 5 upper-middle-income economies (Costa Rica, El Salvador, Indonesia, Paraguay, Peru), and 4 lower-middle-income economies (Cambodia, Ghana, Morocco, the Philippines). Most of the economies in the bottom quintile are low-income (the Central African Republic, Chad, The Gambia, Madagascar, Sierra Leone), with 3 lower-middle-income economies (Côte d'Ivoire, Timor-Leste, Vanuatu) and 2 upper-middle-income economies (Iraq, West Bank and Gaza). These findings should be interpreted with caution, due to the limited geographic coverage of this 2024 report.

Performance by topic

Beyond the pillar performance of economies, B-READY 2024 also presents information on economy performance at the topic level. Table ES.2 provides a visual representation that allows readers to identify the specific topics where economies should improve. To inform detailed policy advice, B-READY also provides much more granular data for each topic and pillar in appendix A and on the project's website (https://www.worldbank.org/en /businessready).

The performance patterns of economies tend to be consistent across various topics, but all economies have room for improvement. While economies exhibit varying degrees of performance across different topics, a consistent pattern emerges. Economies with a favorable business environment in one area (for example, being in a higher quintile group) tend to have a similar performance in other areas (being in higher quintiles). The opposite is also true. Economies in a lower quintile in one area tend to have lower quintile performances across other areas. This trend could be attributed to the fact that topics are interlinked. Policy makers may consider these interlinkages as they devise reform strategies.

To explore the linkages between the topics, the topic scores were ordered from highest to lowest, and the correlations were analyzed based on this ordering. This method, which assesses the association between two variables based on their position rather than their raw values, is particularly useful when comparing how economies belong to specific quintiles.

For example, Market Competition and Business Location are the two topics with the most similarity in the distribution of economies—meaning that the same economies appear in the same performance quintile in both topics. Their correlation is 0.80. Seven economies are present in the top quintile for both (Colombia, Costa Rica, Croatia, Estonia, Hungary, Rwanda, Singapore). Another 5 economies share the second quintile (Hong Kong SAR, China; Mauritius; Portugal; Romania; the Slovak Republic), and 6 appear consistently in the bottom quintile in both (Chad, The Gambia, Iraq, Lesotho, Sierra Leone, Timor-Leste).[19] This suggests that economies that protect fair and efficient allocation of resources between competing firms are also more likely to have regulations and services that reduce market distortion of land and property rights, including clearly defined sets of building regulations and environmental permitting standards.

TABLE ES.2 B-READY 2024 performance, by topic

Economy	Business Entry	Business Location	Utility Services	Labor	Financial Services	International Trade	Taxation	Dispute Resolution	Market Competition	Business Insolvency
Bangladesh	74.08	66.91	62.10	64.01	61.45	53.86	56.36	41.90	42.65	40.39
Barbados	78.23	44.39	62.81	69.64	61.37	57.54	52.34	61.63	39.17	45.42
Bosnia and Herzegovina	55.73	63.83	59.58	69.87	56.41	68.65	46.92	49.92	52.23	61.23
Botswana	92.50	56.78	60.85	63.51	69.30	68.26	50.88	56.06	50.92	38.45
Bulgaria	92.08	71.51	81.10	68.72	68.56	75.82	59.96	68.78	64.34	66.40
Cambodia	43.80	49.00	64.45	68.44	86.03	57.68	58.60	61.76	33.09	19.63
Central African Republic	46.26	44.98	53.02	49.95	33.98	34.82	23.28	38.46	33.84	40.81
Chad	47.48	41.04	43.46	55.67	44.26	43.31	43.39	49.23	32.52	42.24
Colombia	88.62	72.38	74.99	62.08	75.19	54.02	57.71	72.85	64.84	74.49
Costa Rica	71.08	72.99	70.22	58.73	66.14	73.93	42.22	59.91	68.55	45.09
Côte d'Ivoire	63.82	44.21	58.87	69.28	42.19	51.08	53.39	61.44	34.68	50.44
Croatia	78.72	76.24	76.77	75.60	63.28	84.73	39.86	71.84	63.24	76.48
El Salvador	45.86	61.90	65.57	56.19	70.99	61.72	43.03	61.45	49.52	18.01
Estonia	90.75	80.40	72.72	68.89	61.54	85.59	70.72	80.24	64.69	79.22
Gambia, The	46.61	33.42	36.43	49.22	42.20	38.58	39.01	50.69	26.76	43.47
Georgia	80.08	83.01	73.08	83.46	74.97	76.72	68.51	82.09	54.93	75.65
Ghana	40.99	60.39	68.52	68.57	59.86	56.25	56.78	54.85	32.19	64.93
Greece	96.58	57.86	69.30	64.71	58.63	87.04	56.02	65.61	64.18	43.71
Hong Kong SAR, China	85.49	71.17	77.71	68.81	69.96	90.77	70.56	72.67	57.80	46.91
Hungary	85.81	73.52	64.45	81.87	80.70	78.23	59.35	75.20	63.17	65.75
Indonesia	63.72	68.09	70.55	72.20	56.51	64.58	59.91	64.24	52.34	56.96
Iraq	52.22	48.47	54.19	53.66	44.05	42.13	29.40	39.87	21.38	6.74
Kyrgyz Republic	64.83	67.37	71.92	54.35	70.62	60.65	46.59	62.54	52.70	52.31
Lesotho	76.44	45.93	56.05	62.69	54.30	61.39	60.19	50.10	25.53	37.02
Madagascar	62.35	42.44	35.04	50.68	50.66	54.83	51.66	47.71	39.90	35.77

Quintile: Top   Second   Third   Fourth   Bottom

(Continued)

TABLE ES.2 B-READY 2024 performance, by topic (Continued)

Economy	Business Entry	Business Location	Utility Services	Labor	Financial Services	International Trade	Taxation	Dispute Resolution	Market Competition	Business Insolvency
Mauritius	75.58	68.64	41.48	76.60	60.17	74.36	69.22	51.32	57.03	61.02
Mexico	61.53	61.81	76.79	59.74	84.31	63.77	65.56	67.69	51.69	53.93
Montenegro	79.72	66.55	73.63	63.25	63.16	67.20	44.04	68.79	53.12	61.96
Morocco	76.73	77.39	76.64	59.10	62.66	75.51	47.69	43.67	58.14	46.58
Nepal	66.36	60.51	65.39	65.70	70.58	66.77	57.99	64.40	33.06	52.04
New Zealand	84.64	80.38	63.00	79.95	85.04	69.94	71.74	61.07	53.87	59.52
North Macedonia	90.83	55.68	78.44	70.40	73.42	65.34	46.84	61.10	62.26	60.09
Pakistan	91.50	54.25	59.21	53.45	67.97	45.71	57.48	41.99	46.24	48.79
Paraguay	53.92	60.50	53.64	66.23	63.90	64.55	55.27	62.27	48.34	45.33
Peru	63.22	64.89	65.30	64.61	78.41	49.81	49.97	56.61	63.76	61.66
Philippines	48.49	60.27	66.47	75.54	60.70	71.47	56.66	62.88	50.13	45.51
Portugal	92.67	70.17	78.20	73.66	71.12	75.40	52.86	72.41	61.52	79.24
Romania	79.50	69.56	67.61	62.76	73.42	85.80	50.61	74.42	61.06	59.00
Rwanda	85.39	72.01	67.76	60.15	69.28	82.09	66.31	82.87	64.02	80.20
Samoa	73.39	60.10	65.03	70.24	52.09	51.36	56.94	47.82	51.16	23.52
Seychelles	54.49	57.83	53.77	72.71	56.07	61.43	58.35	37.84	35.90	43.72
Sierra Leone	48.44	46.36	60.54	69.02	41.57	37.69	41.45	42.26	30.17	40.26
Singapore	93.57	78.24	81.76	66.83	73.33	79.83	70.39	71.08	62.29	89.69
Slovak Republic	85.62	71.13	86.42	70.87	65.53	80.88	49.85	78.31	60.81	72.59
Tanzania	69.15	53.62	78.73	63.95	57.28	60.11	61.57	63.46	48.29	39.56
Timor-Leste	49.92	40.31	60.19	56.91	24.82	48.61	48.89	36.47	16.69	0.00
Togo	77.26	67.76	65.04	56.45	53.64	60.89	58.68	69.48	41.24	59.45
Vanuatu	44.08	51.63	51.14	54.37	41.24	41.28	50.21	43.04	23.01	21.44
Viet Nam	65.47	62.92	78.73	73.19	57.17	72.39	56.46	64.23	57.67	55.12
West Bank and Gaza	62.47	55.05	57.76	53.14	44.60	49.16	33.09	36.51	25.29	11.99

Quintile: ■ Top ■ Second ■ Third ■ Fourth ■ Bottom

Source: B-READY 2024 data.

Note: The economies are ordered alphabetically. Shades of blue represent the quintiles of the topic scores. The darker the shade, the better the performance.

International Trade and Market Competition are the second most similar topics in terms of economy distribution; their correlation is 0.76. Six economies are present in the top quintile for both (Croatia, Estonia, Greece, Hungary, Rwanda, Singapore). Another 5 economies share the second quintile (Mauritius, Morocco, New Zealand, Portugal, Viet Nam), and 7 appear consistently in the bottom quintile in both (Chad, The Gambia, Iraq, Sierra Leone, Timor-Leste, Vanuatu, West Bank and Gaza).[20] Global trade dynamics and government policies on trade influence competitive practices within markets and vice versa. For example, companies that engage in global trade can adopt innovative practices from other economies, enhancing their competitive capabilities. The exchange of knowledge and diversification of products benefit consumers, while fostering a more dynamic competitive environment.

Another notable example of complementarities is between Dispute Resolution and Business Insolvency, with a correlation of 0.72. These two topics share 8 economies in their top quintile (Colombia, Croatia, Estonia, Georgia, Hungary, Portugal, Rwanda, the Slovak Republic), while 3 economies consistently appear in the second quintile (Indonesia, Montenegro, Togo), and 4 in the bottom quintile (Iraq, Timor-Leste, Vanuatu, West Bank and Gaza).[21] This finding suggests a likely complementarity arising from the characteristics of the judiciary institutions benchmarked within these topics. A favorable business environment in one area also tends to have a good environment in other areas, and overall. In some topics, however, complementarities are limited or nonexistent due to the very different nature of topics, such as Taxation and Utility Services or Labor and Financial Services.[22]

Figure ES.5 presents the distribution of economies in top quintiles. Strong performance is not reserved to a small group of economies. In total, 29 economies score in the top quintile in at least one topic, representing all income levels (1 low-income, 7 lower-middle-income, 10 upper-middle-income, 11 high-income economies) and all global regions (6 economies from East Asia and Pacific; 6 OECD high-income economies; 5 from Europe and Central Asia; 4 from Latin America and the Caribbean; 1 from the Middle East and North Africa; 1 from South Asia; and 6 from Sub-Saharan Africa). This is very encouraging. However, no economy scores in the top quintile across 9 or 10 topics, indicating that there is potential for improvement in every economy across the 10 topics.

FIGURE ES.5 **Strong performance is not confined to a small group of economies, but all have room for improvement**

Distribution of economies in top quintiles

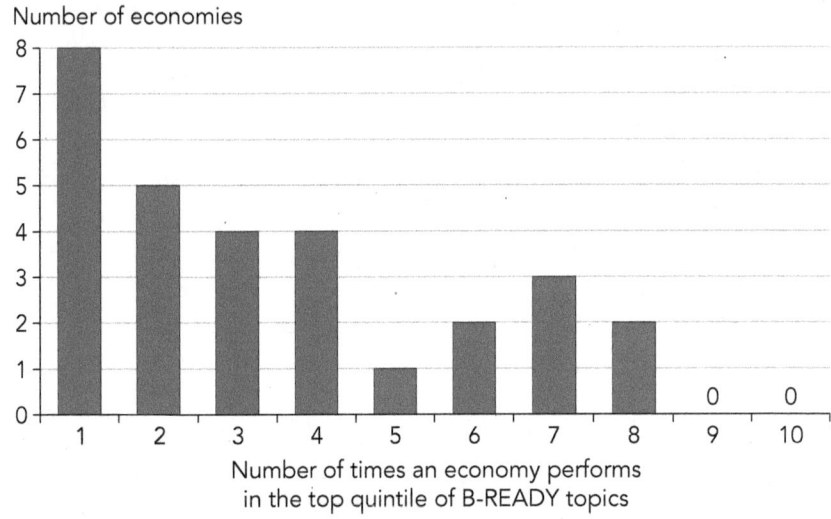

Number of economies

Number of times an economy performs in the top quintile of B-READY topics

Source: B-READY 2024 data.
Note: The sample comprises 50 economies. The distribution is the following: 8 economies (Botswana, Cambodia, Indonesia, Lesotho, Morocco, Pakistan, the Philippines, the Seychelles) are present in the top quintile for any one topic; 5 economies (Costa Rica, Mauritius, Peru, Tanzania, Viet Nam) for any two topics; 4 economies (Greece, Mexico, North Macedonia, Romania) for any three topics; 4 economies (Bulgaria; Hong Kong SAR, China; New Zealand; the Slovak Republic) for any four topics; 1 economy (Portugal) for any five topics; 2 economies (Colombia, Rwanda) for any six topics; 3 economies (Estonia, Croatia, Georgia) for any seven topics; 2 economies (Hungary, Singapore) for any eight topics. No economy scores in the top quintile across any nine topics or across all ten topics.

B-READY 2024 key emerging findings

1. Economies do not need to be rich to develop a good business environment. The three B-READY pillar scores (Regulatory Framework, Public Services, Operational Efficiency) have strong positive associations with GDP per capita (refer to figure ES.6). Nevertheless, some low-income and middle-income economies also achieve relatively high scores. For example, Colombia, Georgia, Rwanda, and Togo perform well on Regulatory Framework. Rwanda also performs well in Public Services. It also excels in Operational Efficiency, along with Georgia, the Kyrgyz Republic, and Nepal.

Figure ES.7 displays performance groups by specific topic and shows the occurrence of low-income and middle-income economies in the top two quintiles of each topic. Low- and middle-income economies appear in the top two quintiles for all the topics covered by B-READY. In all, 29 of the 38 economies classified at these income levels are present in the top two quintiles in at least one B-READY topic. Financial Services and Taxation have the highest number of low- and middle-income economies (14) in the top two groups, followed by Utility Services (13), Business Insolvency (12), and Business Location, Dispute Resolution, and Labor (11 each). These results underscore the point that robust business environments can exist at all income levels, albeit in specific areas.

FIGURE ES.6 The association between B-READY pillar scores and GDP per capita is strong and positive, with notable exceptions

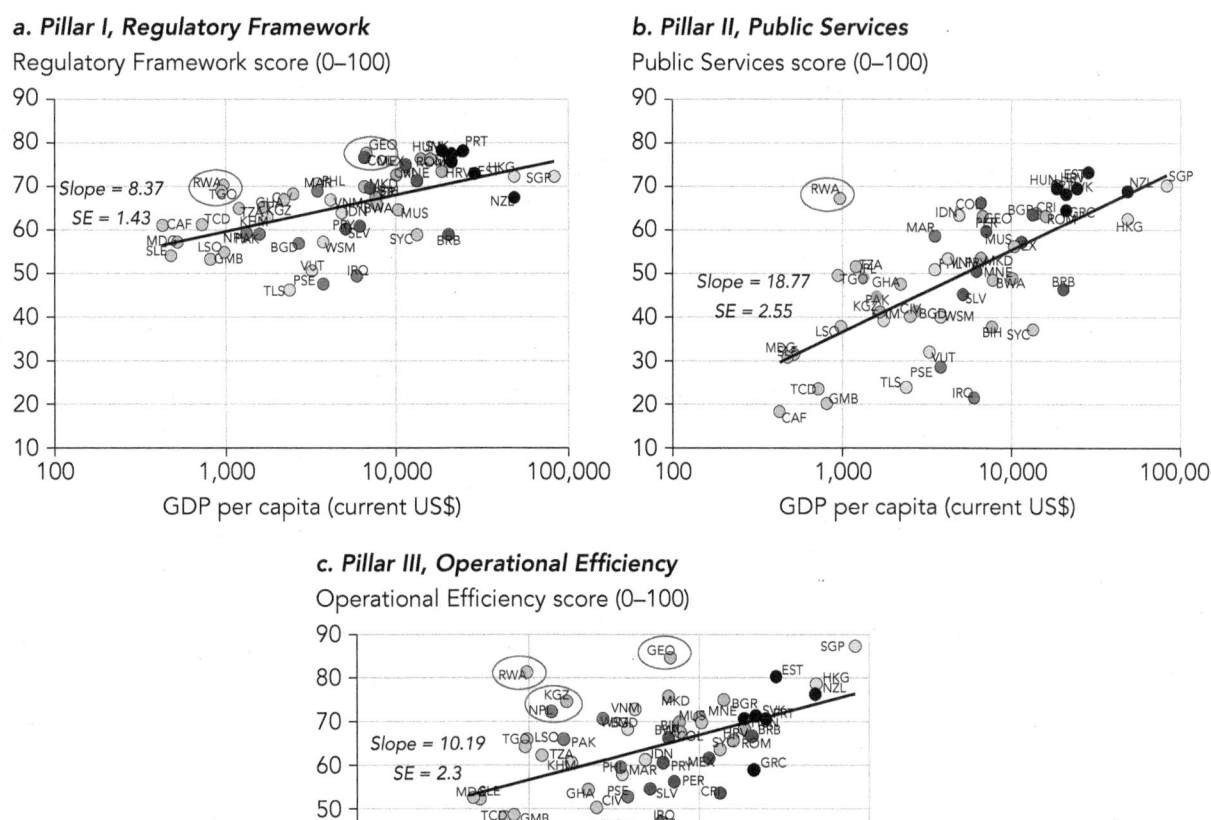

a. Pillar I, Regulatory Framework

b. Pillar II, Public Services

c. Pillar III, Operational Efficiency

Sources: B-READY 2024 data; World Development Indicators 2023.

Note: The sample comprises 50 economies. The statistical relationship between the B-READY pillar scores and GDP per capita is significant at the 1 percent level. The x-axis uses a log scale. A fitted regression line is included for each panel. Economies circled in red are examples of low- and middle-income economies that achieve relatively high scores within their income groups. For economy abbreviations, refer to appendix B and International Organization for Standardization (ISO), https://www.iso.org/obp/ui/#search. GDP = gross domestic product; OECD = Organisation for Economic Co-operation and Development; SE = standard error.

FIGURE ES.7 Low-income and middle-income economies can be found in the top two quintiles in every topic

	Financial Services	Taxation	Utility Services	Business Insolvency	Business Location	Dispute Resolution	Labor	International Trade	Market Competition	Business Entry
14	Botswana									
13	Bulgaria	Bulgaria	Bulgaria							
12	Colombia	Colombia	Colombia	Bosnia and Herzegovina						
11	Costa Rica	Georgia	Costa Rica	Bulgaria	Bulgaria	Bulgaria	Bosnia and Herzegovina			
10	El Salvador	Mauritius	Georgia	Colombia	Colombia	Colombia	Bulgaria	Bosnia and Herzegovina	Bulgaria	
9	Georgia	Mexico	Indonesia	Georgia	Costa Rica	Georgia	Georgia	Botswana	Colombia	Botswana
8	Mexico	Cambodia	Mexico	Indonesia	Georgia	Indonesia	Indonesia	Bulgaria	Costa Rica	Bulgaria
7	North Macedonia	Lesotho	Montenegro	Mauritius	Indonesia	Mexico	Mauritius	Costa Rica	Georgia	Colombia
6	Peru	Nepal	North Macedonia	Montenegro	Mauritius	Montenegro	North Macedonia	Georgia	Mauritius	Georgia
5	Cambodia	Pakistan	Ghana	North Macedonia	Bangladesh	Nepal	Côte d'Ivoire	Mauritius	North Macedonia	Montenegro
4	Kyrgyz Republic	Rwanda	Kyrgyz Republic	Peru	Kyrgyz Republic	Rwanda	Philippines	Morocco	Peru	North Macedonia
3	Nepal	Samoa	Morocco	Ghana	Morocco	Tanzania	Samoa	Philippines	Morocco	Pakistan
2	Pakistan	Tanzania	Tanzania	Rwanda	Rwanda	Togo	Sierra Leone	Rwanda	Rwanda	Rwanda
1	Rwanda	Togo	Viet Nam	Togo	Togo	Viet Nam	Viet Nam	Viet Nam	Viet Nam	Togo

■ Low income and lower middle income   ■ Upper middle income

Source: B-READY 2024.
Note: The sample comprises 50 economies. The income classification data are as of June 2024 to ensure alignment with the latest data collection period.

2. Economies vary the most on Public Services, second on Operational Efficiency, and third on Regulatory Framework. Among the three pillars assessed by B-READY, the Public Services pillar has the widest range of 54.96 points (refer to figure ES.8). Operational Efficiency has a score range of 46.97 points, and Regulatory Framework has a range of 32.02 points. These results indicate that business-supporting institutions and infrastructure vary substantially across economies, as does a firm's experience while complying with regulations and using public services. On the other hand, the regulatory environment appears more homogenous across economies.

FIGURE ES.8 **Public Services is the B-READY pillar with the widest range and weakest performance, on average**

a. Pillar I, Regulatory Framework

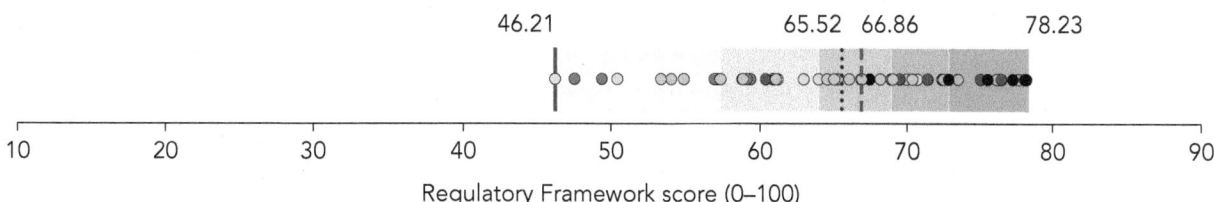

b. Pillar II, Public Services

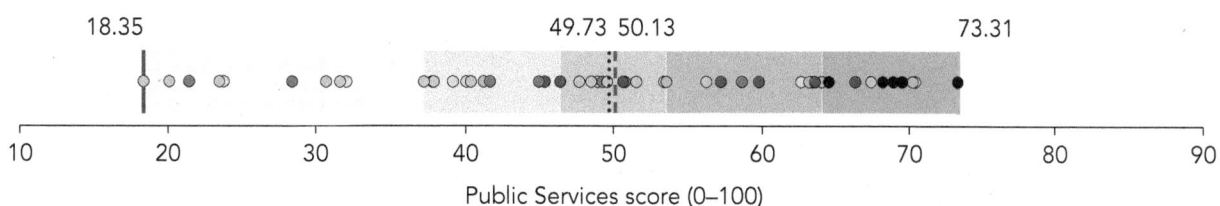

c. Pillar III, Operational Efficiency

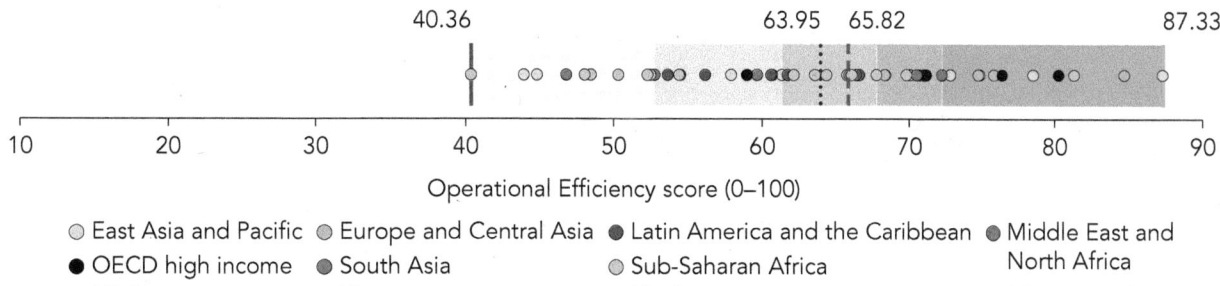

Source: B-READY 2024 data.
Note: For each pillar, the scores are plotted on the graph with minimum, mean, median, and maximum scores indicated by vertical lines, with corresponding scores provided. The dots, representing economies, indicate by color to which regional grouping an economy belongs. The blue panels represent quintiles (with darker shades indicating better performance). OECD = Organisation for Economic Co-operation and Development.

This point is further emphasized in figure ES.9, which presents the pillar scores for each economy. As pillar scores decline from high-performing economies to lower-performing ones, the decline for the Public Services pillar is particularly steep, and the gap between Public Services and Regulatory Framework scores widens significantly for the lower-performing economies. This indicates that disparities in public services contribute substantially to the variation in business environment performance across economies.

3. Economies are better at enacting regulations than providing public services. The B-READY data provide evidence of a "public services gap" across all regional and income groups: that is, a notable difference between the Regulatory Framework score and the Public Services score. Figure ES.10 demonstrates that the Public Services score is lower than the Regulatory Framework score for nearly all economies, as evidenced by its position below the 45-degree line. This gap persists when examining the average scores across all regional and income groups (refer to figure ES.11, panels a and b).

At the regional level, OECD high-income economies exhibit the narrowest public services gap (5.93 points). Economies in Latin America and the

FIGURE ES.9 **Pillar II, Public Services, largely drives the variation in the business environment across economies**

Score (0–100)

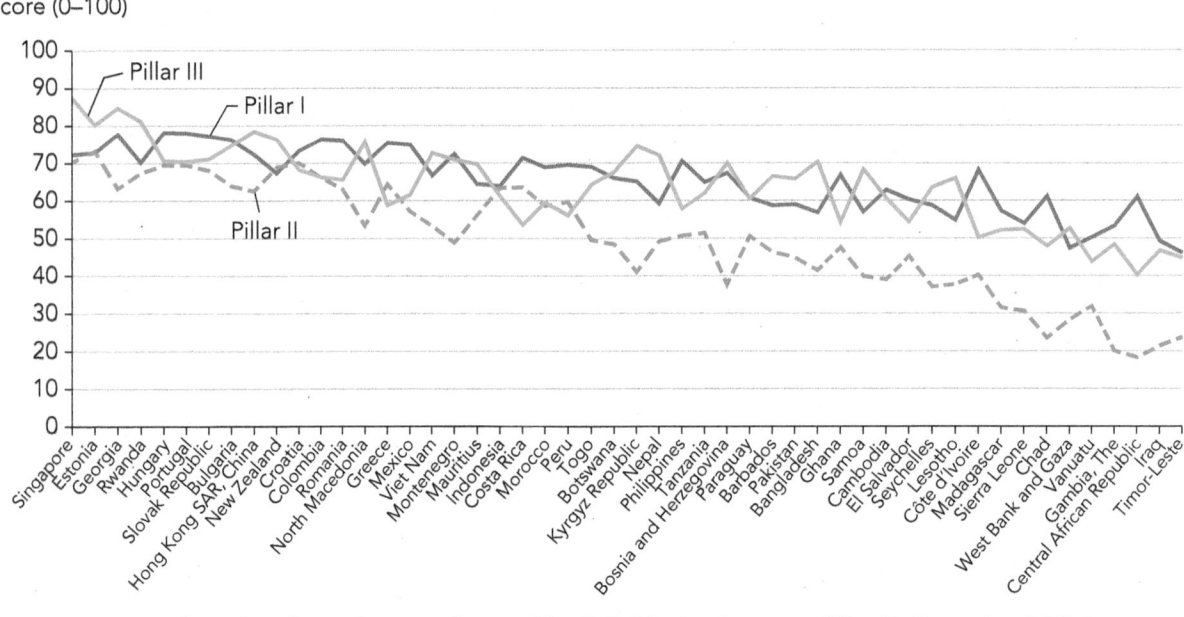

Source: B-READY 2024 data.
Note: The sample comprises 50 economies.

FIGURE ES.10 Most economies suffer from a "public services gap": Their scores for Public Services are lower than their scores for Regulatory Frameworks

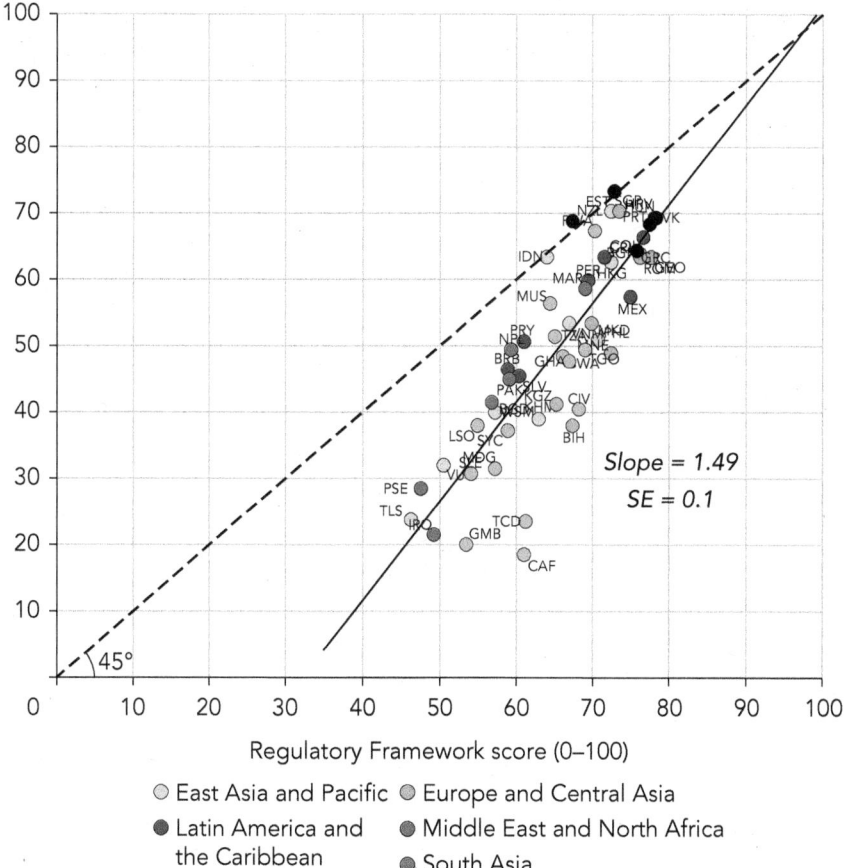

Source: B-READY 2024 data.

Note: The dashed line is set at 45 degrees, and the solid line represents the linear regression of the Public Services pillar score on the Regulatory Framework pillar score. The relationship is significant at the 1 percent level. The dots, representing economies, indicate by color to which regional grouping an economy belongs. The sample comprises 50 economies. The public services gap is represented by the gap as evidenced by the vast majority of economies positioned below the 45-degree line. For economy abbreviations, refer to appendix B and International Organization for Standardization (ISO), https://www.iso.org/obp/ui/#search. OECD = Organisation for Economic Co-operation and Development; SE = standard error.

Caribbean, South Asia, and East Asia and Pacific follow, with considerably larger gaps of 11.89 points, 13.18 points, and 14.13 points, respectively. Economies in Europe and Central Asia stand out with a relatively wider gap of 17.05 points despite performing exceptionally well on average in Pillar I, indicating important areas for improvement in public services provision. The gap is widest for economies in the Middle East and North Africa (19.10 points) and Sub-Saharan Africa (22.16 points).

FIGURE ES.11 The "public services gap" is evident across regions, income levels, and topics

a. By region

Average pillar score (0–100)

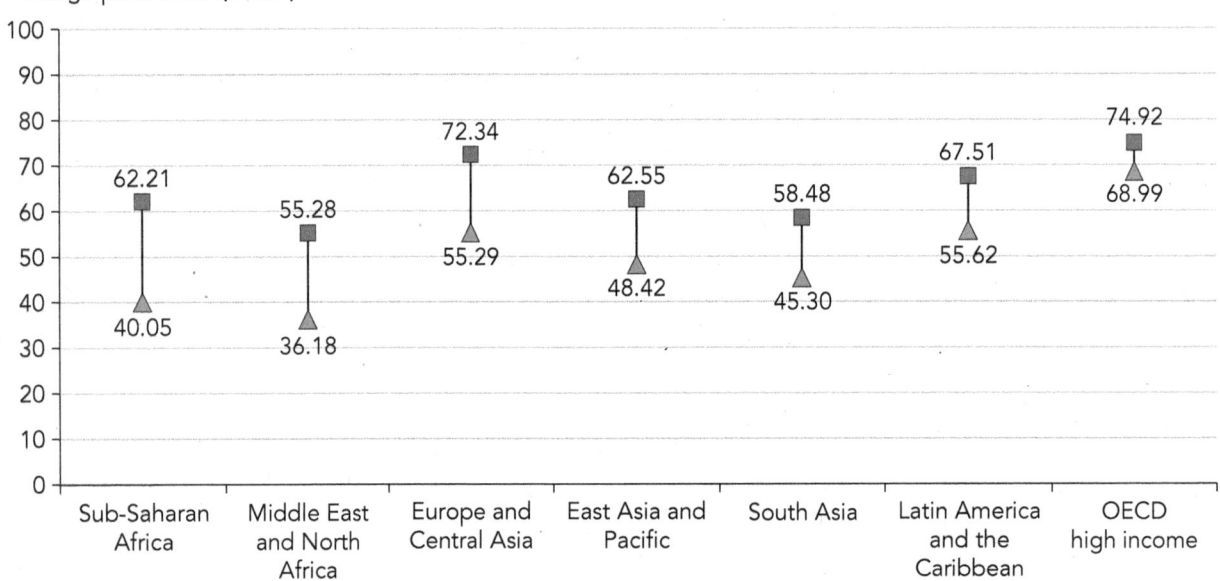

b. By income level

Average pillar score (0–100)

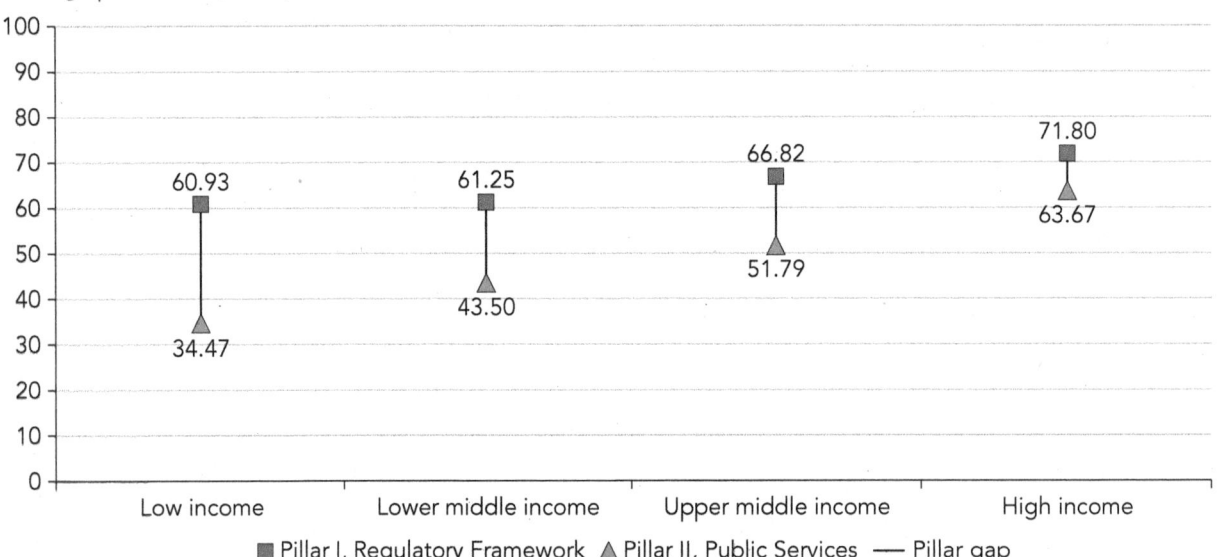

■ Pillar I, Regulatory Framework   ▲ Pillar II, Public Services   — Pillar gap

(Continued)

FIGURE ES.11 **The "public services gap" is evident across regions, income levels, and topics** *(Continued)*

c. By topic

Average pillar score (0–100)

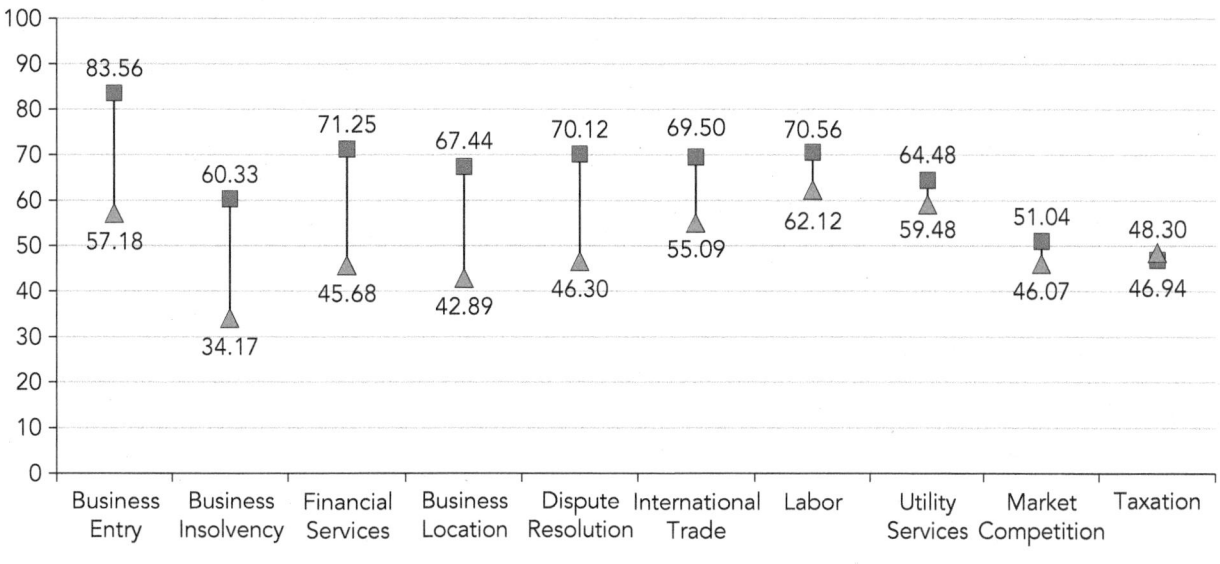

■ Pillar I, Regulatory Framework   ▲ Pillar II, Public Services   —— Pillar gap

Source: B-READY 2024 data.
Note: Data in each panel are arranged from the largest to the smallest gap. OECD = Organisation for Economic Co-operation and Development.

At the income level, high-income economies exhibit the narrowest gap (8.13 points). Moving toward lower-income levels, the gap widens progressively, ranging from 15.03 points in upper-middle-income economies to 17.75 points in lower-middle-income economies, and 26.46 points in low-income economies. Among the various topics (refer to figure ES.11, panel c), the public services gap is most pronounced in Business Entry and nonexistent in Taxation.

However, as the business environment improves, this gap narrows significantly (refer to figure ES.12). Moving from the bottom quintiles to the top quintiles of the two pillars, the public services gap declines from 26.02 and 19.18 points in the bottom and fourth quintiles, respectively, to less than 8 points in the top quintile.

4. Existing firms can be resilient amid poor conditions, but both active and potential firms could thrive if the business environment improves.
Operational Efficiency scores are higher than the average of the other two pillar scores (Regulatory Framework and Public Services) for most economies

FIGURE ES.12 **The "public services gap" closes remarkably as the business environment improves**

Average pillar score (0–100)

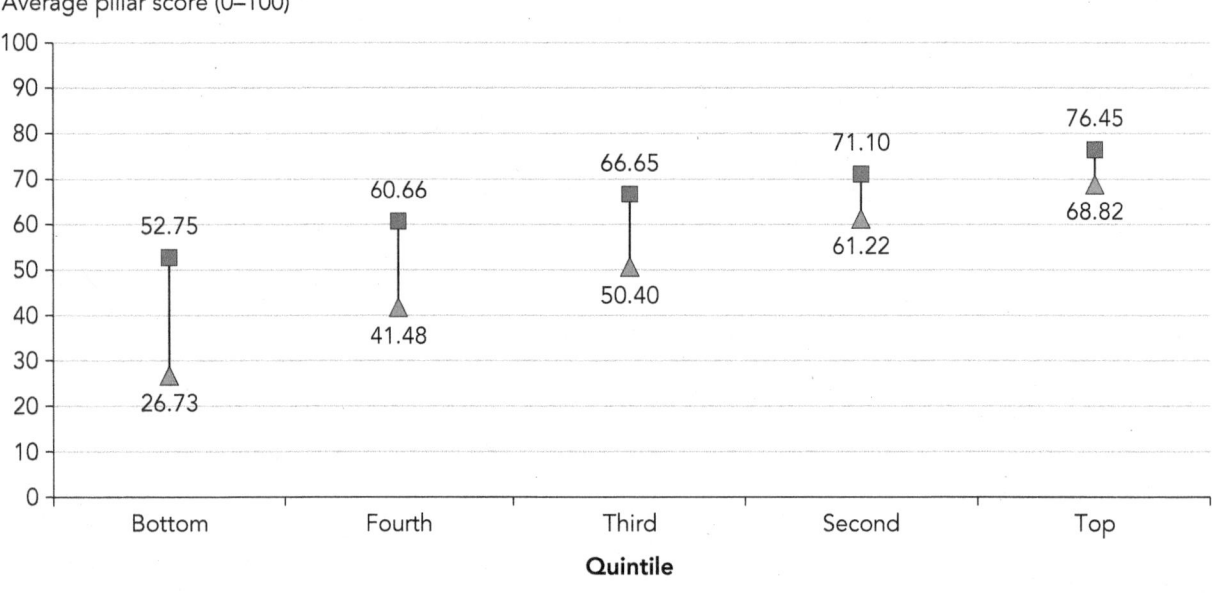

Source: B-READY 2024 data.

Note: The economies in each quintile are determined by the respective scores of the Regulatory Framework and Public Services pillars.

(refer to figure ES.13). Across the 10 topics, the Operational Efficiency pillar outperforms the Public Services pillar on average, and notably so in the topics of Business Location, Utility Services, and Taxation, where the pillar also surpasses the Regulatory Framework pillar (refer to figure ES.14). These patterns highlight the adaptability of firms in environments marked by deficient public services provision, suggesting they may have developed coping mechanisms to navigate their respective business environments.

Although firms exhibit resilience amid challenging conditions, they have the potential to thrive if these conditions improve. Such improvements can also foster market entry for newcomers, essential for cultivating a more dynamic, innovative, and diversified business landscape. A caveat to note in interpreting these data is that firms providing input for Operational Efficiency indicators are sampled from the formal sector and exclude very small or recently established firms. Larger and older firms may be less sensitive to weak regulatory and public services environments.

5. Most economies have room to improve across all B-READY topics. Figure ES.15 offers a concise overview of the score distribution for all the B-READY topics. The topic of Business Entry has the highest average score (69.96 points), followed by Utility Services (65.13 points), and Labor (64.99 points). Conversely, the topics with the lowest average scores are Market Competition (48.04 points), Business Insolvency (49.99 points),

FIGURE ES.13 For most economies, scores on the Operational Efficiency pillar are higher than the average scores on the Regulatory Framework pillar and the Public Services pillar

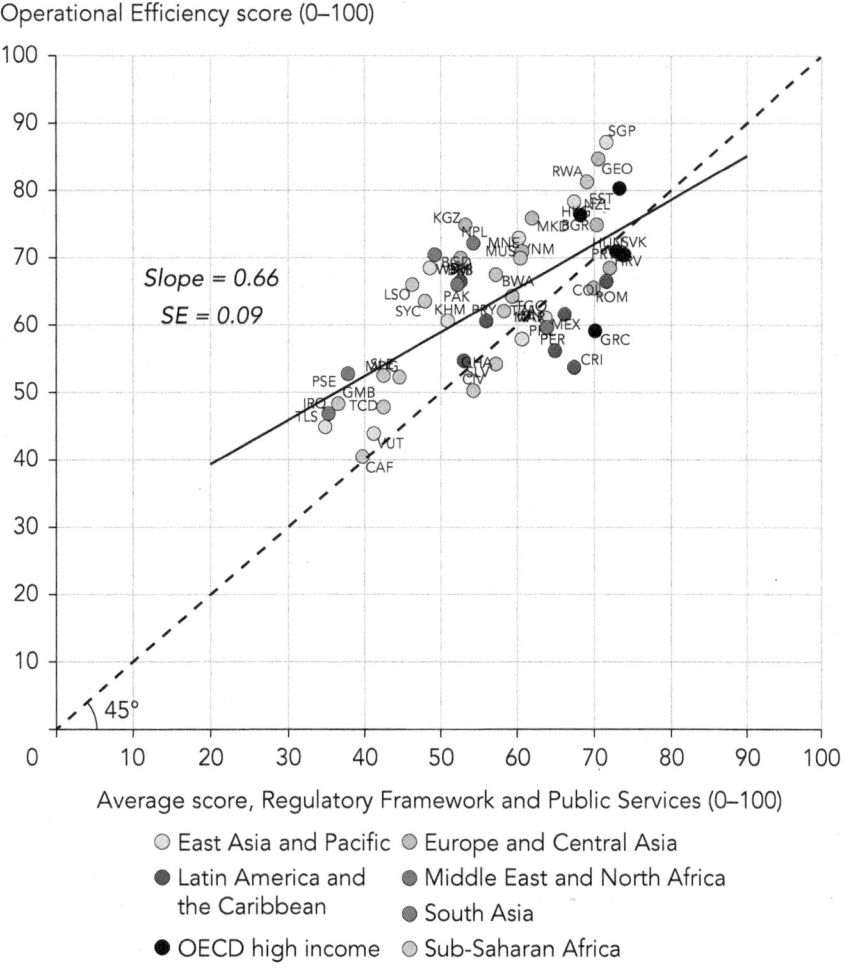

Source: B-READY 2024 data.
Note: The dashed line is set at 45 degrees, and the solid line represents the linear regression of the Operational Efficiency score on the average of the Regulatory Framework score and the Public Services score. The relationship is significant at the 1 percent level. The dots, representing economies, indicate by color to which regional grouping an economy belongs. The sample comprises 50 economies. For economy abbreviations, refer to appendix B and International Organization for Standardization (ISO), https://www.iso.org/obp/ui/#search. OECD = Organisation for Economic Co-operation and Development; SE = standard error.

and Taxation (53.50 points). These patterns suggest a large diversity across economies in adopting good international practices in regulations and public services, and their practical implementation, underscoring potential for enhancement across the board. Furthermore, a notable positive correlation across all topics indicates that economies with a favorable business environment in one area also tend to perform well in others, as shown in figure ES.16. Embracing a comprehensive reform agenda spanning all B-READY topics is essential for driving significant improvements in the overall business landscape.

FIGURE ES.14 Firms are resilient to the "public services gap" across topics

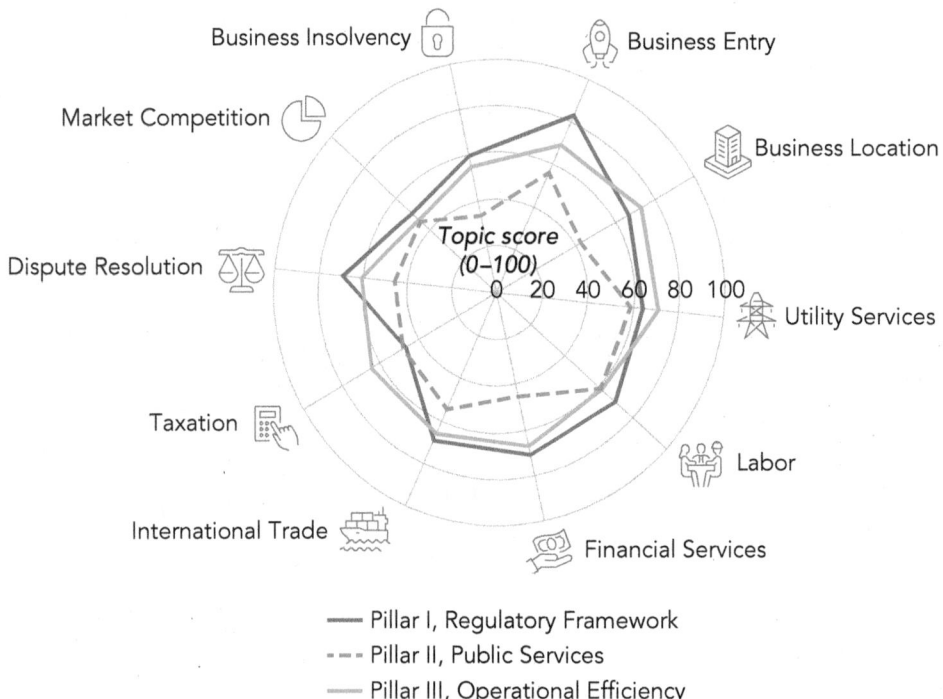

Topic score
(0–100)
0 20 40 60 80 100

—— Pillar I, Regulatory Framework
--- Pillar II, Public Services
—— Pillar III, Operational Efficiency

Source: B-READY 2024 data.
Note: The sample comprises 50 economies.

FIGURE ES.15 The distribution of scores shows scope for improvement across all topics

Topic score (0–100)

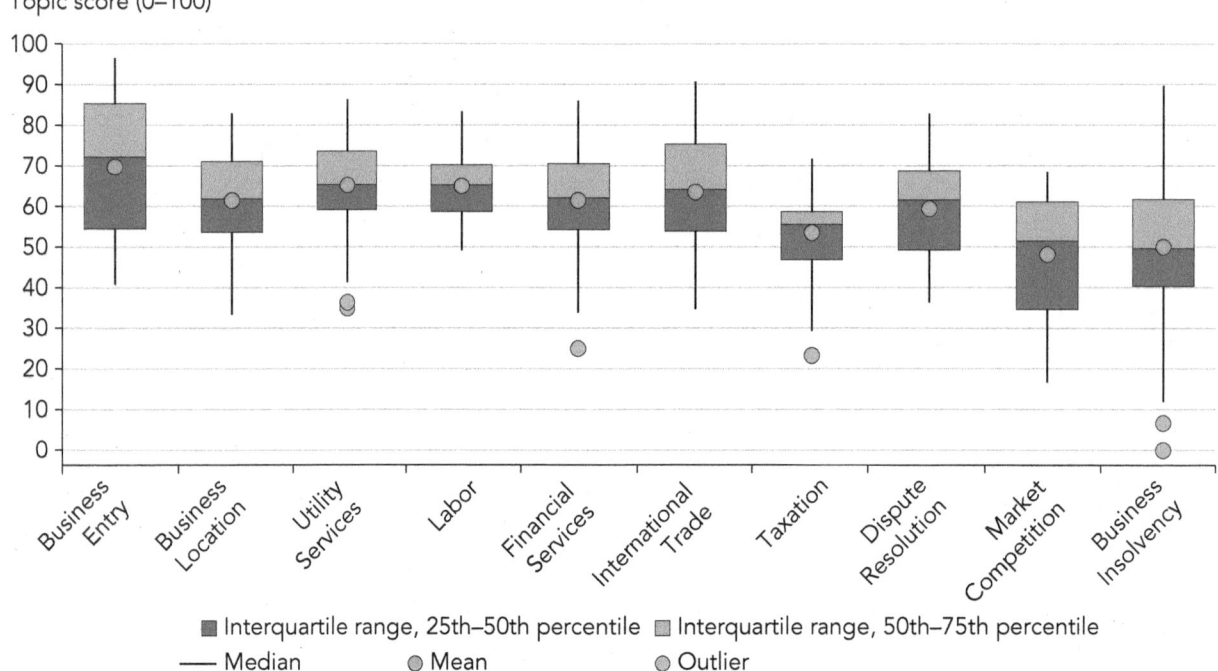

■ Interquartile range, 25th–50th percentile ■ Interquartile range, 50th–75th percentile
— Median ● Mean ◉ Outlier

Source: B-READY 2024 data.
Note: The figure displays the distribution of B-READY topic scores across the 50 sampled economies. It presents the median (horizontal black line dividing the light blue and dark blue boxes), mean (orange dots), the interquartile range (25th–75th percentiles, light blue and dark blue boxes), and standard whiskers. Points outside the whiskers represent outliers for each topic (green dots).

FIGURE ES.16 Economies with a favorable business environment in one topic tend to perform well in others

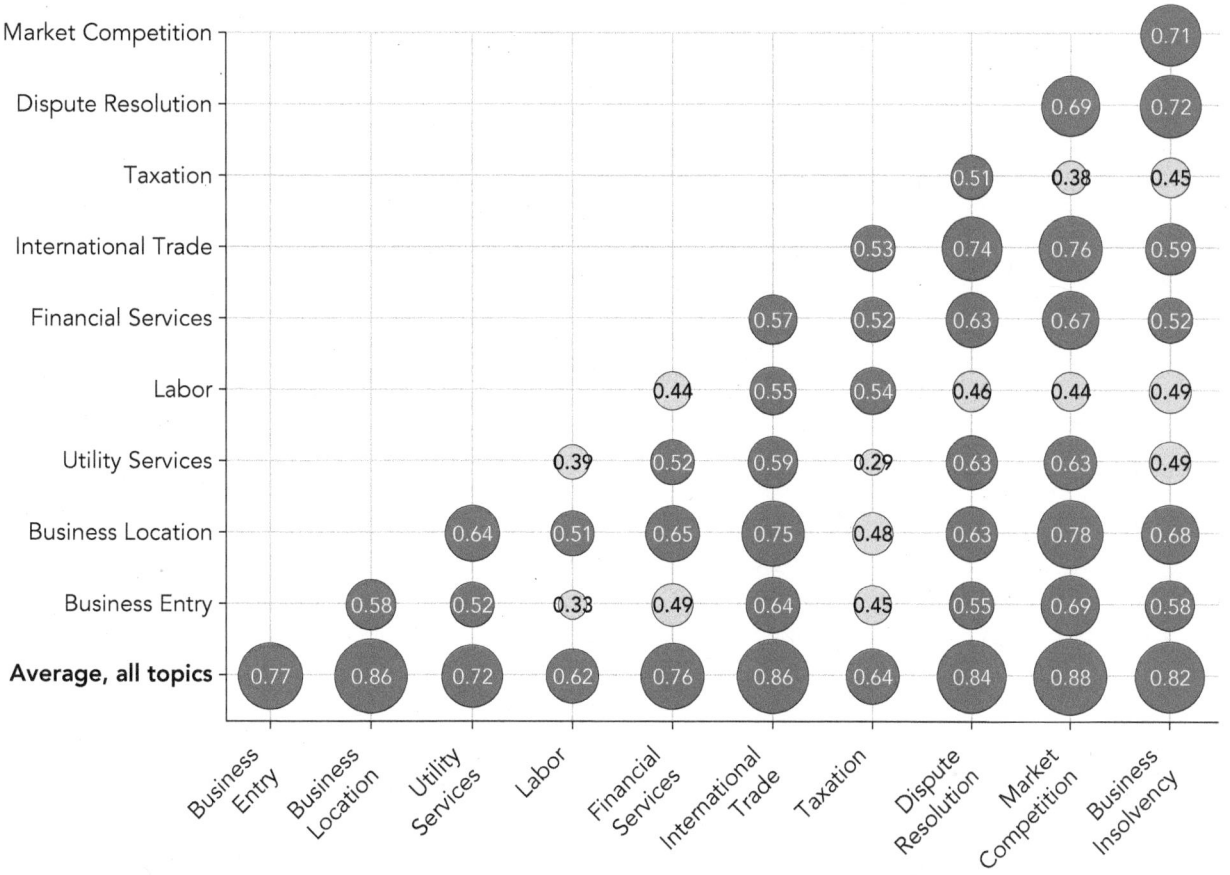

Correlation of topic pairs: ● Above 0.5 ○ Below 0.5

Source: B-READY 2024 data.
Note: The figure is based on the B-READY topic scores across the 50 sampled economies. The blue bubbles indicate a correlation of topic pairs above 0.5, while yellow bubbles indicate a correlation below 0.5. The size of the bubble indicates the relative size of the correlation. All correlations are positive and statistically significant at the 1 percent level.

Findings from the cross-cutting themes of digital adoption, environmental sustainability, and gender

B-READY collects data on three critical cross-cutting themes (digital adoption, environmental sustainability, and gender), which are embedded into topics' corresponding pillars, making them an integral part of topic scores (refer to chapter 4).

Data on digital adoption underscore the variance among economies in the uptake of digital public services, with some services (such as the availability of taxpayer online service portals) more widespread than others (such as electronic court auctions). This pattern suggests that economies still need to develop a wide range of digital services. The adoption of digital public services generally correlates positively with income levels. For instance, firms in high-income economies use e-payments far more frequently than those in low-income economies. However, there is significant variation among economies within the same income bracket, demonstrating that effective digitalization of public services is achievable at any income level.

In the area of environmental sustainability, much remains to be learned. One emerging trend is that many environmentally good practices are not widely implemented. While nearly all economies have adopted national environmental regulations for construction (47 of them require environmental impact assessments), incentives to promote green building standards are notably scarce, with only 10 economies implementing such measures. Sustainable water supply regulations are in place in about half the economies, reflecting a growing yet incomplete commitment to water conservation. These findings indicate an inconsistent progression toward environmental good practices and underscore the need for broader adoption of regulations and business incentives to achieve global sustainability goals.

Regarding gender, the findings indicate a need for improved sex-disaggregated data to effectively measure gender disparities. For example, many economies lack such data on land ownership, as well as on the representation of judges, mediators, and arbitrators by gender. Regarding gender-targeted programs for women entrepreneurs, about half of the surveyed economies offer specialized support, such as incubators and accelerators. However, only a minority have gender-sensitive regulations in procurement and trade. Significant progress is still required across various areas measured by B-READY to advance gender-sensitive policies that promote the inclusion of women-owned businesses.

Next steps for *Business Ready*

B-READY will continue consultations to further enhance the methodology. The B-READY 2024 report presents information about the first of three initial data collection and reporting cycles. The methodology will be subject to refinements as B-READY expands its economy coverage and moves from initial rollout to full-fledged project. As outlined in the B-READY Concept Note, the consultation process with the rest of the World Bank Group will continue to improve subsequent B-READY data and reports, enhancing their relevance for country engagement. Feedback received from stakeholders during dissemination activities will also be considered during this period. Any changes or updates to B-READY processes and methodology will be reported and published in updated versions of the *B-READY Manual and Guide* and the *B-READY Methodology Handbook*,

available on the B-READY website (https://www.worldbank.org/en
/businessready).

B-READY 2025 will entail several updates to enhance data collection
processes and improve the quality of the data. The updates to expert
questionnaires will reflect refinements to the methodology of the topics,
which will be included in the *B-READY Methodology Handbook*. The
updates to the data collection process will consist of more efficient and
streamlined expert recruitment and engagement procedures, which will
be included in the *B-READY Manual and Guide*. B-READY will continue to
have an open and transparent dialogue with governments, civil society, and
private sector organizations. It will provide governments with the possibility
to complete B-READY questionnaires that are used to validate data. It
will make economy profiles and other informational materials available
on the website for everyone to consult. And it will provide opportunities
for knowledge sharing through meetings, conferences, and public
presentations.

Notes

1. Refer to the World Bank mission statement, https://www.worldbank.org/en
   /who-we-are.
2. Loayza and Pennings (2022).
3. Artuc et al. (2020); SIDALC (Alliance of Agricultural Information Services),
   https://www.sidalc.net/search/Record/dig-okr-1098633289/Description.
4. USAID (2021).
5. World Development Indicators (WDI) 2024 (https://databank.worldbank.org
   /source/world-development-indicators). The figure was derived by dividing
   the five-year average of "Gross fixed capital formation, private sector (% of
   GDP)" by the five-year average of "Gross fixed capital formation (% of GDP)"
   for all economies and taking the average across all low- and middle-income
   economies. Five-year averages use the data available for 2018 to 2022.
6. IMF (2024). The figure was derived by averaging "General government total
   expenditure (as a % of GDP)" in 2022 across all low- and middle-income
   countries and subtracting from overall GDP.
7. UNECA (2020).
8. World Bank (2024a).
9. "The World Bank in Africa, Overview," https://www.worldbank.org/en/region
   /afr/overview.
10. World Bank (2022b).
11. World Bank (2024b).
12. UN Climate Change (2024).
13. B-READY Concept Note, Annex III b (World Bank 2022a) provides
    further information on the initially planned gradual expansion of
    the number of economies: https://thedocs.worldbank.org/en/doc
    /2250b12dfe798507f7b42064378cc616-0540012022/original/BEE-Concept

14. -Note-December-2022.pdf. The B-READY website also provides up-to-date information on the economies covered and planned to be covered: https://www.worldbank.org/en/businessready/covered-economies.
14. B-READY Concept Note, Annex III a, Main Expert Contributors per Topic (World Bank 2022a), https://thedocs.worldbank.org/en/doc /2250b12dfe798507f7b42064378cc616-0540012022/original/BEE-Concept -Note-December-2022.pdf.
15. For more information about the Enterprise Surveys, refer to https://www .enterprisesurveys.org/en/methodology (World Bank 2023c).
16. World Bank (2023a).
17. World Bank (2023b).
18. For more details about the three-year rollout, refer to chapter 1 and the B-READY website: https://www.worldbank.org/en/businessready.
19. Similarities between Market Competition and Business Location extend to the third quintile, where 6 economies are grouped in both topics (Bosnia and Herzegovina, El Salvador, Mexico, Montenegro, Paraguay, the Philippines) and another 4 economies appear in the fourth quintile (Cambodia, Pakistan, the Seychelles, Tanzania).
20. Similarities between International Trade and Market Competition extend to the third quintile, where 5 economies can be found in both topics (El Salvador, Indonesia, Mexico, Montenegro, Paraguay), and the fourth quintile, where 6 economies are present in both (Bangladesh, Barbados, Cambodia, Côte d'Ivoire, Madagascar, Tanzania).
21. Similarities between Dispute Resolution and Business Insolvency extend to the third quintile, where 4 economies jointly appear (Barbados, Côte d'Ivoire, Kyrgyz Republic, the Philippines), and to the fourth quintile, where 2 economies appear in both topics (Chad, The Gambia).
22. The correlation between Taxation and Utility Services is 0.27 (the lowest among all topic correlations). The correlation between Labor and Financial Services is 0.29 (the second-lowest among all topic correlations).

References

Artuc, E., R. Cull, S. Dasgupta, R. Fattal Jaef, D. Filmer, X. Gine, H. Jacoby, D. Jolliffe, H. Looi Kee, L. Klapper, A. C. Kraay, N. Loayza, D. McKenzie, B. Özler, V. Rao, B. Rijkers, S. Schmukler, M. Toman, A. Wagstaff, and M. Woolcock. 2020. "Toward Successful Development Policies: Insights from Research in Development Economics." Policy Research Working Paper 9133, World Bank, Washington, DC.

IMF (International Monetary Fund). 2024. *World Economic Outlook*, April 2024. *Steady but Slow: Resilience Amid Divergence*. Washington, DC: IMF.

Loayza, N., and S. Pennings. 2022. *The Long-Term Growth Model: Fundamentals, Extensions, and Applications*. Washington, DC: World Bank.

UN Climate Change. 2024. "From Vision to Reality: Getting the Job Done: Executive Secretary Speech." Speech by UN Climate Change Executive Secretary Simon Stiell at ADA University, Baku, Azerbaijan, February 2, 2024.

UNECA (United Nations Economic Commission on Africa). 2020. "The Private Sector in Africa." Chapter 2 in *Economic Report on Africa 2020: Innovative Finance for Private Sector Development in Africa*. Addis Ababa, Ethiopia: UNECA.

USAID (United States Agency for International Development). 2021. "Private Sector Engagement Policy." USAID, Washington, DC. https://www.usaid.gov/policy/private-sector-engagement.

World Bank. 2021. "Doing Business: External Panel Review: Final Report." World Bank, Washington, DC. https://www.worldbank.org/content/dam/doingBusiness/pdf/db-2021/Final-Report-EPR-Doing-Business.pdf.

World Bank. 2022a. "Concept Note: Business Enabling Environment." World Bank, Washington, DC. https://thedocs.worldbank.org/en/doc/2250b12dfe798507f7b42064378cc616-0540012022/original/BEE-Concept-Note-December-2022.pdf.

World Bank. 2022b. *Poverty and Shared Prosperity 2022: Correcting Course*. Washington, DC: World Bank.

World Bank. 2023a. *Business Ready (B-READY): Manual and Guide*. Washington, DC: World Bank. https://thedocs.worldbank.org/en/doc/5d79ca28ad482b1a9bc19b9c3a9c9e19-0540012023/original/B-READY-Manual-and-Guide.pdf.

World Bank. 2023b. *Business Ready: Methodology Handbook*. Washington, DC: World Bank. https://thedocs.worldbank.org/en/doc/357a611e3406288528cb1e05b3c7dfda-0540012023/original/B-READY-Methodology-Handbook.pdf.

World Bank. 2023c. *Enterprise Surveys: Manual and Guide*. Washington, DC: World Bank. https://www.worldbank.org/content/dam/enterprisesurveys/documents/methodology/Enterprise%20Surveys_Manual%20and%20Guide.pdf.

World Bank. 2024a. *Global Economic Prospects, January 2024*. Washington, DC: World Bank.

World Bank. 2024b. *World Development Report 2024: The Middle-Income Trap*. Washington, DC: World Bank.

ABBREVIATIONS

ADR	alternative dispute resolution
B-READY	*Business Ready*
CDD	customer due diligence
FDI	foreign direct investment
GDP	gross domestic product
OECD	Organisation for Economic Co-operation and Development
OHADA	Organization for the Harmonisation of Business Law in Africa
SAR	special administrative region
SMEs	small and medium enterprises
VAT	value added tax
WBL	*Women, Business and the Law*

INTRODUCTION

Around the world, the private sector is the engine of long-term economic growth and a vital catalyst for social and economic development. When functioning well, the private sector promotes innovation and entrepreneurship, improves access to and the quality of economic opportunities, and supports the sustainable use of natural resources (Artuc et al. 2020; Loayza and Pennings 2022). In developing economies, it generates about 90 percent of jobs (USAID 2021), 75 percent of investment (World Bank 2024),[1] more than 70 percent of output (IMF 2024),[2] and more than 80 percent of government revenue (UNECA 2020).

However, the private sector must become more dynamic and resilient to meet the formidable development challenge. In the coming decade alone, the world must create jobs for 44 million young people each year, with 30 percent of them in Africa.[3] To end extreme poverty within a decade, most low-income economies will need to achieve gross domestic product (GDP) per capita growth of about 9 percent each and every year (World Bank 2022b). To escape the "middle-income trap," developing economies will need to achieve GDP per capita growth of more than 5 percent a year over extended periods of time (World Bank 2024). To tackle climate change and achieve other key global development goals by 2030, they need to secure a hefty increase in investment—about US$2.4 trillion per year (UN Climate Change 2024).

Private sector development is, therefore, critical for achieving the goals of poverty alleviation, collective prosperity, and a sustainable ecosystem.

A reproducibility package is available for this book in the Reproducible Research Repository at https://reproducibility.worldbank.org/index.php/catalog/187.

The private sector is driven by the efforts and ingenuity of entrepreneurs and workers, but it is profoundly affected by public policies and regulations that, when working well, can create a conducive business environment. The private sector needs an enabling business environment to thrive, and governments can play a major positive role in creating it.

What is *Business Ready*?

Business Ready (B-READY) is a new data collection and analysis project of the World Bank Group to assess the business and investment climate worldwide, accompanied by an annual corporate flagship report. It is a key instrument of the World Bank Group's new strategy to facilitate private investment, generate employment, and improve productivity to help economies accelerate development in inclusive and sustainable ways. B-READY replaces and improves upon the World Bank Group's earlier *Doing Business* project. It reflects a more balanced and more transparent approach toward evaluating an economy's business and investment climate, building on recommendations from hundreds of experts inside and outside the World Bank Group, including governments, the private sector, and civil society organizations (refer to box 1.1).[4] The project aims to balance de jure and de facto measures, ensuring that the data produced are both comparable across economies and representative within each economy.

BOX 1.1

Comparison of the key features of *Doing Business* and B-READY

On September 16, 2021, the senior management of the World Bank Group decided to discontinue the *Doing Business* report and data collection. It also announced the development of a new approach for assessing the business and investment climate: the *Business Ready* (B-READY) project. This new project draws on advice from experts in the World Bank Group and recommendations from qualified academics and practitioners outside the institution, including the External Panel Review on *Doing Business* methodology (World Bank 2021), as well as feedback from an extensive consultation process with potential users in government, the private sector, and civil society.

While the focus of the *Doing Business* project was on assessing the business environment for small and medium enterprises, the B-READY project targets private sector development as a whole. *Doing Business* centered on the regulatory burden for firms, with some attention to public services. In contrast, B-READY evaluates the regulatory burden as well as the quality of regulations and provision of related public services, along with the ease of compliance with the regulatory framework and the effective use of public services directly relevant to firms. All topics examined by B-READY are structured under three pillars: (I) Regulatory Framework,

(Continued)

BOX 1.1

Comparison of the key features of *Doing Business* and B-READY *(Continued)*

(II) Public Services, and (III) Operational Efficiency. Furthermore, the new project assesses not only the ability to conduct business for individual firms (firm flexibility), but also the inclusive and sustainable aspects of private sector development (social benefits). To gather data, B-READY uses 21 questionnaires, compared with 11 questionnaires used by *Doing Business*. In its first year, it collected data on almost 1,200 indicators (from about 2,000 data points) per economy. It also covers all major topics related to a firm's life cycle, whereas *Doing Business* sometimes omitted critical areas such as labor.

Doing Business collected data through expert consultations and extensive case studies with strict assumptions, covering either de jure or de facto regulations, but not both uniformly. In contrast, B-READY combines expert consultations and firm surveys to capture a balanced view of de jure and de facto aspects. This allows B-READY to achieve a better balance between data comparability across economies.

Doing Business assessed economies' performance based on rankings and scores, focusing on aggregate rankings to drive public interest and motivate reforms. B-READY uses quantifiable disaggregated indicators, aggregating points into scores by topic and pillar. This approach identifies specific areas for reform and encourages reforms without overhyping economywide rankings.

While *Doing Business* covered the main business city in 191 economies and the second-largest business city in 11 economies, B-READY aims for wide coverage within and across economies, with coverage for different topics based on whether regulations are national or local.

Like *Doing Business*, B-READY updates data each year for indicators based on expert consultations. For data derived from firm-level surveys, it updates data for different sets of economies each year, resulting in stable data for each economy over a three-year cycle.

B-READY assessments aim to improve the private sector, not only by advancing the interests of individual firms but also by elevating the interests of workers, consumers, potential new enterprises, and the natural environment. B-READY aims to achieve this objective by focusing on three main areas:

- *Reform advocacy*. B-READY advocates for policy reform through the effective communication of international benchmarking, opening the door for knowledge sharing and policy dialogue for governments, the private sector, the World Bank Group, and other development institutions.

- *Policy guidance.* B-READY guides specific policy change through comprehensive and relevant data and information, showing how and by how much each economy lags international good practice.

- *Analysis and research.* B-READY provides granular data for research and analysis, shedding light on the drivers and mechanisms of private sector development.

This strategy is illustrated in figure 1.1.

FIGURE 1.1 **B-READY's comprehensive approach to private sector development**

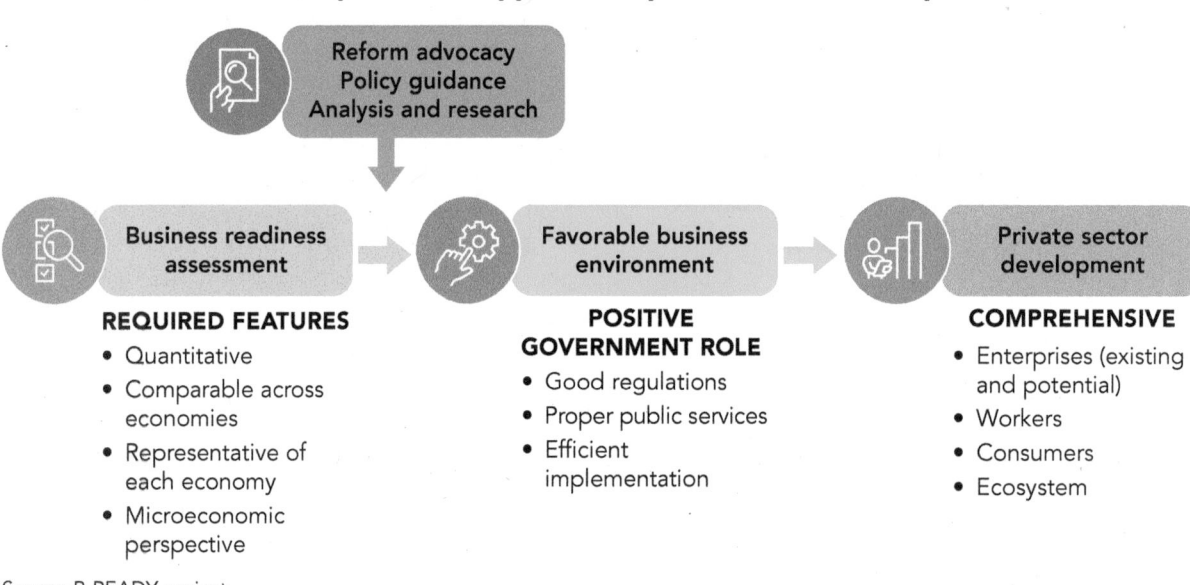

Source: B-READY project.

As a new project, B-READY is in a three-year rollout phase, spanning 2024 to 2026. During this period, the project will grow in geographic coverage and refine its process and methodology. This 2024 report is the first of three during the rollout. It covers 50 economies that represent all income levels and geographic regions around the world. Due to the limited number of economies included in this first report, the regional and income trends are suggestive, not definitive. Likewise, the methodology remains open to refinement and may evolve through subsequent studies. The second report, expected to be released in September 2025, will cover more than 100 economies. The third report, expected to be released in September 2026, will assess about 180 economies, bringing the rollout phase to conclusion and providing a full global benchmark for future business readiness assessments. There is no straightforward advantage or disadvantage to an economy being in one round versus another. In fact, there are pros and cons to participating either earlier or later in the project.

Earlier participation will bring data faster for potential attention and action, whereas later participation will bring a more refined methodology and broader economy coverage for enhanced benchmarking.[5]

Topics and pillars

B-READY is organized according to topics that correspond to various stages of the life cycle of a firm and its participation in the market while opening, operating (or expanding), and closing (or reorganizing) a business. The topics have been selected based on their relevance to private sector development, value added to fill an existing data gap, and complementarity between topics to inform comprehensive reforms. B-READY provides a comprehensive assessment for each of 10 topics: Business Entry, Business Location, Utility Services, Labor, Financial Services, International Trade, Taxation, Dispute Resolution, Market Competition, and Business Insolvency.

Across the 10 topics, the assessment includes data on three cross-cutting themes increasingly important in modern economies: digital adoption, environmental sustainability, and gender. B-READY looks at digital adoption, either by governments or businesses, anchored in specific areas of the business environment. For environmental sustainability, B-READY assesses relevant indicators that reflect environmental regulatory provisions affecting business operations. For gender, the report focuses on the collection and availability of anonymized data disaggregated by sex, as well as measuring the implementation and targeting of programs and gender-sensitive regulations affecting businesses in economies around the world. The 10 topics and cross-cutting themes are illustrated in figure 1.2.

FIGURE 1.2 B-READY topics correspond to various stages of the life cycle of a firm and examine three cross-cutting themes

Source: B-READY project.

Note: Although Business Entry and Business Insolvency are the clear beginning and end stages of a firm's life cycle, the remaining eight topics can occur in varying sequences during a firm's operating and expanding stages. The topics are interconnected. This figure is not intended to represent a linear progression in a firm's life cycle or to suggest strictly that these ought to be the exact phases, but to give an overall assessment of the business environment of the typical stages of the life cycle of a firm.

For each of the 10 topics, B-READY considers three pillars (refer to figure 1.3):

- *Pillar I, Regulatory Framework,* covers the rules and regulations that firms must follow as they open, operate (or expand), and close (or reorganize) a business.

- *Pillar II, Public Services,* spans the facilities that governments provide to support compliance with regulations and the institutions and infrastructure that enable business activities.

- *Pillar III, Operational Efficiency,* captures the ease of compliance with the regulatory framework and the effective use of public services directly relevant to firms.

By enacting high-quality regulations and providing essential public services, governments can play a positive role, enhancing firms' operational efficiency and profitability, while contributing to broader economic development and social well-being.

FIGURE 1.3 B-READY pillars define the scope of the project

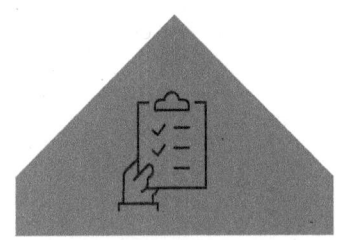  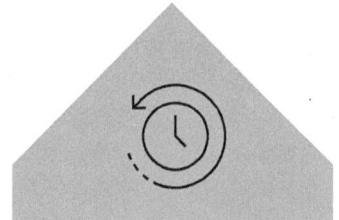

Pillar I	Pillar II	Pillar III
Regulatory Framework	**Public Services**	**Operational Efficiency**
Rules and regulations that firms must follow as they open, operate, and close a business	Facilities to support regulatory compliance and institutions and infrastructure to enable business activities	Ease of regulatory compliance and effective use of public services directly relevant to firms

Source: B-READY project.

B-READY's structure—by topics and pillars related to the life cycle of the firm—reflects its scope as well as its limitations. The business environment is the set of conditions beyond a firm's control that have a significant influence on how businesses behave and perform throughout their life cycle. This set of conditions can be quite broad, ranging from macroeconomic policy to microeconomic rules. To differentiate the B-READY benchmarking exercise from other well-established international measures, B-READY concentrates on the regulatory framework and public service provision at the microeconomic level—that is, as enacted and implemented to directly affect the behavior and performance of active and potential enterprises.

Across all topics and pillars, B-READY analyzes more than 1,200 indicators (refer to box 1.2). The selection of topic indicators relies on the same criteria as the topics themselves: relevance, value added, and complementarity. B-READY indicators have five characteristics:

- They focus on issues in which there is an established good practice.

- They are quantifiable and point to areas that are actionable—that is, they are subject to change through policy reform.

- They seek to provide a balance between de jure and de facto measures within each topic.

- They produce data that balance comparability across economies and representativeness within each economy.

- They are based on primary data collected specifically for the B-READY project, spanning the most relevant aspects of each topic.

BOX 1.2
Scoring

For each economy, B-READY produces two sets of scores: one consisting of 10 topic scores and another comprising 3 pillar scores. Topic and pillar scores can range from a minimum of 0 to a maximum of 100.

For topic scores, every score is generated by averaging the scores assigned to each of the three pillars (Regulatory Framework, Public Services, Operational Efficiency) for that topic. Within these pillars, common features inform the grouping into a particular *category*. Each category contains a number of *subcategories*. In turn, each subcategory contains a number of *indicators*.

Points are allocated to each indicator according to its contribution to firm flexibility (that is, ease of business from a firm's perspective) and/or social benefits (that is, the impact to the broader private sector). Indicator points are then compiled to determine the total points for the subcategory, category, and ultimately, the pillar. Categories and subcategories are weighted to reflect their significance and relevance to that pillar. Each pillar score in a topic is standardized to potentially range from 0 to 100.

For pillar scores, each score is generated by averaging the scores assigned to that pillar (Regulatory Framework, Public Services, Operational Efficiency) across 10 topics. For more details, refer to the *B-READY Methodology Handbook* (World Bank 2023b).

For the Regulatory Framework pillar, indicators distinguish between rules and regulations that promote clarity, fairness, and the sustainability of the business environment and those that unnecessarily inhibit entrepreneurial activity.

For the Public Services pillar, the indicators emphasize digitalization, interoperability, transparency, and adequacy of services directed at easing regulatory compliance and enabling business activities. Indicators in this pillar measure the availability of online public services, without precluding other means of providing public services. The availability of electronic services is a key factor in enhancing accessibility and efficiency. Indicators are limited to the scope of the business environment in areas related to the life cycle of a firm.

For the Operational Efficiency pillar, the indicators across topics assess firms' experience in practice with respect to the business environment. They encompass both the ease of compliance with the regulatory framework and the effective use of public services directly relevant to firms.

By emphasizing good regulatory practices, and the importance of public service provision, B-READY indicators propose an active but strategic role for governments to improve the business environment. This role lies primarily in adopting effective rules and regulations that adhere to internationally recognized good practices, as well as enabling institutions for the private sector that stimulate business activity, reduce uncertainty and risks, reinforce the rule of law, and promote responsible business conduct.

B-READY does not cover other aspects of the business environment that are well covered by other indicators, including macroeconomic conditions (such as the World Bank's Global Economic Prospects), government corruption and accountability (such as the World Bank's Worldwide Governance Indicators), human capital (such as the World Bank's Human Capital Index), or conflict, crime, and violence (such as statistics from the United Nations Office on Drugs and Crime). Although B-READY does not measure informality or collect data directly from informal firms, including the self-employed and household businesses,[6] it helps address informality by assessing the issues that incentivize firms to formalize or prevent firms from formalizing, as well as issues that affect the workers to be employed by expanding formal firms.

Data collection and governance

B-READY combines primary data collected from thousands of specialists—each an expert in the private sector of a specific economy—with data collected directly from businesses operating in that economy. To accomplish this, B-READY uses expert questionnaires tailored to the B-READY project and World Bank Enterprise Surveys featuring questions designed to feed into the B-READY assessment (refer to figure 1.4).[7]

Through expert questionnaires, the project obtains detailed information from specialists in each topic for indicators in the Regulatory Framework and Public Services pillars. The questionnaires are administered to three to five experts per questionnaire and economy. Topic specialists include accountants, architects, customs brokers, freight forwarders, engineers, lawyers, and notaries, among other relevant experts in a particular economy.[8] All private sector experts contributing to these questionnaires undergo a rigorous selection process. That process includes initial identification of the relevant private sector experts by B-READY topic teams, distribution of screening questionnaires to the identified experts to determine their level of expertise, and final selection of three to five qualified expert contributors per questionnaire and economy.

Using the World Bank Enterprise Surveys, the project gathers data directly from businesses for indicators in the Operational Efficiency pillar. The respondents to these surveys are business owners and top managers of formal (registered) firms with at least 1 percent private ownership and with five or more employees in the nonextractive and nonagricultural private sector. The firms are selected through stratified random sampling to ensure representativeness of businesses across each economy.[9] The project also uses expert questionnaires to collect data on Operational Efficiency indicators not routinely faced by firms themselves in topics such as Business Entry and Business Insolvency because ad hoc surveys would be prohibitively expensive.

The complementary use of expert questionnaires and firm-level surveys is an important innovation that capitalizes on the synergies between the two data collection modes and represents a significant increase in the data available to policy makers, development practitioners, and researchers. For each economy, expert questionnaire data will be updated every year, while Enterprise Surveys data will be updated every three years (refer to figure 1.4). The World Bank Enterprise Surveys program has been expanded from 15 to about 60 surveys per year to accommodate the data collection effort. Box 1.3 provides information about data validation and quality assurance.

FIGURE 1.4 **B-READY relies on data obtained directly from experts and enterprises**

Expert questionnaires	World Bank Enterprise Surveys
• Data from experts, all in the private sector except for credit registries, who regularly deal with business regulations and related public services and institutions. • Provide de jure information (Pillar I) and de facto information (Pillars II–III). • Data collection through 21 questionnaires, filled in by three to five experts per questionnaire and economy. • Updated annually for each economy.	• Data from the owners or managers of a representative sample of registered firms. • Provide de facto information (Pillar III). • Data collection embedded in the World Bank Enterprise Surveys program (expanded from 15 to about 60 surveys per year). • Updated every three years for each economy.

Source: B-READY project.

BOX 1.3

Data validation and quality assurance

Data collected through both expert consultations and Enterprise Surveys are subject to rigorous validation and quality assurance processes. When discrepancies arise in questionnaire responses in data collected through expert consultations—such as divergence in private sector responses, divergence between private sector responses and government inputs, or misalignment in the unit of measurement for numerical variables—questionnaires are returned to relevant experts through the survey software, providing them an opportunity to review and change the response if needed.

The Enterprise Surveys also follow a robust quality control process, which includes several aspects to monitor the order for contacting firms, weekly progress reports, and data quality checks (refer to *Enterprise Surveys: Manual and Guide* [World Bank 2023c]).

Following data validation and quality assurance processes, the individual data are aggregated to economy-level variables, applying standard aggregation methods of taking the median, mean, or mode, depending on the question type (refer to the *B-READY Methodology Handbook* [World Bank 2023b]). This step is critical for transforming individual expert and firm insights into a coherent, economywide perspective.

B-READY attempts to achieve a balance between data comparability across economies and data representativeness within each economy. Expert questionnaires address this balance by using broad parameters instead of narrow case studies to measure the business environment that most firms face, while retaining comparability across economies. Firm-level surveys address the balance by using representative samples of registered firms, allowing for comparison of the average or typical experience of actual firms. B-READY, therefore, covers information relevant to firms of different sizes and locations, various economic sectors, and foreign and domestic ownership.

B-READY is designed for benchmarking across economies and over time. This requires the application of a homogeneous methodology across economies in different geographic locations and at different income levels. It also requires quantifying the business environment conditions into comparable scores. The chapters that follow provide more insights into the B-READY data, pillar scores, and topic scores, and how they relate to development.

B-READY is governed by the highest data integrity standards, including sound data-gathering processes, robust data safeguards, and clear approval protocols. Two B-READY foundational documents are publicly available on its website: the *B-READY Manual and Guide*, specifying the protocols and safeguards to ensure the integrity of the assessments (World Bank 2023a), and the *B-READY Methodology Handbook*, detailing the project's topics, indicators, and scoring approach (World Bank 2023b). The documents will be updated and improved as the three-year rollout of the project progresses (refer to figure 1.5).

Transparency and replicability are the cornerstones of B-READY governance. All the granular data used for scoring are made publicly available on the B-READY website (https://www.worldbank.org/en /businessready), and all results presented in B-READY reports are replicable using straightforward toolkits made available on the same website.

FIGURE 1.5 B-READY will roll out over a three-year period

B-READY 1 2024	B-READY 2 2025	B-READY 3 2026
50 economies with new (2024) data from expert questionnaires	**112 economies** with new (2025) data from expert questionnaires	**184 economies** with new (2026) data from expert questionnaires
50 economies with new (2024) data from Enterprise Surveys	**62 economies** with new (2025) data from Enterprise Surveys	**72 economies** with new (2026) data from Enterprise Surveys
	50 economies with Enterprise Surveys data from B-READY 1 (2024)	**62 economies** with Enterprise Surveys data from B-READY 2 (2025)
		50 economies with Enterprise Surveys data from B-READY 1 (2024)

Source: B-READY project.

Organization of the report

The B-READY 2024 report is organized as follows. Chapter 2 presents a summary of the B-READY data based on the economies' performance across the three pillars and 10 topics. The chapter describes how economies can improve, while exploring differences and similarities between income levels. Chapter 3 presents the results by pillar across economies, pulling together information across topics and examining how pillar scores compare with one another. Chapter 4 explores each of the 10 topics, discussing their motivation and methodology, presenting their specific scores, and comparing them with one another. Chapter 5 briefly describes lessons learned and what is next for the project. Appendix A provides scores for each of the 10 B-READY topics, both overall and by pillar. Appendix B presents economies' characteristics and auxiliary data, including population and GDP per capita. The project website (https://www.worldbank.org/en/businessready) includes economy-specific profiles, along with a range of data visualizations.

Notes

1. The figure was derived by dividing the five-year average of the gross fixed capital formation of the private sector (percentage of GDP) by the five-year average of the gross fixed capital formation for all economies (percentage of GDP) and taking the average across all low- and middle-income economies. Five-year averages use the data available for 2018–22.
2. The figure was derived by averaging the general government total expenditure (as a percentage of GDP) in 2022 across all low- and middle-income countries and subtracting from overall GDP.
3. "The World Bank in Africa, Overview," https://www.worldbank.org/en/region/afr/overview.
4. The B-READY Concept Note (box I.2 and annex IC) explains in detail the difference between *Doing Business* and B-READY (World Bank 2022a).
5. Refer to the B-READY Concept Note (annex IIIB), which provides further information on the initially planned gradual expansion of the number of economies (World Bank 2022a). The B-READY website also provides up-to-date information on the economies covered and those that tentatively will be covered (https://www.worldbank.org/en/businessready/covered-economies).
6. Informal businesses are assessed in several cities around the world by the Enterprise Analysis Unit by means of the Informal Sector Enterprise Surveys (https://www.enterprisesurveys.org/en/informal-businesses). The survey on informal businesses has not yet been expanded to a global scale.
7. World Bank Enterprise Surveys (database), https://www.enterprisesurveys.org/en/enterprisesurveys.
8. Refer to the B-READY Concept Note, annex IIIA, Main Expert Contributors per Topic (World Bank 2022a).

9. For more information about the Enterprise Surveys, refer to https://www
   .enterprisesurveys.org/en/methodology. The surveys are stratified by sector
   of activity, firm size, and geographic location. Stratification by firm size divides
   the population of firms into three strata: small firms (5–19 employees); medium
   firms (20–99 employees); and large firms (100 or more employees). In very large
   economies, a fourth size stratum is added: the top 1 percent of firms by size.
   Geographic stratification reflects the distribution of nonagricultural economic
   activity, usually covering main urban centers where most economic activity
   is concentrated. Stratification by sector of activity depends on the size of the
   economy as measured by the gross national income. Very small economies are
   divided into manufacturing and services. Small economies add retail. Medium
   economies further differentiate manufacturing. Large economies include more
   detailed subsectors while preserving residual categories. In addition, the
   B-READY report acknowledges that survivorship bias is one of the caveats for the
   interpretation of results obtained from firm-level surveys. However, the data from
   firm-level surveys are used to measure the efficiency of the provision of services,
   provided that the services were used. The data are not meant to quantify these
   services for hypothetical firms (counterfactuals) should the business environment
   be different. The information provided by existing firms contains valuable
   information on the business environment they actually face, including the
   obstacles they must overcome.

References

Artuc, E., R. Cull, S. Dasgupta, R. N. Fattal Jaef, D. P. Filmer, X. Gine, H. G. Jacoby, D. M. Jolliffe, H. L. Kee, L. Klapper, A. C. Kraay, N. V. Loayza, D. J. McKenzie, B. Ozler, V. Rao, B. Rijkers, S. L. Schmukler, M. A. Toman, A. Wagstaff, and M. Woolcock. 2020. "Toward Successful Development Policies: Insights from Research in Development Economics." Policy Research Working Paper 9133, World Bank, Washington, DC.

IMF (International Monetary Fund). 2024. *World Economic Outlook, April 2024. Steady but Slow: Resilience Amid Divergence.* Washington, DC: IMF.

Loayza, N., and S. Pennings. 2022. *The Long Term Growth Model: Fundamentals, Extensions, and Applications.* Washington, DC: World Bank.

UN Climate Change. 2024. "From Vision to Reality: Getting the Job Done: Executive Secretary Speech." Speech by UN Climate Change Executive Secretary Simon Stiell at ADA University, Baku, Azerbaijan, February 2, 2024.

UNECA (United Nations Economic Commission for Africa). 2020. "The Private Sector in Africa." Chapter 2 in *Economic Report on Africa 2020: Innovative Finance for Private Sector Development in Africa.* Addis Ababa: UNECA.

USAID (US Agency for International Development). 2021. "Private Sector Engagement Policy." USAID, Washington, DC. https://www.usaid.gov/policy /private-sector-engagement.

World Bank. 2021. "Doing Business: External Panel Review: Final Report." World Bank, Washington, DC. https://www.worldbank.org/content/dam /doingBusiness/pdf/db-2021/Final-Report-EPR-Doing-Business.pdf.

World Bank. 2022a. "Concept Note: Business Enabling Environment." World Bank, Washington, DC. https://thedocs.worldbank.org/en/doc/2250b12 dfe798507f7b42064378cc616-0540012022/original/BEE-Concept-Note -December-2022.pdf.

World Bank. 2022b. *Poverty and Shared Prosperity 2022: Correcting Course.* Washington, DC: World Bank.

World Bank. 2023a. *Business Ready (B-READY): Manual and Guide.* Washington, DC: World Bank. https://thedocs.worldbank.org/en/doc/5d79ca28ad482b1a9bc 19b9c3a9c9e19-0540012023/original/B-READY-Manual-and-Guide.pdf.

World Bank. 2023b. *Business Ready: Methodology Handbook.* Washington, DC: World Bank. https://thedocs.worldbank.org/en/doc/357a611e3406288528cb 1e05b3c7dfda-0540012023/original/B-READY-Methodology-Handbook.pdf.

World Bank. 2023c. *Enterprise Surveys: Manual and Guide.* Washington, DC: World Bank. https://www.worldbank.org/content/dam/enterprisesurveys /documents/methodology/Enterprise%20Surveys_Manual%20and%20 Guide.pdf.

World Bank. 2024. *World Development Report 2024: The Middle-Income Trap.* Washington, DC: World Bank.

B-READY 2024 DATA AND SUMMARY RESULTS

Introduction

B-READY granular data provide a wealth of information that can be used to guide specific policy reform. These data are presented in the main body of the report, and in more detail on the B-READY website (https://www.worldbank.org/en/businessready) through different accessible facilities and tools, including economy profiles.

To facilitate international benchmarking, the granular data are used to obtain topic-specific pillar scores, topic scores, and overall pillar scores. A *topic-specific pillar score* is built from the points assigned to sets of indicators, organized in categories by subject matter. Each score can range from 0 to 100 (where 100 represents the best possible performance). Within each topic, there are three topic-specific pillars: Regulatory Framework, Public Services, and Operational Efficiency. The average of the three topic-specific pillar scores, in turn, equals the *topic score*. Each *overall pillar score* is the average of the corresponding topic-specific pillar scores across the 10 B-READY topics.

Performance by pillar

B-READY divides economies into five equal groupings (quintiles), from highest to lowest performers, based on their scores within each pillar, and presents data by quintile. This approach enhances the understanding

A reproducibility package is available for this book in the Reproducible Research Repository at https://reproducibility.worldbank.org/index.php/catalog/187.

of the distribution of the data, facilitates the identification of patterns and trends, and improves the ease of communication. It allows readers to observe absolute performance (pillar score) and relative performance (quintile groups). It also can help policy makers readily identify the areas for improvement in their economy in terms of regulations, public services, and operational efficiency. The B-READY data by quintile for the 50 economies featured in the 2024 report are summarized in table 2.1.

TABLE 2.1 B-READY 2024 performance, by pillar

Pillar I Regulatory Framework		Pillar II Public Services		Pillar III Operational Efficiency	
Hungary	78.23	Estonia	73.31	Singapore	87.33
Portugal	78.11	Singapore	70.40	Georgia	84.75
Georgia	77.67	Croatia	70.24	Rwanda	81.31
Slovak Republic	77.29	Portugal	69.53	Estonia	80.28
Colombia	76.50	Hungary	69.50	Hong Kong SAR, China	78.52
Bulgaria	76.33	New Zealand	68.91	New Zealand	76.39
Romania	76.19	Slovak Republic	68.17	North Macedonia	75.81
Greece	75.60	Rwanda	67.37	Bulgaria	74.82
Mexico	75.07	Colombia	66.28	Kyrgyz Republic	74.71
Croatia	73.48	Greece	64.51	Viet Nam	72.78
Estonia	72.84	Bulgaria	64.03	Nepal	72.21
Montenegro	72.48	Costa Rica	63.58	Slovak Republic	71.14
Hong Kong SAR, China	72.40	Indonesia	63.44	Montenegro	71.03
Singapore	72.37	Georgia	63.33	Hungary	70.68
Costa Rica	71.41	Romania	63.19	Portugal	70.53
Philippines	70.68	Hong Kong SAR, China	62.64	Bangladesh	70.49
Rwanda	70.35	Peru	59.76	Bosnia and Herzegovina	70.05
North Macedonia	69.95	Morocco	58.66	Mauritius	69.79
Peru	69.51	Mexico	57.25	Samoa	68.32
Togo	69.03	Mauritius	56.28	Croatia	68.31
Morocco	68.92	North Macedonia	53.56	Botswana	67.73
Côte d'Ivoire	68.16	Viet Nam	53.41	Barbados	66.55
Bosnia and Herzegovina	67.45	Tanzania	51.56	Colombia	66.38
New Zealand	67.45	Philippines	50.80	Lesotho	66.06
Ghana	66.91	Paraguay	50.68	Pakistan	65.90
Viet Nam	66.81	Togo	49.58	Romania	65.74
Botswana	66.01	Nepal	49.29	Togo	64.36
Kyrgyz Republic	65.22	Montenegro	48.92	Seychelles	63.57
Tanzania	65.00	Botswana	48.52	Tanzania	62.15
Mauritius	64.55	Ghana	47.67	Mexico	61.73

Quintile: ■ Top ■ Second ■ Third ▪ Fourth   Bottom

(Continued)

TABLE 2.1 **B-READY 2024 performance, by pillar** *(Continued)*

Pillar I Regulatory Framework		Pillar II Public Services		Pillar III Operational Efficiency	
Indonesia	63.98	Barbados	46.40	Indonesia	61.31
Cambodia	62.94	El Salvador	45.36	Cambodia	60.66
Chad	61.22	Pakistan	44.97	Paraguay	60.60
Central African Republic	61.11	Bangladesh	41.64	Morocco	59.66
Paraguay	60.90	Kyrgyz Republic	41.23	Greece	58.98
El Salvador	60.38	Côte d'Ivoire	40.34	Philippines	57.95
Nepal	59.34	Samoa	40.04	Peru	56.20
Pakistan	59.10	Cambodia	39.14	El Salvador	54.53
Seychelles	58.85	Lesotho	37.89	Ghana	54.42
Barbados	58.81	Bosnia and Herzegovina	37.81	Costa Rica	53.66
Madagascar	57.38	Seychelles	37.21	West Bank and Gaza	52.75
Samoa	57.13	Vanuatu	32.06	Sierra Leone	52.51
Bangladesh	56.99	Madagascar	31.64	Madagascar	52.29
Lesotho	54.94	Sierra Leone	30.73	Côte d'Ivoire	50.31
Sierra Leone	54.09	West Bank and Gaza	28.42	Gambia, The	48.44
Gambia, The	53.37	Timor-Leste	23.80	Chad	48.05
Vanuatu	50.44	Chad	23.51	Iraq	46.79
Iraq	49.39	Iraq	21.45	Timor-Leste	44.83
West Bank and Gaza	47.54	Gambia, The	20.11	Vanuatu	43.94
Timor-Leste	46.21	Central African Republic	18.35	Central African Republic	40.36

Quintile: ■ Top ■ Second ■ Third ▨ Fourth   Bottom

Source: B-READY 2024 data.
Note: The economies are ordered according to their scores in each of the three pillars: Pillar I, Regulatory Framework; Pillar II, Public Services; and Pillar III, Operational Efficiency. They are further grouped into quintiles, which are marked with varying shades of blue (with darker shades representing better performance).

Top quintile. Economies in the top quintile (indicated by the darkest shade of blue in table 2.1) demonstrate the highest performance in each pillar, ranging from the 80th percentile to the maximum value. This top quintile represents the leading 20 percent of economies, showcasing effective implementation of good practices in all three pillars.

In the Regulatory Framework pillar within this top quintile, Hungary ranks highest with a score of 78.23 points, while Croatia has the lowest score of 73.48 points. The average score in this pillar is 76.45 points. This pillar has the narrowest range among all pillars (4.75 points). This narrow range shows that economies within this quintile maintain similar high standards, demonstrating a widespread adoption of internationally recognized good practices in the Regulatory Framework pillar.

In the Public Services pillar, Estonia emerges as the top performer with a score of 73.31 points, while Greece holds the lowest score of 64.51 points within the top quintile. This pillar has the lowest average score across all pillars (68.82 points), with a range of 8.80. The moderate range indicates some variability in the quality of public services, though most economies still offer superior support for businesses through enhanced transparency, digitalization, and interoperability of government services. For example, top-performing economies in this pillar are recognized for their user-friendly online platforms, which simplify business interactions with government agencies, reduce bureaucracy, and improve overall service delivery. This digitalization not only facilitates smoother operations but also builds trust between businesses and government, fostering a more conducive business environment for economic growth. However, the fact that this pillar has the lowest average score among all pillars suggests that there is still room for improvement in delivering high-quality public services.

In the Operational Efficiency pillar, Singapore stands out as the top performer with a score of 87.33 points, while Viet Nam has the lowest score of 72.78 points within the top quintile. The average score in this pillar is 78.67 points, the highest among the pillars. However, scores also have the most significant variation among all pillars, with a range of 14.55 points. This relatively wide range indicates uneven performance levels among top-performing economies.

Overall, economies in the top quintile perform well across multiple pillars, often ranking highly across various topics. For instance, Estonia scores in the top quintile of economies in 7 of the 10 topics and Rwanda is present in the first quintile in 6 of the 10 topics. This strong performance across pillars showcases the broad strengths of these economies, though it also reveals specific areas where further improvements could enhance their overall competitiveness.

Second quintile. Economies in the second quintile represent the next 20 percent of the data, from the 60th to the 80th percentile. These economies are characterized by having adopted many de jure international good practices and high levels of de facto public services and operational efficiency as experienced by firms. They have above-average scores across most topics, but also show potential for improvements. Within this quintile, the Regulatory Framework pillar has the highest average score of 71.10 among the three pillars, coupled with the narrowest range (3.81 points), indicating a relatively consistent performance across these economies and adherence to regulatory good practices. Estonia leads this pillar within the second quintile, achieving a score of 72.84 points, while Togo has the lowest score of 69.03 points. Despite being in the second quintile for the Regulatory Framework pillar, Estonia demonstrates its overall strength by ranking in the top quintile for both the Public Services and Operational Efficiency pillars. This positioning reflects Estonia's ability to translate its regulatory framework into efficient public services and a business environment where firms experience the ease of compliance with the regulations and the effective use of public services. This contrast between Estonia's placement in the second quintile for the Regulatory Framework and its top-quintile achievements in other pillars suggests that while the regulatory framework is robust, there may still be room for refinement to fully match the efficiency and service quality seen in its other strengths. By continuing to fine-tune its regulatory environment, Estonia has the potential to further elevate its overall economic performance, ensuring that all aspects of its business environment are aligned at the highest level.

In the Public Services pillar, within the second quintile, Bulgaria achieves the highest score of 64.03 points while Mauritius scores the lowest at 56.28 points. Similar to Estonia, Bulgaria, despite being in the second quintile for Public Services, excels in the top quintile for both the Regulatory Framework and Operational Efficiency pillars. This suggests that while Bulgaria maintains a strong regulatory framework that enhances the operational efficiency for businesses, there remains a need for improvement in its public services to achieve exceptional overall business environment performance. It is also notable that the Public Services pillar has the lowest average score (61.22 points) with the widest range (7.75 points) among the three pillars. This broader range highlights disparities in the quality of public services among economies in this quintile that could be addressed to further elevate these economies.

The Operational Efficiency pillar shows a relatively higher average score of 70.26 points compared to the Public Services pillar in the second quintile, with a narrower range of 3.90 points. While most economies in this quintile demonstrate strong operational efficiency, slight disparities suggest that targeted reforms could enhance efficiency further. Nepal leads this pillar with a score of 72.21 points, and Croatia scores the lowest at 68.31 points. While Nepal excels in the Operational Efficiency pillar, its scores are lower in the other pillars. This pattern may be explained by the adaptability of existing firms to the poor regulatory environment and deficient public services. The disparities in Nepal's performance across different pillars underscores the need for substantial reforms even if the country performs relatively well in the Operational Efficiency pillar. Addressing these gaps could enhance overall business conditions and support more sustainable economic growth.

Third quintile. This quintile covers the middle 20 percent of economies, ranging from the 40th to the 60th percentile. These economies exhibit a mix of strengths and weaknesses in their business environment. In the Regulatory Framework pillar, the average score of the third quintile is 66.65 points, with Morocco achieving the highest score of 68.92 points, and Mauritius the lowest at 64.55 points within the third quintile. The Operational Efficiency pillar follows closely, with an average score of 65.02 points, led by Botswana at 67.73 points, while Mexico has the lowest score of 61.73. The Public Services pillar has the lowest average score among the three, at 50.40 points, with North Macedonia scoring the highest at 53.56 points and Ghana the lowest at 47.67 points.

In the third quintile, the range between the highest and lowest scores across all pillars is relatively similar, indicating a consistent level of performance within each pillar among these economies. While these economies may have established good laws and regulations, deficiencies in public services and a lack of transparency of information may be hindering them from developing a stronger private sector. To improve their overall business environment, these economies should continue reform efforts in topics where they perform well. At the same time, they should address weakness in the topics and pillars where they currently underperform.

Fourth quintile. Economies in the fourth quintile include the penultimate 20 percent of the data, from the 20th percentile up to the 40th percentile. These economies grapple with a challenging business environment characterized by relatively weak regulatory frameworks and public services, which constrains the operational efficiency of their businesses.

Among the pillars in the fourth quintile, the Public Services pillar stands out with the lowest average score (41.48 points), reflecting the relatively low level of support available to businesses. In this pillar, Barbados achieves the highest score of 46.40, while Bosnia and Herzegovina scores lowest at 37.81 points. The Operational Efficiency pillar comes next, with an average of 57.80 points. Here, Indonesia leads with a score of 61.31 points, while Costa Rica has the lowest score at 53.66 points. The Regulatory Framework pillar has the highest average score within the quintile, at 60.66 points, with Indonesia scoring the highest at 63.98 points and Barbados at the lower end with 58.81 points. These relatively low scores highlight the pressing need for improvement in these economies to foster a more conducive business environment.

Bottom quintile. Economies in the bottom quintile (lightest shade of blue in table 2.1) represent the lowest performance in each pillar, from the minimum value to the 20th percentile. These economies face significant challenges, particularly in the Public Services pillar, which has an average score of just 26.73 points. In contrast, their average scores are relatively higher in the Regulatory Framework pillar (52.75 points) and Operational Efficiency pillar (48.03 points).

The range between the highest and lowest scores within pillars is the widest in this quintile, highlighting the significant disparities in performance. For example, Madagascar achieves the highest score in this group for the Regulatory Framework pillar, with 57.38 points, while Timor-Leste scores the lowest with 46.21 points. Similarly, in the Public Services pillar, the Seychelles scores the highest, with 37.21 points, whereas the Central African Republic records the lowest with 18.35 points. In the Operational Efficiency pillar, West Bank and Gaza attains the highest score of 52.75 points, while the Central African Republic scores 40.36 points.

This wide range of scores reveals that while some economies in the bottom quintile manage to maintain moderately stable regulatory and operational frameworks, others fall severely behind, especially in public service delivery. Entrepreneurs in these economies, many of which are fragile and conflict-affected, need to show remarkable resilience in conducting their operations. The pronounced disparities in pillar performance underscores the uneven development within these economies and points to critical areas that require urgent attention and reform.

There is significant diversity in the distribution of economies by income level across the three pillars. Figure 2.1 shows how economies in each of the quintiles are distributed by income across the three pillars. These patterns yield several important insights.

Economies of varying income levels can adopt strong regulatory frameworks (refer to figure 2.1, panel a). The top quintile in the Regulatory Framework pillar consists mostly of high-income economies, with notable examples such as Hungary, Portugal, and the Slovak Republic, but 40 percent are upper-middle-income economies, including Bulgaria, Colombia, Georgia, and Mexico. The second quintile features all income levels: 3 high-income economies (Estonia; Hong Kong SAR, China; Singapore); 4 upper-middle-income economies (Costa Rica, Montenegro, North Macedonia, Peru); 1 lower-middle-income economy (the Philippines); and 2 low-income economies (Rwanda, Togo). Such regional and income-level diversity emphasizes the potential for any economy to establish a robust legal and regulatory framework that can boost its business climate. Additionally, it presents an opportunity for mutual learning among peers. The third quintile mainly consists of lower-middle-income economies, with the inclusion of 1 high-income economy (New Zealand) and 3 upper-middle-income economies (Bosnia and Herzegovina, Botswana, Mauritius). The fourth quintile spans all income levels, while the bottom quintile is mostly lower-middle-income, with 2 upper-middle-income economies (Iraq, West Bank and Gaza) and 3 low-income economies (The Gambia, Madagascar, Sierra Leone).

FIGURE 2.1 The distribution of economies by income level varies considerably across pillars and by performance

a. Pillar I, Regulatory Framework

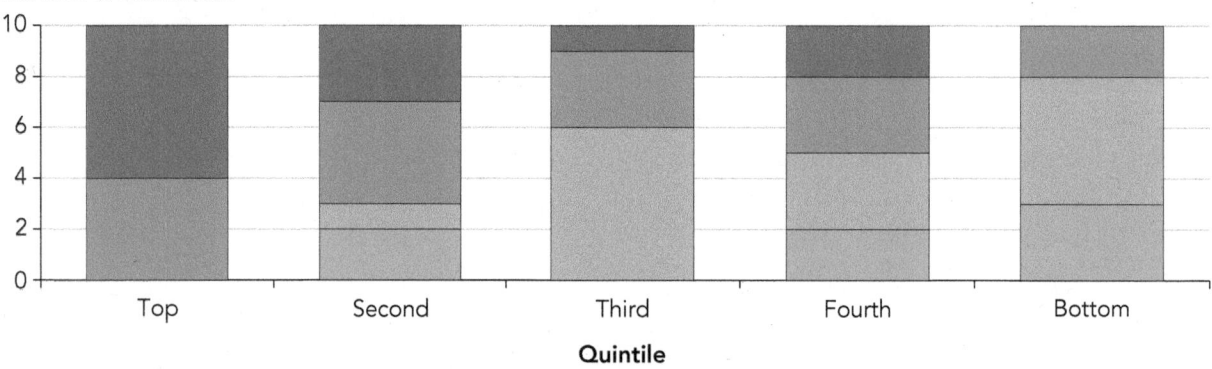

b. Pillar II, Public Services

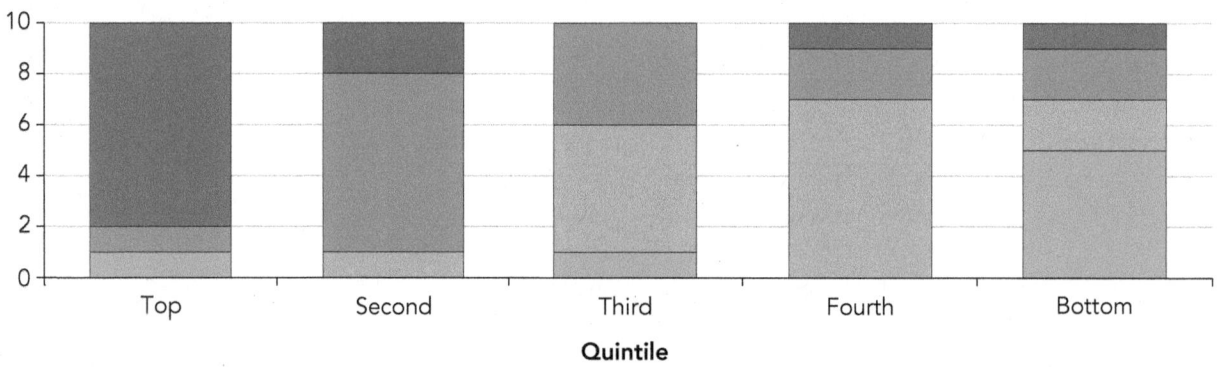

c. Pillar III, Operational Efficiency

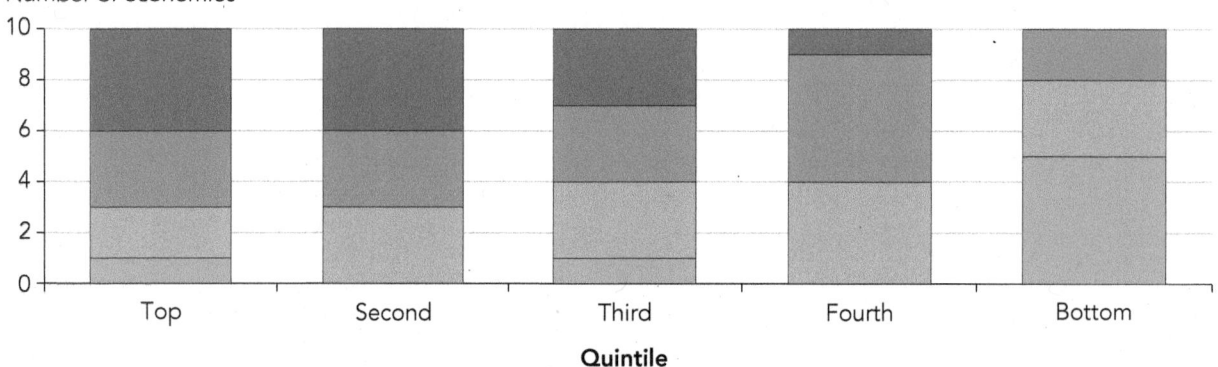

Source: B-READY 2024 data.
Note: The income classification data are as of June 2024 to ensure alignment with the latest data collection period.

High-income economies tend to provide higher quality public services to support businesses, but all income levels are represented across top quintiles (refer to figure 2.1, panel b). The Public Services pillar shows higher diversity of income levels across the quintiles. High-income economies make up 80 percent of the top quintile; however, the group also includes 1 upper-middle-income economy (Colombia) and 1 low-income economy (Rwanda), indicating that high-quality public services to support businesses are not solely provided by high-income economies. The second quintile is diverse, with 2 high-income economies (Hong Kong SAR, China; Romania); 7 upper-middle-income economies; and 1 lower-middle-income economy (Morocco). The third quintile reflects a broad spectrum, with 4 upper-middle-income economies (Botswana, Montenegro, North Macedonia, Paraguay); 5 lower-middle-income economies (Ghana, Nepal, the Philippines, Tanzania, Viet Nam); and 1 low-income economy (Togo). The fourth quintile follows suit and consists of 1 high-income economy (Barbados); 2 upper-middle-income economies (Bosnia and Herzegovina, El Salvador); and 7 lower-middle-income economies. The bottom quintile is evenly split between low-income economies (the Central African Republic, Chad, The Gambia, Madagascar, Sierra Leone) and those from other income levels (Iraq, the Seychelles, Timor-Leste, Vanuatu, West Bank and Gaza).

Economies across all income levels can facilitate operational efficiency for firms (refer to figure 2.1, panel c). High-income economies comprise 40 percent of the top quintile in the Operational Efficiency pillar (Estonia; Hong Kong SAR, China; New Zealand, Singapore); 30 percent are upper-middle-income (Bulgaria, Georgia, North Macedonia); 20 percent are lower-middle-income (the Kyrgyz Republic, Viet Nam); and the last 10 percent is low-income (Rwanda). This distribution demonstrates the potential for any economy to achieve operational efficiency within its business environment. In the second quintile, 40 percent of economies are high-income (Croatia, Hungary, Portugal, the Slovak Republic), with the rest split equally between upper-middle-income (Bosnia and Herzegovina, Mauritius, Montenegro) and lower-middle-income (Bangladesh, Nepal, Samoa). The third quintile has equal representation from high-income (Barbados, Romania, the Seychelles), upper-middle-income (Botswana, Colombia, Mexico), and lower-middle-income economies (Lesotho, Pakistan, Tanzania), with 1 low-income economy (Togo). The fourth quintile consists of 1 high-income economy (Greece); 5 upper-middle-income economies (Costa Rica, El Salvador, Indonesia, Paraguay, Peru); and 4 lower-middle-income economies (Cambodia, Ghana, Morocco, the Philippines). Most of the economies in the bottom quintile are low-income (the Central African Republic, Chad, The Gambia, Madagascar, Sierra Leone), with 3 lower-middle economies (Côte d'Ivoire, Timor-Leste, Vanuatu) and 2 upper-middle-income economies (Iraq, West Bank and Gaza). These findings should be interpreted with caution, due to the limited geographic coverage of this 2024 report.

Performance by topic

Beyond the pillar performance of economies, presented in table 2.1, B-READY 2024 also presents information on economy performance at the topic level. Table 2.2 provides a visual representation that allows readers to identify the specific topics where economies should improve. This table presents topic scores for each economy, with shades of blue indicating the quintile of the economy's topic-specific score. Darker shades of blue represent better performance. To inform detailed policy advice, B-READY also provides much more granular data for each topic and pillar in appendix A and on the project's website (https://www.worldbank.org/en /businessready).

The performance patterns of economies tend to be consistent across various topics, but all economies have room for improvement. Economies with a favorable business environment in one area (for example, being in a higher quintile group) tend to have a similar performance in other areas (being in higher quintiles). The opposite is also true. Economies in a lower quintile in one area tend to have lower quintile performance across other areas. This trend could be attributed to the fact that topics are interlinked. Policy makers may consider these interlinkages as they devise reform strategies.

Examining relationships between topics

To explore the linkages between the topics, the topic scores were ordered from highest to lowest, and the correlations were analyzed based on this ordering. This method, which assesses the association between two variables based on their position, rather than their raw values, is particularly useful when comparing how economies belong to specific quintiles.

Market Competition and Business Location are the two topics with the highest similarities in the distribution of economies—meaning that the same economies appear in the same performance quintile in both topics. Their correlation is 0.80. Seven economies are present in the top quintile for both (Colombia, Costa Rica, Croatia, Estonia, Hungary, Rwanda, Singapore). Another 5 economies share the second quintile (Hong Kong SAR, China; Mauritius; Portugal; Romania; the Slovak Republic); and 6 appear consistently in the bottom quintile in both (Chad, The Gambia, Iraq, Lesotho, Sierra Leone, Timor-Leste).[1] This suggests that economies that protect fair and efficient allocation of resources between competing firms, are also more likely to have regulations and services that reduce market distortion of land and property rights, including clearly defined sets of building regulations and environmental permitting standards.

TABLE 2.2 B-READY 2024 performance, by topic

Economy	Business Entry	Business Location	Utility Services	Labor	Financial Services	International Trade	Taxation	Dispute Resolution	Market Competition	Business Insolvency
Bangladesh	74.08	66.91	62.10	64.01	61.45	53.86	56.36	41.90	42.65	40.39
Barbados	78.23	44.39	62.81	69.64	61.37	57.54	52.34	61.63	39.17	45.42
Bosnia and Herzegovina	55.73	63.83	59.58	69.87	56.41	68.65	46.92	49.92	52.23	61.23
Botswana	92.50	56.78	60.85	63.51	69.30	68.26	50.88	56.06	50.92	38.45
Bulgaria	92.08	71.51	81.10	68.72	68.56	75.82	59.96	68.78	64.34	66.40
Cambodia	43.80	49.00	64.45	68.44	86.03	57.68	58.60	61.76	33.09	19.63
Central African Republic	46.26	44.98	53.02	49.95	33.98	34.82	23.28	38.46	33.84	40.81
Chad	47.48	41.04	43.46	55.67	44.26	43.31	43.39	49.23	32.52	42.24
Colombia	88.62	72.38	74.99	62.08	75.19	54.02	57.71	72.85	64.84	74.49
Costa Rica	71.08	72.99	70.22	58.73	66.14	73.93	42.22	59.91	68.55	45.09
Côte d'Ivoire	63.82	44.21	58.87	69.28	42.19	51.08	53.39	61.44	34.68	50.44
Croatia	78.72	76.24	76.77	75.60	63.28	84.73	39.86	71.84	63.24	76.48
El Salvador	45.86	61.90	65.57	56.19	70.99	61.72	43.03	61.45	49.52	18.01
Estonia	90.75	80.40	72.72	68.89	61.54	85.59	70.72	80.24	64.69	79.22
Gambia, The	46.61	33.42	36.43	49.22	42.20	38.58	39.01	50.69	26.76	43.47
Georgia	80.08	83.01	73.08	83.46	74.97	76.72	68.51	82.09	54.93	75.65
Ghana	40.99	60.39	68.52	68.57	59.86	56.25	56.78	54.85	32.19	64.93
Greece	96.58	57.86	69.30	64.71	58.63	87.04	56.02	65.61	64.18	43.71
Hong Kong SAR, China	85.49	71.17	77.71	68.81	69.96	90.77	70.56	72.67	57.80	46.91
Hungary	85.81	73.52	64.45	81.87	80.70	78.23	59.35	75.20	63.17	65.75
Indonesia	63.72	68.09	70.55	72.20	56.51	64.58	59.91	64.24	52.34	56.96
Iraq	52.22	48.47	54.19	53.66	44.05	42.13	29.40	39.87	21.38	6.74
Kyrgyz Republic	64.83	67.37	71.92	54.35	70.62	60.65	46.59	62.54	52.70	52.31
Lesotho	76.44	45.93	56.05	62.69	54.30	61.39	60.19	50.10	25.53	37.02
Madagascar	62.35	42.44	35.04	50.68	50.66	54.83	51.66	47.71	39.90	35.77

Quintile: ■ Top ■ Second ■ Third ■ Fourth ■ Bottom

(Continued)

TABLE 2.2 B-READY 2024 performance, by topic (Continued)

Economy	Business Entry	Business Location	Utility Services	Labor	Financial Services	International Trade	Taxation	Dispute Resolution	Market Competition	Business Insolvency
Mauritius	75.58	68.64	41.48	76.60	60.17	74.36	69.22	51.32	57.03	61.02
Mexico	61.53	61.81	76.79	59.74	84.31	63.77	65.56	67.69	51.69	53.93
Montenegro	79.72	66.55	73.63	63.25	63.16	67.20	44.04	68.79	53.12	61.96
Morocco	76.73	77.39	76.64	59.10	62.66	75.51	47.69	43.67	58.14	46.58
Nepal	66.36	60.51	65.39	65.70	70.58	66.77	57.99	64.40	33.06	52.04
New Zealand	84.64	80.38	63.00	79.95	85.04	69.94	71.74	61.07	53.87	59.52
North Macedonia	90.83	55.68	78.44	70.40	73.42	65.34	46.84	61.10	62.26	60.09
Pakistan	91.50	54.25	59.21	53.45	67.97	45.71	57.48	41.99	46.24	48.79
Paraguay	53.92	60.50	53.64	66.23	63.90	64.55	55.27	62.27	48.34	45.33
Peru	63.22	64.89	65.30	64.61	78.41	49.81	49.97	56.61	63.76	61.66
Philippines	48.49	60.27	66.47	75.54	60.70	71.47	56.66	62.88	50.13	45.51
Portugal	92.67	70.17	78.20	73.66	71.12	75.40	52.86	72.41	61.52	79.24
Romania	79.50	69.56	67.61	62.76	73.42	85.80	50.61	74.42	61.06	59.00
Rwanda	85.39	72.01	67.76	60.15	69.28	82.09	66.31	82.87	64.02	80.20
Samoa	73.39	60.10	65.03	70.24	52.09	51.36	56.94	47.82	51.16	23.52
Seychelles	54.49	57.83	53.77	72.71	56.07	61.43	58.35	37.84	35.90	43.72
Sierra Leone	48.44	46.36	60.54	69.02	41.57	37.69	41.45	42.26	30.17	40.26
Singapore	93.57	78.24	81.76	66.83	73.33	79.83	70.39	71.08	62.29	89.69
Slovak Republic	85.62	71.13	86.42	70.87	65.53	80.88	49.85	78.31	60.81	72.59
Tanzania	69.15	53.62	78.73	63.95	57.28	60.11	61.57	63.46	48.29	39.56
Timor-Leste	49.92	40.31	60.19	56.91	24.82	48.61	48.89	36.47	16.69	0.00
Togo	77.26	67.76	65.04	56.45	53.64	60.89	58.68	69.48	41.24	59.45
Vanuatu	44.08	51.63	51.14	54.37	41.24	41.28	50.21	43.04	23.01	21.44
Viet Nam	65.47	62.92	78.73	73.19	57.17	72.39	56.46	64.23	57.67	55.12
West Bank and Gaza	62.47	55.05	57.76	53.14	44.60	49.16	33.09	36.51	25.29	11.99

Quintile: ■ Top ■ Second ■ Third ■ Fourth ■ Bottom

Source: B-READY 2024 data.
Note: The economies are ordered alphabetically. Shades of blue represent the quintiles of the topic scores. The darker the shade, the better the performance.

International Trade and Market Competition are the second most similar topics in terms of economy distribution: their correlation is 0.76. Six economies are present in the top quintile for both (Croatia, Estonia, Greece, Hungary, Rwanda, Singapore). Another 5 economies share the second quintile (Mauritius, Morocco, New Zealand, Portugal, Viet Nam), and 7 appear consistently in the bottom quintile in both (Chad, The Gambia, Iraq, Sierra Leone, Timor-Leste, Vanuatu, West Bank and Gaza).[2] Global trade dynamics and government policies on trade influence competitive practices within markets, and vice versa. For example, companies that engage in global trade can adopt innovative practices from other countries, enhancing their competitive capabilities. The exchange of knowledge and diversification of products benefits consumers, while fostering a more dynamic competitive environment.

Another notable example of complementarities is between Dispute Resolution and Business Insolvency, with a correlation of 0.72. These two topics share 8 economies in their top quintile (Colombia, Croatia, Estonia, Georgia, Hungary, Portugal, Rwanda, the Slovak Republic), while 3 economies consistently appear in the second quintile (Indonesia, Montenegro, Togo) and 4 in the bottom quintile (Iraq, Timor-Leste, Vanuatu, West Bank and Gaza).[3] This finding suggests a likely complementarity arising from the characteristics of the judiciary institutions benchmarked within these topics. A favorable business environment in one area also tends to be associated with a good environment in other areas. In some topics, however, complementarities are limited or nonexistent due to the very different nature of topics, such as Taxation and Utility Services or Labor and Financial Services.[4]

Figure 2.2 presents the distribution of economies in top quintiles. Strong performance is not reserved to a small group of economies. Eight economies (Botswana, Cambodia, Indonesia, Lesotho, Morocco, Pakistan, the Philippines, the Seychelles) score in the top quintile in any one topic, while 2 economies (Hungary, Singapore) score in 8 topics. In total, 29 economies score in the top quintile in at least one topic, representing all income levels (1 low-income economy; 7 lower-middle-income; 10 upper-middle-income, 11 high-income economies) and all global regions (6 economies from East Asia and Pacific; 6 from the OECD high-income region; 5 from Europe and Central Asia; 4 from Latin America and the Caribbean; 1 from Middle East and North Africa; 1 from South Asia; 6 from Sub-Saharan Africa). This is very encouraging. However, no economy is present in the top quintile across 9 or all 10 topics, indicating that there is potential for improvement in every economy across and within topics.

FIGURE 2.2 **Strong performance is not confined to a small group of economies, but all have room for improvement**

Distribution of economies in top quintiles

Number of economies

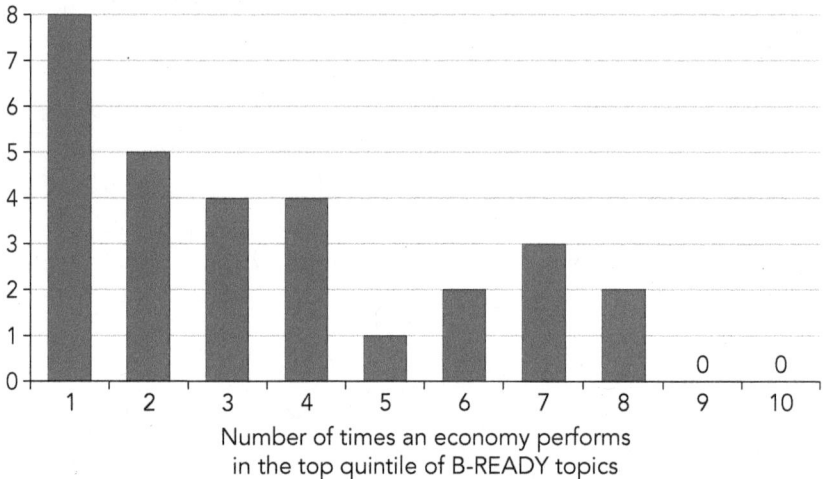

Number of times an economy performs
in the top quintile of B-READY topics

Source: B-READY 2024 data.
Note: The sample comprises 50 economies. The distribution is the following: 8 economies (Botswana, Cambodia, Indonesia, Lesotho, Morocco, Pakistan, the Philippines, the Seychelles) are present in the top quintile for any one topic; 5 economies (Costa Rica, Mauritius, Peru, Tanzania, Viet Nam) for any two topics; 4 economies (Greece, Mexico, North Macedonia, Romania) for any three topics; 4 economies (Bulgaria; Hong Kong SAR, China; New Zealand; the Slovak Republic) for any four topics; 1 economy (Portugal) for any five topics; 2 economies (Colombia, Rwanda) for any six topics; 3 economies (Estonia, Croatia, Georgia) for any seven topics; 2 economies (Hungary, Singapore) for any eight topics. No economy scores in the top quintile across any nine topics or across all ten topics.

Performance across topics by quintile

Performance across topics varies widely from the highest to the lowest performers. The maximum score across all topics is 96.58 points in Business Entry, followed by International Trade with 90.77 points, and Business Insolvency with 89.69 points. Business Insolvency is the only topic in which the minimum is 0.00, indicating that there is at least one economy with no practice in judicial reorganization and judicial liquidation, as measured by the topic. The second lowest minimum is in Market Competition with 16.69 points, followed by Taxation with 23.28 points.

Top quintile. The top quintile economies, across all topics, have regulatory frameworks that align closely with international good practice, reliable public services, and solid signals from firms that businesses operate generally efficiently. For example, in Business Entry, all 10 economies in the top quintile have streamlined company registration processes that enable information exchange between public sector agencies and provide electronic signature, electronic authentication, and electronic search for all company records. This makes the company incorporation process simpler and more time-efficient. Similarly, in Business Location, the economies in the top quintile have established a sound regulatory framework by allowing regulatory flexibility on property lease and ownership, along with a clearly defined set of building regulations and environmental permitting standards.

Second quintile. Among economies in the second quintile, adoption of internationally good practices is generally very high, but some weaknesses are observable at the pillar level. For example, in Utility Services, for economies in the second quintile, performance in one of the three pillars is considerably weaker than in the other two. Colombia's Utility Services' Pillar II (Public Services) and Pillar III (Operational Efficiency) scores are very high, while its Pillar I (Regulatory Framework) score is weaker, suggesting that policy makers may need to consider improving the regulatory framework. Similarly, the Kyrgyz Republic's Pillar III and Pillar I scores are 89.83 and 73.30 points, respectively, while its Pillar II score is 52.63 points. This suggests that the area of public services is lagging the most within the three pillars. In Labor, the economies in the second quintile have established balanced laws and regulations based on recommendations by the International Labour Organization, but are deficient in the availability of public services such as government-provided unemployment protection.

Third quintile. Third quintile economies display medium performance across pillars, with notable deficiencies in public services in certain topics. For example, in Financial Services, access to credit data for borrowers (both individuals and firms) is limited, and effective collateral registries that can facilitate lending decisions and protect the rights of borrowers and lenders have not been implemented. Similarly in International Trade, most economies have poor public services. For example, electronic systems for international trade have only limited functionalities and do not integrate all relevant border control agencies. Physical equipment and facilities are lacking in at least one of the main borders assessed. Trusted trader programs do not cover all economic operators working on trade, are not recognized by all relevant agencies, and do not offer a streamlined certification process for renewals.

Fourth quintile. Fourth quintile economies show considerably weaker performance in two pillars out of the three. For example, while Romania achieves a higher score of 61.45 points in Taxation in Pillar III, it scores lower in Pillar I and Pillar II, with 48.50 points and 41.88 points, respectively. This performance suggests that while Romania has established efficient operational practices, it needs to address shortcomings in its regulatory framework and public service provision to achieve a more cohesive and comprehensive taxation system. Similarly, Botswana's Dispute Resolution Pillar I score is 79.00 points, compared with 43.14 points and 46.05 points in Pillars II and III, respectively. This sends a signal to policy makers about the specific gaps in the country between what exists in the letter of the law (de jure) and how those rules are implemented in practice (de facto).

Bottom quintile. Finally, the bottom quintile economies are characterized by weaker performance across all pillars and no practice or nearly no practice in some areas such as Business Insolvency and Market Competition. Regardless of the area, entrepreneurs in these economies need to show remarkable resilience when conducting their operations.

Relationship between business readiness and economic indicators

The discussion that follows examines the relationship between business readiness and several economic indicators: gross domestic product (GDP) per capita; foreign direct investment (FDI); and income level, focusing on the relative performance of low-income and middle-income economies.

Relationship with GDP

The three B-READY pillar scores (Regulatory Framework, Public Services, Operational Efficiency) are strongly associated with GDP per capita (refer to figure 2.3). However, the intensity of this association varies across the different pillars.[5] The same difference in GDP per capita between two economies is associated with a larger difference in their scores for Pillar II than for Pillars I and III. While these correlations do not imply causation, they show that economies with higher levels of income are more likely to have better business regulations, public services, and operational efficiency.

Economies do not need to be rich to develop a strong business environment. Some low-income and middle-income economies also achieve relatively high scores. For example, Colombia, Georgia, Rwanda, and Togo are present in the top two quintiles of the Regulatory Framework pillar. Rwanda is in the top quintile in Public Services. It also excels in Operational Efficiency, along with Georgia, the Kyrgyz Republic, and Nepal.

FIGURE 2.3 **The association between B-READY pillar scores and GDP per capita is strong and positive, with notable exceptions**

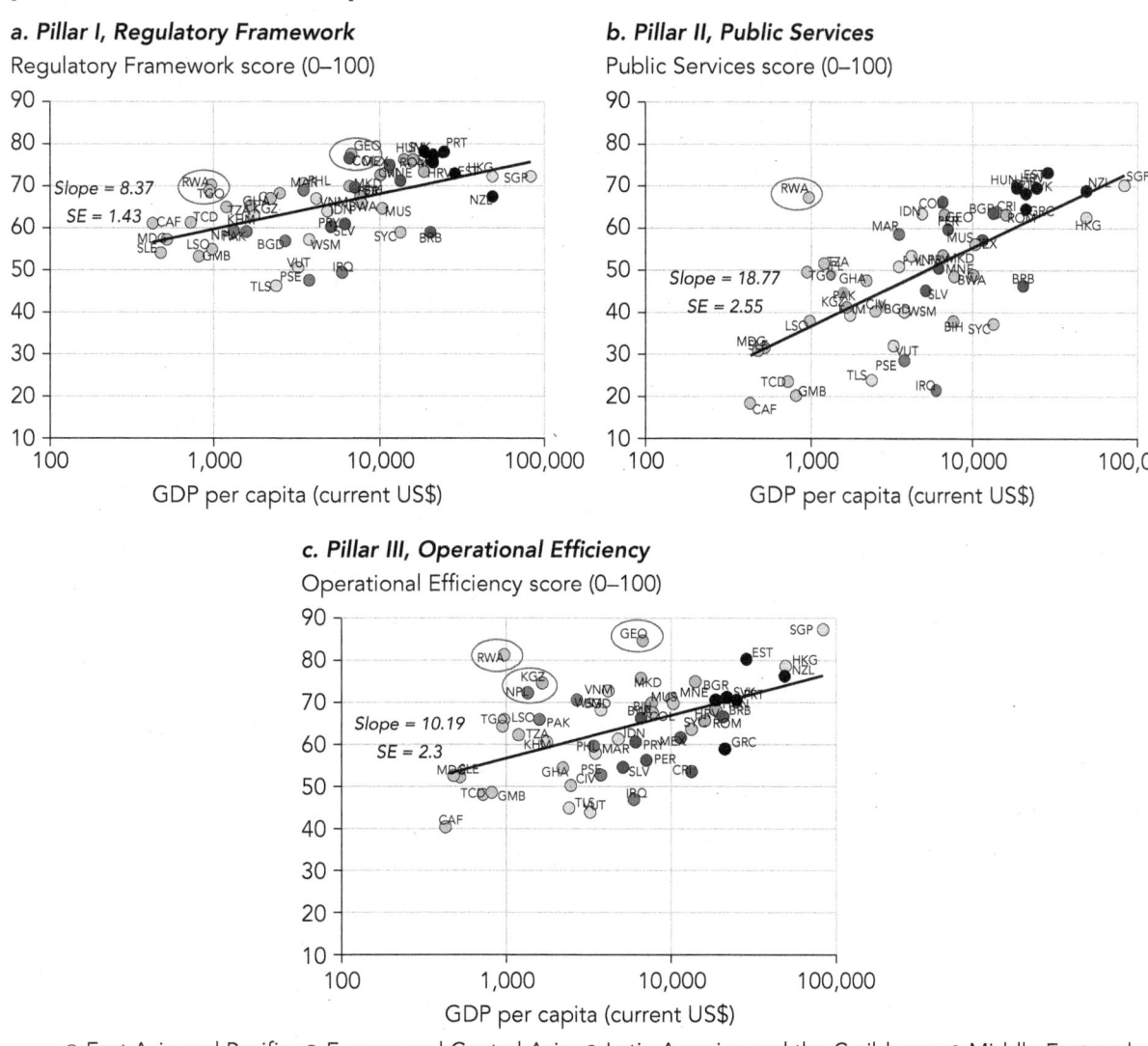

a. Pillar I, Regulatory Framework

Regulatory Framework score (0–100)

b. Pillar II, Public Services

Public Services score (0–100)

c. Pillar III, Operational Efficiency

Operational Efficiency score (0–100)

○ East Asia and Pacific   ○ Europe and Central Asia   ● Latin America and the Caribbean   ● Middle East and North Africa
● OECD high income   ● South Asia   ○ Sub-Saharan Africa

Sources: B-READY 2024 data; World Development Indicators 2023.
Note: The sample comprises 50 economies. The statistical relationship between the B-READY pillar scores and GDP per capita is significant at the 1 percent level. The x-axis uses a log scale. A fitted regression line is included for each panel. Economies circled in red are examples of low- and middle-income economies that achieve relatively high scores within their income groups. For economy abbreviations, refer to appendix B and International Organization for Standardization (ISO), https://www.iso.org/obp/ui/#search. GDP = gross domestic product; OECD = Organisation for Economic Co-operation and Development; SE = standard error.

Relationship with foreign direct investment

B-READY pillar scores are also associated with other development measures, such as FDI.[6] While these findings also do not imply causation, they show that economies with more efficient business regulations and public services tend to attract more FDI (refer to figure 2.4, panels a and b). The relationship with operational efficiency is also significant, but weaker (panel c). A favorable regulatory environment not only enhances the competitiveness and growth of domestic firms but also signals to foreign investors that the economy is an attractive investment destination. Research shows that regulatory constraints, specifically credit constraints, determine whether a firm chooses to export or import (Muûls 2015). In the context of Sub-Saharan Africa in particular, the presence of trade relationships depends not only on favorable market access conditions, but also on how these compare relative to foreign competitors (Nicita and Rollo 2015).

Relationship with income levels: Performance of low-income and middle-income economies

Figure 2.5 displays the low-income and middle-income economies in the top two quintiles in each of the 10 B-READY topics: the strongest performers in those topics. In all, 29 of 38 low-income and middle-income economies in the 2024 B-READY sample are present in the top two quintiles of at least one B-READY topic. Financial Services and Taxation have the highest number of low- and middle-income economies (14) in the top two groups; followed by Utility Services (13); Business Insolvency (12); and Business Location, Dispute Resolution, and Labor (11 each). These results underscore the point that *robust business environments can exist at all income levels, albeit in specific areas.*

Rwanda is the only economy at the low-income and lower-middle-income levels that appears in the top two quintiles in most topics (Business Entry, Business Location, Financial Services, International Trade, Taxation, Dispute Resolution, Market Competition, Business Insolvency), followed by Togo and Viet Nam, which appear in five topics each.

FIGURE 2.4 **There is a strong association between B-READY pillar scores and foreign direct investment**

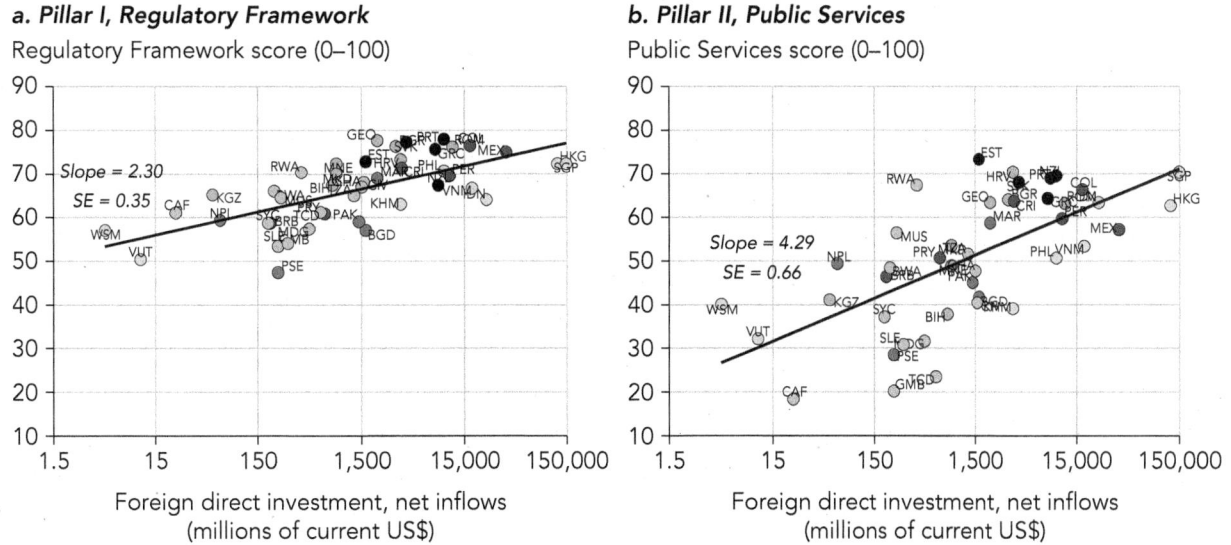

a. Pillar I, Regulatory Framework

Regulatory Framework score (0–100)

Slope = 2.30
SE = 0.35

Foreign direct investment, net inflows
(millions of current US$)

b. Pillar II, Public Services

Public Services score (0–100)

Slope = 4.29
SE = 0.66

Foreign direct investment, net inflows
(millions of current US$)

c. Pillar III, Operational Efficiency

Operational Efficiency score (0–100)

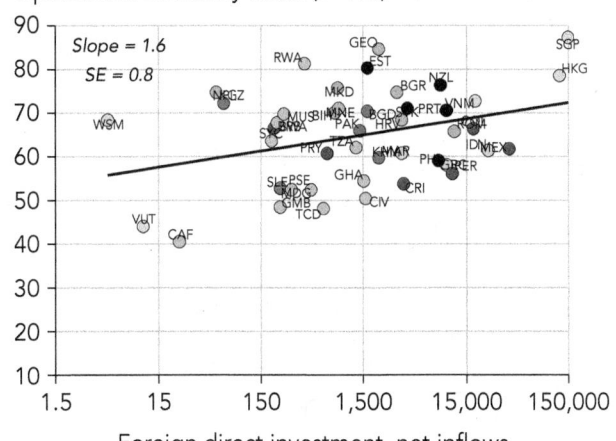

Slope = 1.6
SE = 0.8

Foreign direct investment, net inflows
(millions of current US$)

○ East Asia and Pacific ○ Europe and Central Asia ● Latin America and the Caribbean ● Middle East and North Africa
● OECD high income ● South Asia ○ Sub-Saharan Africa

Sources: B-READY 2024 data; World Development Indicators 2023.
Note: The sample comprises 50 economies. The statistical relationship between the B-READY pillar scores and the natural log of foreign direct investment net inflows, in current US dollars (US$), is significant at the 1 percent level for Pillars I and II, and at the 10 percent level for Pillar III, after removing El Salvador, Hungary, Iraq, Lesotho, Timor-Leste, and Togo due to negative values. The x-axis uses a log scale. A fitted regression line is included for each panel. For economy abbreviations, refer to appendix B and International Organization for Standardization (ISO), https://www.iso.org/obp/ui/#search. OECD = Organisation for Economic Co-operation and Development; SE = standard error.

FIGURE 2.5 Low-income and middle-income economies can be found in the top two quintiles in every topic

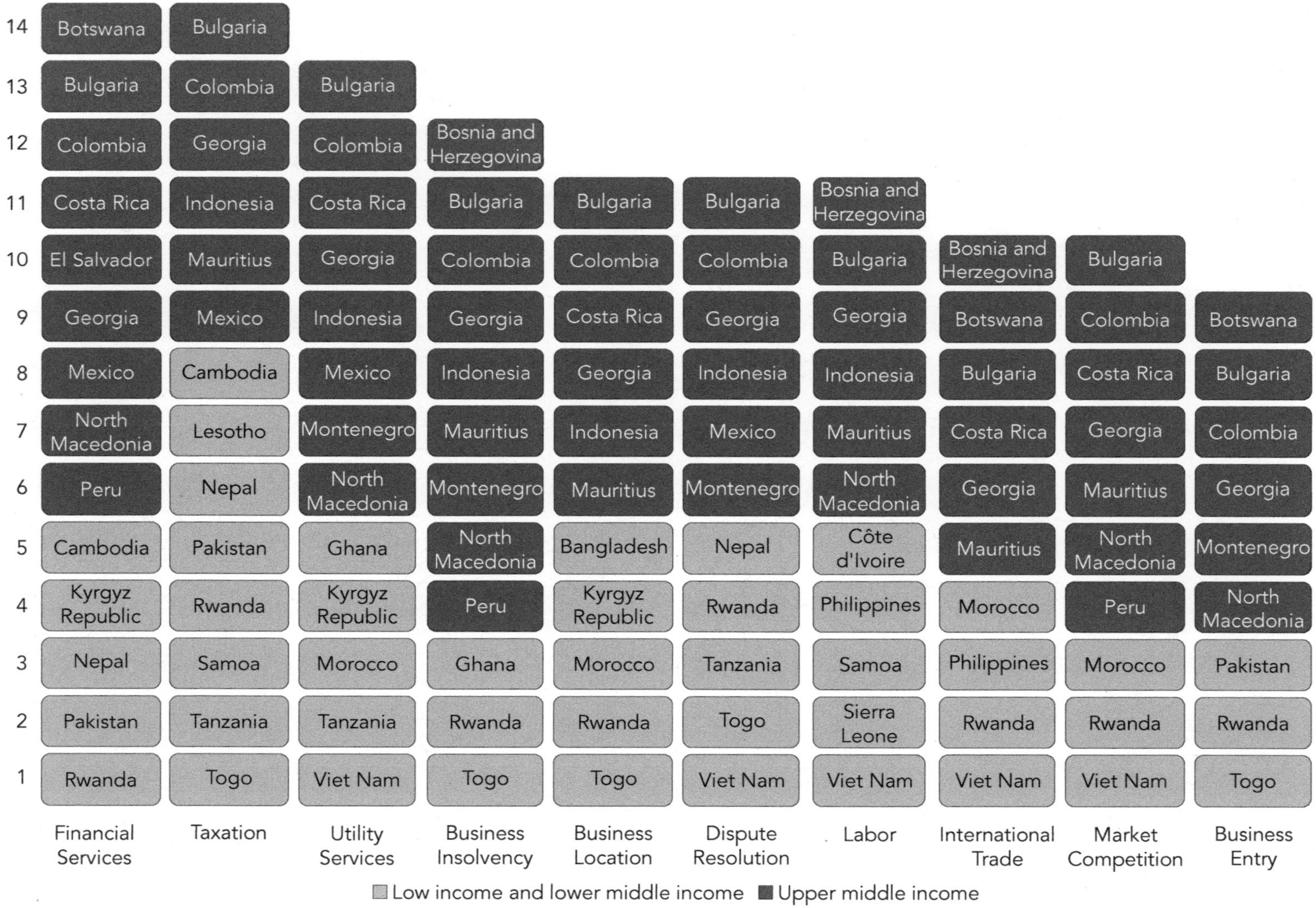

#	Financial Services	Taxation	Utility Services	Business Insolvency	Business Location	Dispute Resolution	Labor	International Trade	Market Competition	Business Entry
14	Botswana	Bulgaria								
13	Bulgaria	Colombia								
12	Colombia	Georgia	Bulgaria	Bosnia and Herzegovina						
11	Costa Rica	Indonesia	Colombia	Bulgaria	Bulgaria	Bulgaria	Bosnia and Herzegovina			
10	El Salvador	Mauritius	Costa Rica	Colombia	Colombia	Colombia	Bulgaria	Bosnia and Herzegovina	Bulgaria	Botswana
9	Georgia	Mexico	Georgia	Georgia	Costa Rica	Georgia	Georgia	Botswana	Colombia	Bulgaria
8	Mexico	Cambodia	Indonesia	Indonesia	Georgia	Indonesia	Indonesia	Bulgaria	Costa Rica	Colombia
7	North Macedonia	Lesotho	Mexico	Mauritius	Indonesia	Mexico	Mauritius	Costa Rica	Georgia	Georgia
6	Peru	Nepal	Montenegro	Montenegro	Mauritius	Montenegro	North Macedonia	Georgia	Mauritius	Montenegro
5	Cambodia	Pakistan	North Macedonia	North Macedonia	Bangladesh	Nepal	Côte d'Ivoire	Mauritius	North Macedonia	North Macedonia
4	Kyrgyz Republic	Rwanda	Ghana	Peru	Kyrgyz Republic	Rwanda	Philippines	Morocco	Peru	Pakistan
3	Nepal	Samoa	Kyrgyz Republic	Ghana	Morocco	Tanzania	Samoa	Philippines	Morocco	Rwanda
2	Pakistan	Tanzania	Morocco	Rwanda	Rwanda	Togo	Sierra Leone	Rwanda	Rwanda	Rwanda
1	Rwanda	Togo	Tanzania	Togo	Togo	Viet Nam	Viet Nam	Viet Nam	Viet Nam	Togo
			Viet Nam							

Legend: ▓ Low income and lower middle income ▓ Upper middle income

Source: B-READY 2024.

Note: The sample comprises 50 economies. The income classification data are as of June 2024 to ensure alignment with the latest data collection period.

Comparison of economies' B-READY pillar scores with their performance on *Doing Business* metrics

As discussed in chapter 1, B-READY improves upon the discontinued *Doing Business* report,[7] striking a better balance along the most salient aspects of the business environment (refer to box 2.1).

BOX 2.1

Balancing dual perspectives: Measuring firm flexibility and social benefits

B-READY introduces a novel and balanced approach to measuring the business environment. It acknowledges that certain business regulations may be burdensome for individual firms; nonetheless, they can benefit private sector development overall. B-READY addresses this tradeoff through a scoring methodology that assigns points based on the impact of good practices on the flexibility of individual firms to conduct business and the social benefits for the entire private sector. An indicator is scored under *firm flexibility* if it increases the benefits or reduces the costs of running a business. An indicator is scored under *social benefits* if its effects go beyond the firm and extend to socially desirable outcomes, such as environmental protection, workers' welfare, market competition, consumer protection, fiscal sustainability, equal access to business opportunities, and information externalities. The *B-READY Methodology Handbook* provides comprehensive details on the methodology used to derive and analyze these indicators, including the scoring of firm flexibility and social benefits (World Bank 2023).

Specifically, points will only be assigned to measures that have a clear effect on firms (under firm flexibility) and/or society (under social benefits), based on internationally recognized and well-established good practices. Measures that have an ambiguous impact on firm flexibility because they benefit some firms at the expense of others (for example, subsidies

for specific exporting sectors) are not assigned firm flexibility points. Similarly, measures that have an ambiguous impact on social benefits (for example, restrictions on firing employees that may benefit incumbent formal workers but harm the prospects of unemployed and informal workers) are not assigned social benefits points. Some indicators may merit both firm flexibility and social benefits points. For example, clear building codes and property transaction standards benefit both individual firms (by simplifying compliance) and society more generally (by strengthening trust and social contracts). In these cases, when points on firm flexibility and social benefits are allocated, they are added together.

For all topics, the process of identifying and categorizing indicators based on their impact on firm flexibility and social benefits is conducted at the indicator level, considering the perspective of each specific topic and respective pillar.

Interesting insights can be observed by analyzing the distribution of firm flexibility and social benefits scores. This analysis can provide a deeper understanding of how economies' performance is influenced by the selection of good practices that have different policy goals. To this end, examining the relationship between aggregate firm flexibility scores and social benefits scores at the pillar level can be particularly valuable. Figure B2.1.1 presents this analysis graphically.

(Continued)

BOX 2.1

Balancing dual perspectives: Measuring firm flexibility and social benefits *(Continued)*

FIGURE B2.1.1 **Firm flexibility and social benefits scores for Pillars I and II**

a. Pillar I, Regulatory Framework

Firm flexibility points

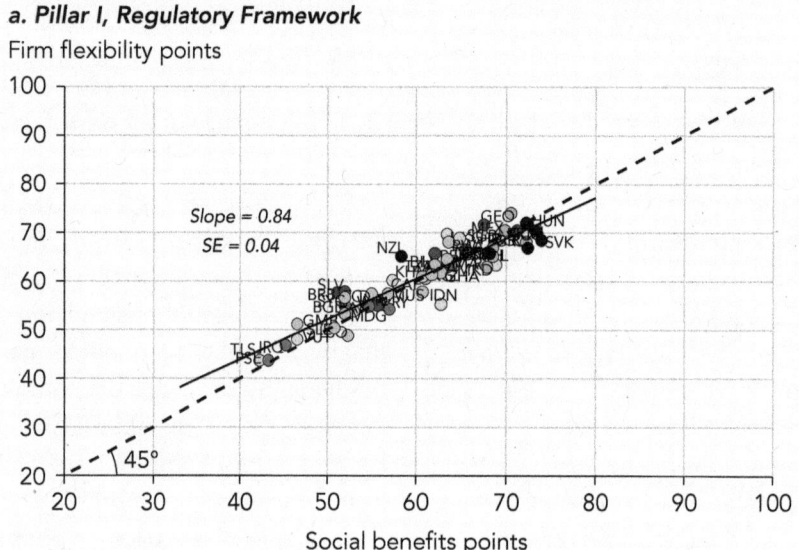

b. Pillar II, Public Services

Firm flexibility points

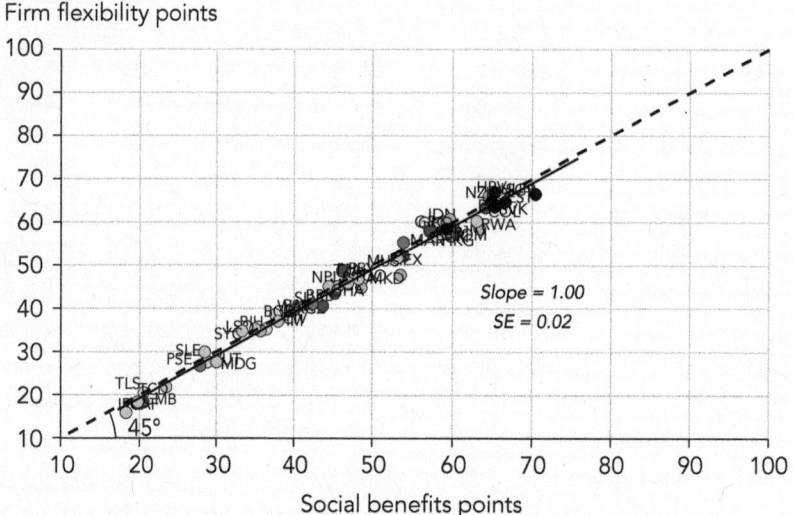

○ East Asia and Pacific ○ Europe and Central Asia ● Latin America and the Caribbean ● Middle East and North Africa
● OECD high income ● South Asia ○ Sub-Saharan Africa

Source: B-READY 2024 data.
Note: Each B-READY pillar score is obtained by taking the total firm flexibility and social benefits score awarded on an indicator level. In this figure, firm flexibility points and social benefits points are aggregated separately for each pillar. The dashed line represents the 45-degree line, while the solid line represents the linear regression of firm flexibility on social benefits points. For economy abbreviations, refer to appendix B and International Organization for Standardization (ISO), https://www.iso.org/obp/ui/#search. OECD = Organisation for Economic Co-operation and Development; SE = standard error.

(Continued)

BOX 2.1

Balancing dual perspectives: Measuring firm flexibility and social benefits *(Continued)*

Panel a depicts the relationship between firm flexibility and social benefits for Pillar I, which focuses on the regulatory framework. The distribution of economies along the 45-degree line varies, with some economies positioned above and others below. This distribution highlights that Pillar I includes regulations that, in some cases, may add only to social benefits without similarly enhancing firm flexibility, and vice versa. Panel b focuses on the provision of public services that facilitate regulatory compliance and business activities. In contrast to the distribution in panel a, economies are mostly scattered along the 45-degree line. This indicates that providing public services contributes to fostering both firm flexibility and social benefits. The separation of firm flexibility and social benefits does not apply to Pillar III, where operational efficiency deals with the ease of compliance and use of public services as they stand.

To further illustrate the tradeoff between firm flexibility and social benefits, consider the Labor and Taxation topics. Labor regulations that protect workers' rights (such as the right to collective bargaining or the minimum legal age for employment) are scored under the social benefits category because of their positive impact on workers' welfare; however, they do not directly contribute to firm flexibility and are thus not scored under that category. On the other hand, regulations that minimize hiring

costs (such as no legal mandate for firms to pay for unemployment protection directly) or reduce bureaucratic hurdles for firms (such as no requirements for third-party approval to dismiss individual workers) are scored under the firm flexibility category. They have an ambiguous impact on social benefits by improving the welfare of prospective and informal workers at the expense of incumbent formal workers and are therefore not scored under that category. For example, while Hungary and Mauritius both perform above average on the Labor topic, Mauritius scores a larger share of points from social benefits, whereas Hungary scores more points on firm flexibility.

In Taxation, the clarity and transparency of tax regulations can simplify compliance and strengthen social contracts; thus, this feature is scored in both the firm flexibility and social benefits categories. Similarly, the digitalization of tax administration, which streamlines filing and payment processes and improves general trust in tax systems and the use of limited tax administration resources, is scored for both firm flexibility and social benefits. However, environmental taxes are exclusively scored under social benefits due to their positive impact on society by promoting sustainable practices and reducing negative environmental externalities. They are not scored under firm flexibility because their impact on individual businesses is ambiguous.

Economies that were performing well on *Doing Business* metrics could be expected to perform well in the B-READY pillar scores. Indeed, the association between *Doing Business* scores and B-READY pillar scores is positive and significant (refer to figure 2.6). However, economies are consistently further away from the best practices in B-READY's Public Services pillar compared to the *Doing Business* metric, while the comparison is more mixed for the Regulatory Framework and Operational Efficiency pillars.

FIGURE 2.6 The correlation between B-READY pillar scores and *Doing Business* scores is high

a. Pillar I, Regulatory Framework

Regulatory Framework score (0–100)

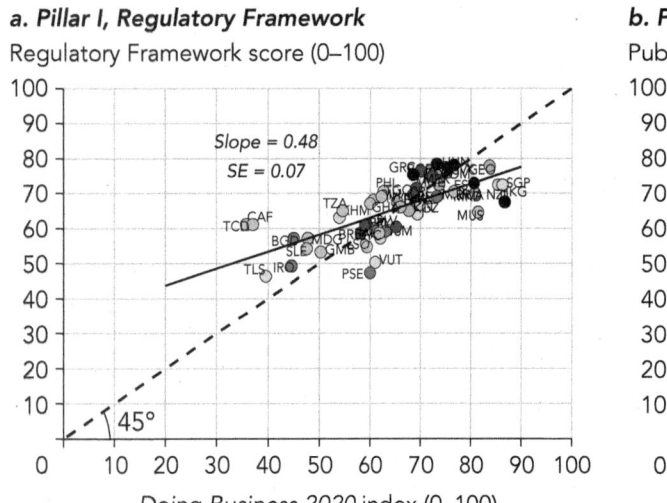

b. Pillar II, Public Services

Public Services score (0–100)

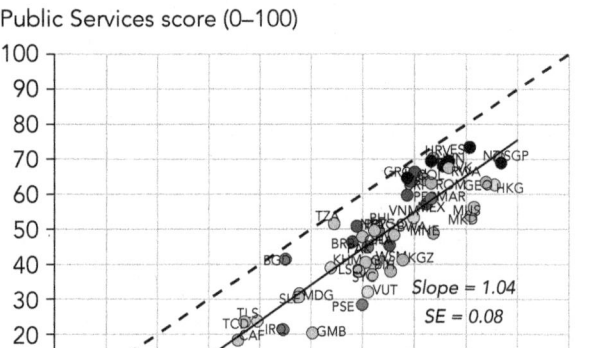

c. Pillar III, Operational Efficiency

Operational Efficiency score (0–100)

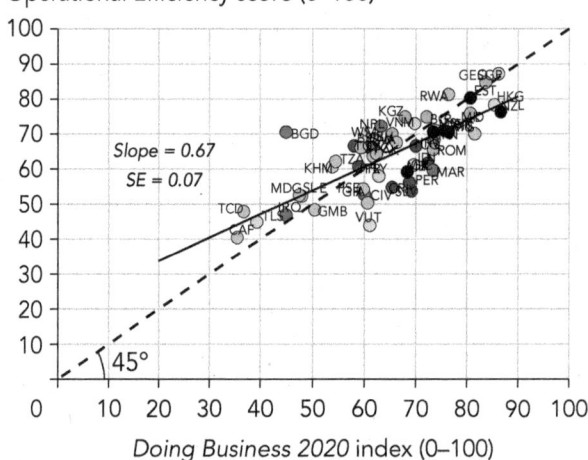

○ East Asia and Pacific ○ Europe and Central Asia ● Latin America and the Caribbean ● Middle East and North Africa
● OECD high income ● South Asia ○ Sub-Saharan Africa

Sources: B-READY 2024 data; *Doing Business* 2020.
Note: The dashed line represents the 45-degree line, while the solid line represents the linear regression of the B-READY 2024 pillar score on the *Doing Business* 2020 score. The association between the B-READY 2024 pillar score and *Doing Business* 2020 score is significant at the 1 percent level for all three pillars. The sample comprises 50 economies. For economy abbreviations, refer to appendix B and International Organization for Standardization (ISO), https://www.iso.org/obp/ui/#search. OECD = Organisation for Economic Co-operation and Development; SE = standard error.

The B-READY project aims to foster a more informed debate not only about the laws and regulations crucial for private sector development, but also about aspects of public services, which are less systematically understood. Effective policies and regulatory frameworks, alongside reliable public services, can provide the foundation for firm growth and productivity, benefiting both workers and markets while reducing the regulatory burden and compliance costs for entrepreneurs (refer to chapter 1).

Notes

1. Similarities between Market Competition and Business Location extend to the third quintile, where 6 economies are grouped in both topics (Bosnia and Herzegovina, El Salvador, Mexico, Montenegro, Paraguay, the Philippines) and another 4 economies appear in the fourth quintile (Cambodia, Pakistan, the Seychelles, Tanzania).
2. Similarities between International Trade and Market Competition extend to the third quintile, where 5 economies can be found in both topics (El Salvador, Indonesia, Mexico, Montenegro, Paraguay); and the fourth quintile, where 6 economies are present in both (Bangladesh, Barbados, Cambodia, Côte d'Ivoire, Tanzania, Madagascar).
3. Similarities between Dispute Resolution and Business Insolvency extend to the third quintile, where 4 economies jointly appear (Barbados, Côte d'Ivoire, the Kyrgyz Republic, the Philippines), and the fourth quintile, where 2 economies appear in both topics (Chad, The Gambia).
4. The correlation between Taxation and Utility Services is 0.29 (the lowest among all topic correlations). The correlation between Labor and Financial Services is 0.29 (the second lowest among all topic correlations).
5. R-squared is as follows: 0.29 for Pillar I; 0.47 for Pillar II; and 0.27 for Pillar III.
6. The association between the B-READY 2024 pillar score and log of FDI (foreign direct investment, net inflows balance of payments, current US$) is significant at the 1% level for Pillars I and II. Several other associations were also tested. The association between the B-READY 2024 pillar score and Trade (as percentage of GDP) is significant at the 5% level for all pillars. The association between the B-READY 2024 pillar score and the labor force participation rate (total, percentage of total population ages 15–64, modeled ILO estimate) is also significant at the 10% level for Pillars I and II.
7. *Doing Business* was discontinued in September 2021. Refer to https://archive.doingbusiness.org/en/doingbusiness.

References

Muûls, M. 2015. "Exporters, Importers and Credit Constraints." *Journal of International Economics* 95 (2): 333–43.

Nicita, A., and V. Rollo. 2015. "Market Access Conditions and Sub-Saharan Africa's Exports Diversification." *World Development* 68 (C): 254–63.

World Bank. 2023. *Business Ready: Methodology Handbook*. Washington, DC: World Bank. https://thedocs.worldbank.org/en/doc/357a611e3406288528 cb1e05b3c7dfda-0540012023/original/B-READY-Methodology -Handbook.pdf.

B-READY PILLAR RESULTS

Introduction

B-READY is built on three pillars—Regulatory Framework, Public Services, and Operational Efficiency—all essential to understanding the strength of a business environment. The pillars are critical to fostering a thriving business ecosystem, facilitating the entry of competitive firms and the orderly exit of noncompetitive ones, and enabling firms to comply with regulations efficiently and operate effectively throughout their life cycle.

The Regulatory Framework pillar measures the rules and regulations that firms must follow as they open, operate, and close a business. Policies and regulations that create a conducive business environment are imperative for private sector development. They can encourage the creation of new firms (Klapper, Lewin, and Quesada Delgado 2011), including by attracting foreign investment. They can also facilitate the operation and expansion of existing businesses, promote market competition and innovation, and foster the formalization of firms and workers, thereby supporting growth and job creation (Bruhn and McKenzie 2014; Loayza and Servén 2010). The Regulatory Framework pillar consists of de jure measures, reflecting those measures as they are mandated by law and regulations.

The Public Services pillar includes both the facilities that governments provide directly or through private firms to support compliance with regulations and the critical institutions and infrastructure

---

A reproducibility package is available for this book in the Reproducible Research Repository at https://reproducibility.worldbank.org/index.php/catalog/187.

that enable business activities. Effective public institutions and government facilities supported by digital technologies streamline the bureaucratic procedures for firms, promote transparency and accountability (World Bank 2016), and reduce information asymmetries (Al-Sadiq 2021). The public services considered by B-READY are limited to the scope of the business environment areas related to the life cycle of a firm.

The Operational Efficiency pillar reflects both the ease of compliance with the regulatory framework and the effective use of public services directly relevant to firms. The Public Services and Operational Efficiency pillars capture de facto measures representing the business environment as actually experienced by experts and firms.

Business Ready: Methodology Handbook presents in detail the methodology used to derive, score, and analyze these pillars, including the motivation, indicators, questionnaires, and scoring guidelines for each topic and pillar (World Bank 2023).

How do pillar scores offer insights into where reform is most needed?

This B-READY 2024 report presents the performance of economies by pillar, thereby helping policy makers identify and address the specific areas that would benefit from improvement in their economies, while learning from the experience of others in the same region, and at a similar level of development.

Each B-READY pillar is scored on a scale of 0 (worst performance) to 100 (best performance). B-READY pillar scores are obtained by taking the simple average of the corresponding pillar scores across the 10 B-READY topics. In turn, the score of each topic is built from the points assigned to sets of indicators, organized by subject matter. Table 3.1 presents the three pillar scores for each of the 50 economies in the B-READY 2024 sample. Economies are divided into five equal groupings (quintiles) based on their pillar performance, from highest to lowest performers (for more on quintiles, refer to chapter 2).

TABLE 3.1 **B-READY 2024 pillar scores**

Economy	Pillar I Regulatory Framework	Pillar II Public Services	Pillar III Operational Efficiency
Bangladesh	56.99	41.64	70.49
Barbados	58.81	46.40	66.55
Bosnia and Herzegovina	67.45	37.81	70.05
Botswana	66.01	48.52	67.73
Bulgaria	76.33	64.03	74.82
Cambodia	62.94	39.14	60.66
Central African Republic	61.11	18.35	40.36
Chad	61.22	23.51	48.05
Colombia	76.50	66.28	66.38
Costa Rica	71.41	63.58	53.66
Côte d'Ivoire	68.16	40.34	50.31
Croatia	73.48	70.24	68.31
El Salvador	60.38	45.36	54.53
Estonia	72.84	73.31	80.28
Gambia, The	53.37	20.11	48.44
Georgia	77.67	63.33	84.75
Ghana	66.91	47.67	54.42
Greece	75.60	64.51	58.98
Hong Kong SAR, China	72.40	62.64	78.52
Hungary	78.23	69.50	70.68
Indonesia	63.98	63.44	61.31
Iraq	49.39	21.45	46.79
Kyrgyz Republic	65.22	41.23	74.71
Lesotho	54.94	37.89	66.06
Madagascar	57.38	31.64	52.29
Mauritius	64.55	56.28	69.79
Mexico	75.07	57.25	61.73
Montenegro	72.48	48.92	71.03
Morocco	68.92	58.66	59.66
Nepal	59.34	49.29	72.21
New Zealand	67.45	68.91	76.39
North Macedonia	69.95	53.56	75.81
Pakistan	59.10	44.97	65.90
Paraguay	60.90	50.68	60.60
Peru	69.51	59.76	56.20
Philippines	70.68	50.80	57.95
Portugal	78.11	69.53	70.53
Romania	76.19	63.19	65.74
Rwanda	70.35	67.37	81.31
Samoa	57.13	40.04	68.32

Quintile: ■ Top ■ Second ■ Third ▫ Fourth   Bottom

(Continued)

TABLE 3.1 **B-READY 2024 pillar scores** *(Continued)*.

Economy	Pillar I Regulatory Framework	Pillar II Public Services	Pillar III Operational Efficiency
Seychelles	58.85	37.21	63.57
Sierra Leone	54.09	30.73	52.51
Singapore	72.37	70.40	87.33
Slovak Republic	77.29	68.17	71.14
Tanzania	65.00	51.56	62.15
Timor-Leste	46.21	23.80	44.83
Togo	69.03	49.58	64.36
Vanuatu	50.44	32.06	43.94
Viet Nam	66.81	53.41	72.78
West Bank and Gaza	47.54	28.42	52.75

Quintile: ■ Top ■ Second ▨ Third ▨ Fourth Bottom

Source: B-READY 2024 data.
Note: Scores range from 0 (lowest) to 100 (highest). Shades of blue represent the quintiles of the pillar scores. The darker the shade, the better the performance.

Pillar I. The Regulatory Framework pillar measures good practices as prescribed in laws and regulations. Hungary has the highest score in Pillar I (78.23 points), with Portugal (78.11 points), Georgia (77.67 points), the Slovak Republic (77.29 points), and Colombia (76.50 points) also at the forefront (refer to figure 3.1, panel a). These economies exhibit strong regulatory frameworks in which good practices have been introduced comprehensively in most areas covered by the report, thereby providing businesses and investors with greater confidence, clarity, and enhanced risk management. In Business Entry, for example, in Portugal, Hungary, and the Slovak Republic legislation requires entrepreneurs to register information about beneficial ownership.[1] This is a good practice because it can help prevent the misuse of corporate vehicles for illicit purposes. Similarly, in Taxation, Hungary, Georgia, and the Slovak Republic, follow good practices by codifying tax audit and dispute resolution procedures in a single legislative act and by being transparent in publishing future tax plans ahead of the period covered by those plans.

The lowest scores on Pillar I are observed for Timor-Leste (46.21 points), West Bank and Gaza (47.54 points), Iraq (49.39 points), Vanuatu (50.44 points), and The Gambia (53.37 points). The scores reflect weaker regulatory frameworks in which good practices have not been adopted comprehensively or in which regulations that pose unnecessary restrictions and obstacles to firms and entrepreneurs remain prevalent. For example, Timor-Leste does not exhibit the presence of regulatory good practices as measured by Business Insolvency, making it difficult for firms and creditors to recover from financial distress. Similarly, West Bank and Gaza has not adopted any regulatory good practices in Taxation as measured by B-READY, contributing to unclear tax regulations and higher compliance costs for firms.

FIGURE 3.1 B-READY 2024 scores: Pillars I, II, and III

a. Pillar I, Regulatory Framework

Regulatory Framework score (0–100)

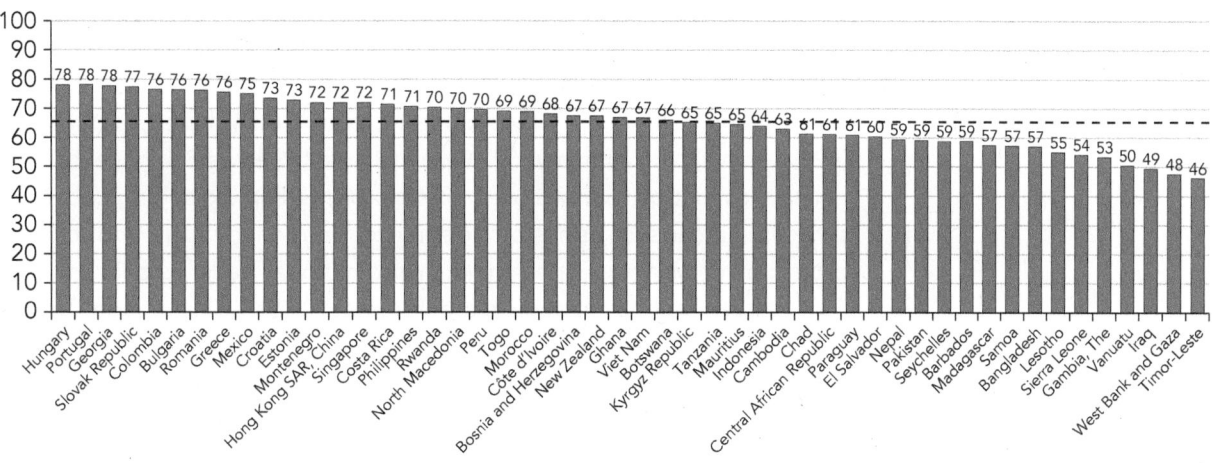

b. Pillar II, Public Services

Public Services score (0–100)

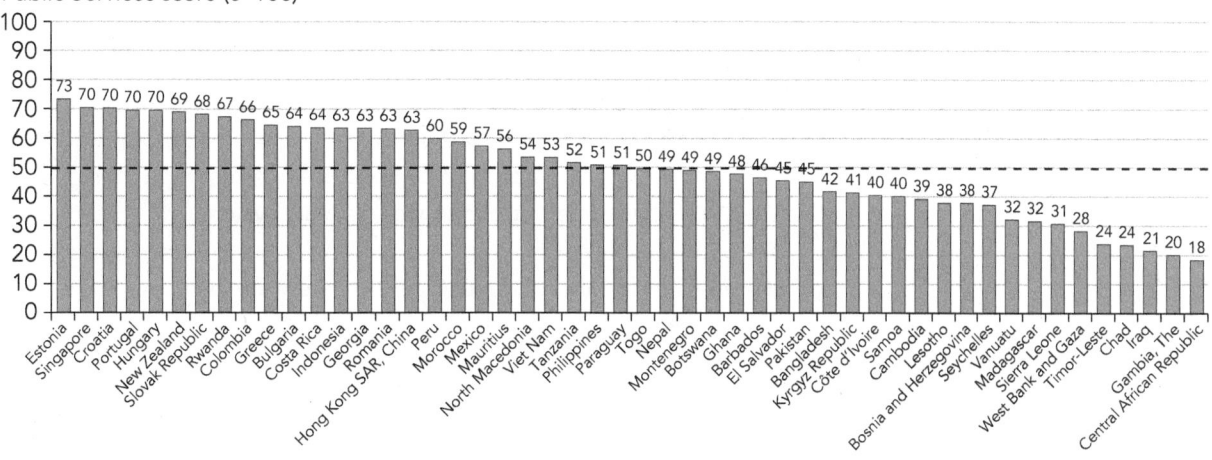

c. Pillar III, Operational Efficiency

Operational Efficiency score (0–100)

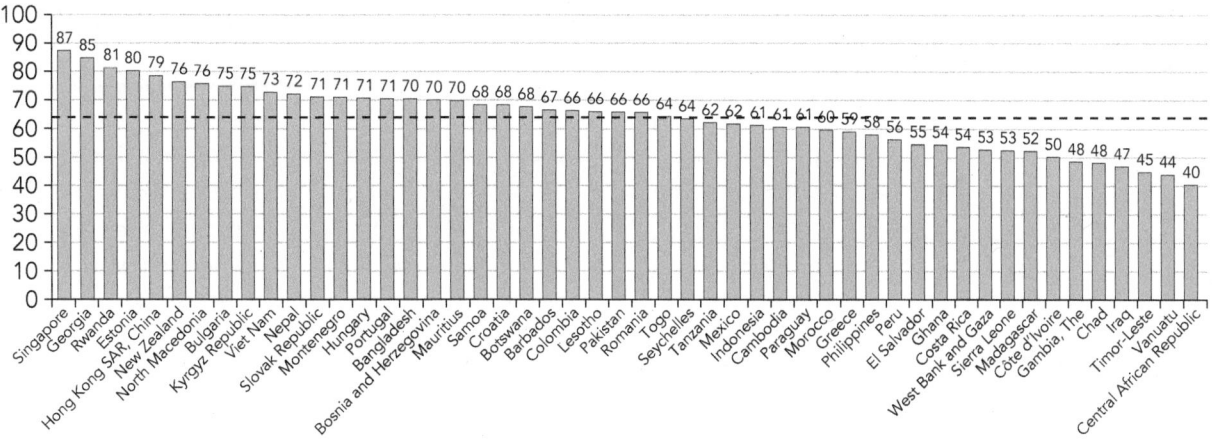

Source: B-READY 2024 data.

Note: The dashed horizontal line represents the average pillar score across economies. Scores have been rounded.

Pillar II. The Public Services pillar measures institutional provisions, including both the facilities that governments provide to support compliance with regulations and the institutions and infrastructure that enable business activities.

Few economies score strongly in this pillar. Those that do are Estonia (73.31 points), Singapore (70.40 points), Croatia (70.24 points), Portugal (69.53 points), and Hungary (69.50 points) (refer to figure 3.1, panel b). The economies that perform well demonstrate prowess in digitalizing public services in areas such as customs clearance, payment of taxes, and social protection of workers. For example, in International Trade, Estonia and Croatia have well-developed electronic systems that facilitate trade. These systems streamline clearance procedures and reduce compliance costs, while increasing the transparency, compliance, and security of a transaction. In Financial Services, the topic's leading economies are distinguished by their advanced digital systems, highlighting the importance of digital development in driving financial progress. Borrowers (firms and individuals), as well as banks and other financial institutions, have online access to data from credit reporting agencies and collateral registries, thereby facilitating lending decisions and improving access to finance. Digitalization not only enhances the operational efficiency of service provision but also promotes accessibility for small and medium enterprises across an economy and improves transparency and accountability—possibly creating a more inclusive, more streamlined public service delivery system.

A substantial number of economies demonstrate weak performance in the Public Services pillar, indicating significant challenges in supporting businesses in their regulatory compliance and firm operations. The lowest scores in Pillar II are observed in the Central African Republic (18.35 points), The Gambia (20.11 points), Iraq (21.45 points), Chad (23.51 points), and Timor-Leste (23.80 points). These scores reflect a near absence of public services and a lack of infrastructure to underpin the business environment, posing challenges for firms attempting to comply with regulations and expand their business activities. For example, Iraq lacks an operational competition authority, hindering its ability to effectively promote and protect a level playing field among firms. Some upper-middle-income and high-income economies also exhibit notable weaknesses in public service provision, including the Seychelles (37.21 points), Bosnia and Herzegovina (37.81 points), and El Salvador (45.36 points). The Seychelles does not have electronic public procurement systems, as measured by Market Competition, which restricts access and adds transaction costs for firms. El Salvador lacks specialized judicial proceedings for reorganization, as well as electronic services and case management systems in liquidation and reorganization proceedings under Business Insolvency.

Pillar III. The Operational Efficiency pillar measures both the ease of compliance with the regulatory framework and the effective use of public services as experienced by experts and firms. Many economies show strong performance in this pillar, indicating that businesses can operate in diverse economic and regional landscapes (refer to figure 3.1, panel c). For example, among the higher-performing economies are Singapore (87.33 points), Georgia (84.75 points), Rwanda (81.31 points), Estonia (80.28 points), and Hong Kong SAR, China (78.52 points). Strong performers frequently excel at operating businesses efficiently and at significantly reducing a firm's transaction costs. Rwanda, for example, is able to register new domestic companies at a relatively low cost to entrepreneurs, as measured in Business Entry. In Singapore, both liquidation and reorganization proceedings, as measured in Business Insolvency, are efficiently resolved in a timely manner at little cost. In International Trade, firms in Hong Kong SAR, China, can efficiently comply with all import requirements in three days because it is a free port where all shipments are under document inspection and only a few undergo physical inspection. Georgia shows remarkable efficiency in Business Location, taking only 14.6 days to complete the entire process of transferring the ownership of a commercial property from one business to another.

Few economies exhibit weak performance in Pillar III. The lowest scores on Pillar III are observed in the Central African Republic (40.36 points), Vanuatu (43.94 points), Timor-Leste (44.83 points), Iraq (46.79 points), and Chad (48.05 points). Businesses operating in these economies face relatively greater challenges than other economies in conducting their day-to-day operations. For example, in Vanuatu it takes 73 days to register a new domestic company, as measured in Business Entry. In the Central African Republic, it takes 32 days to obtain a loan, as measured in Financial Services. In Iraq, there have been no completed (closed) cases of judicial reorganization or judicial liquidation proceedings involving corporate debtors over the last three years, as measured in Business Insolvency.

Comparisons across pillars. Looking across pillars offers insights into areas in which reforms are most needed to enhance business readiness. Figure 3.2 displays the distribution of scores for each of the three pillars. The average score in Pillar I across all economies is 65.52 points, followed by the average scores in Pillar III (63.95 points) and Pillar II (49.73 points). The 15.79-point difference between Pillar I and Pillar II scores indicates a lag in the implementation of public services related to the adoption of good practices in the regulatory framework. In other words, economies are better at enacting regulations that are conducive for businesses than at providing related institutional support through public services.

FIGURE 3.2 Public Services is the B-READY pillar with the widest range and weakest performance, on average

a. Pillar I, Regulatory Framework

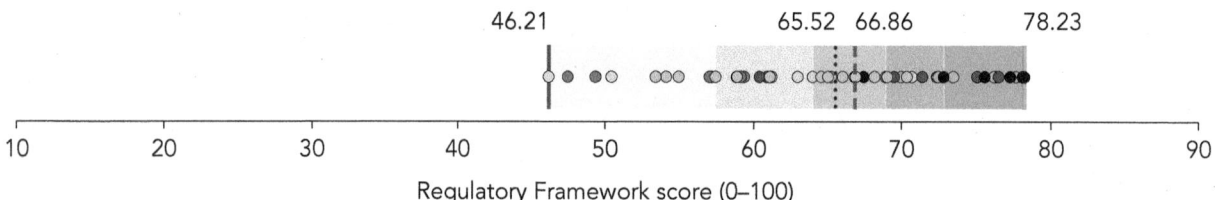

Regulatory Framework score (0–100)

b. Pillar II, Public Services

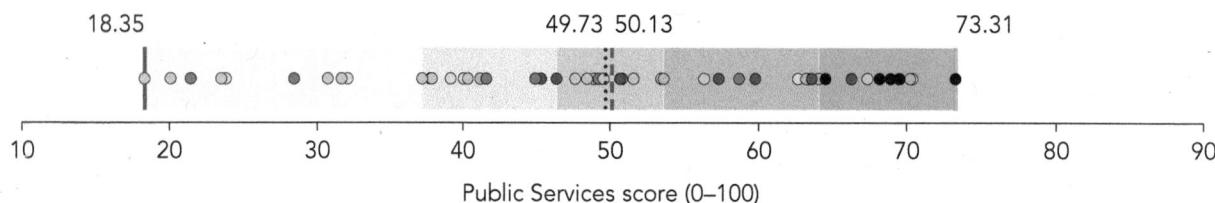

Public Services score (0–100)

c. Pillar III, Operational Efficiency

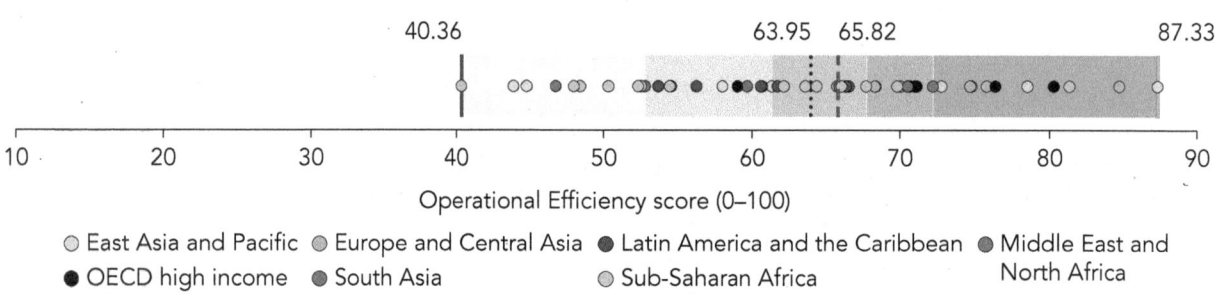

Operational Efficiency score (0–100)

○ East Asia and Pacific ○ Europe and Central Asia ● Latin America and the Caribbean ● Middle East and North Africa
● OECD high income ● South Asia ○ Sub-Saharan Africa
— Minimum ······ Mean - - - Median — Maximum

Source: B-READY 2024 data.
Note: For each pillar, the scores are plotted on the graph with minimum, mean, median, and maximum scores indicated by vertical lines, with corresponding scores provided. The dots, representing economies, indicate by color to which regional grouping an economy belongs. The blue panels represent quintiles (with darker shades indicating better performance). OECD = Organisation for Economic Co-operation and Development.

Economies vary the most in Public Services, second in Operational Efficiency, and third in Regulatory Framework. This variation highlights the greater challenges economies face in implementing de facto measures assessed in the Public Services and Operational Efficiency pillars than in establishing de jure regulations under the Regulatory Framework pillar. Figure 3.2 also reveals that the widest variation is found in the Public Services pillar, with scores ranging from 18.35 points (lowest, Central African Republic) to 73.31 points (highest, Estonia). The Operational Efficiency pillar follows with minimum and maximum scores of 40.36 points (Central African Republic) and 87.33 points (Singapore), respectively. The smallest variation is observed for the Regulatory Framework pillar, with a minimum score of 46.21 points (Timor-Leste) and a maximum score of 78.23 points (Hungary).

The 54.96-point range in Pillar II scores suggests that firms operating in different economies have very different experiences with public services and how they are implemented. It also underscores that economies can improve substantially in this area. Conversely, the Regulatory Framework's position as the pillar with the lowest score variability suggests that many economies have enshrined a good number of internationally recognized good practices in their laws. For example, in Labor, most economies have regulations pertaining to the International Labour Organization Declaration on Fundamental Principles and Rights at Work.[2] Specifically, 49 economies grant all workers the right of freedom of association and assembly and the right to collective bargaining. The same number of economies have a regulation that prohibits forced labor or compulsory labor. Forty-eight economies have regulations that prohibit children from performing work that is likely to harm their health, safety, or morals, and 48 economies also have national occupational safety and health legislation.

Similarly, in Business Insolvency, most economies have regulations pertaining to insolvency administrators. Specifically, in 48 economies the legal framework establishes a mechanism for the selection and appointment of an insolvency administrator, while in 49 economies the law sets out the cases in which an insolvency administrator may be disqualified. In 46 economies, the legal framework provides for an automatic stay of proceedings, including measures that prevent the commencement, or suspend the continuation, of judicial, administrative, or other individual actions related to a debtor's assets, rights, obligations, or liabilities. These findings suggest that there is a degree of regulatory convergence among economies at different levels of development. Possible explanations include regional harmonization efforts, such as those in the European Union, or the adoption and dissemination of international agreements and harmonized laws, such as those by the Organization for the Harmonisation of Business Law in Africa (OHADA).

The variation in scores is further illustrated in figure 3.3, which presents graphically the scores for the three pillars for each economy. All economies except New Zealand and Estonia have higher scores in Pillar I than in Pillar II. In New Zealand, the score for Pillar II is 1.46 points higher than for Pillar I; in Estonia, the difference is only 0.47 points. As pillar scores decline from high-performing economies to lower-performing ones, the Public Services pillar exhibits a particularly steep decline, and the gap between the Public Services and Regulatory Framework scores widens significantly for the lower-performing economies. This finding indicates that de facto disparities in public services contribute substantially to the variation in business environment performance across economies.

FIGURE 3.3 **Pillar II, Public Services, largely drives the variation in the business environment across economies**

Score (0–100)

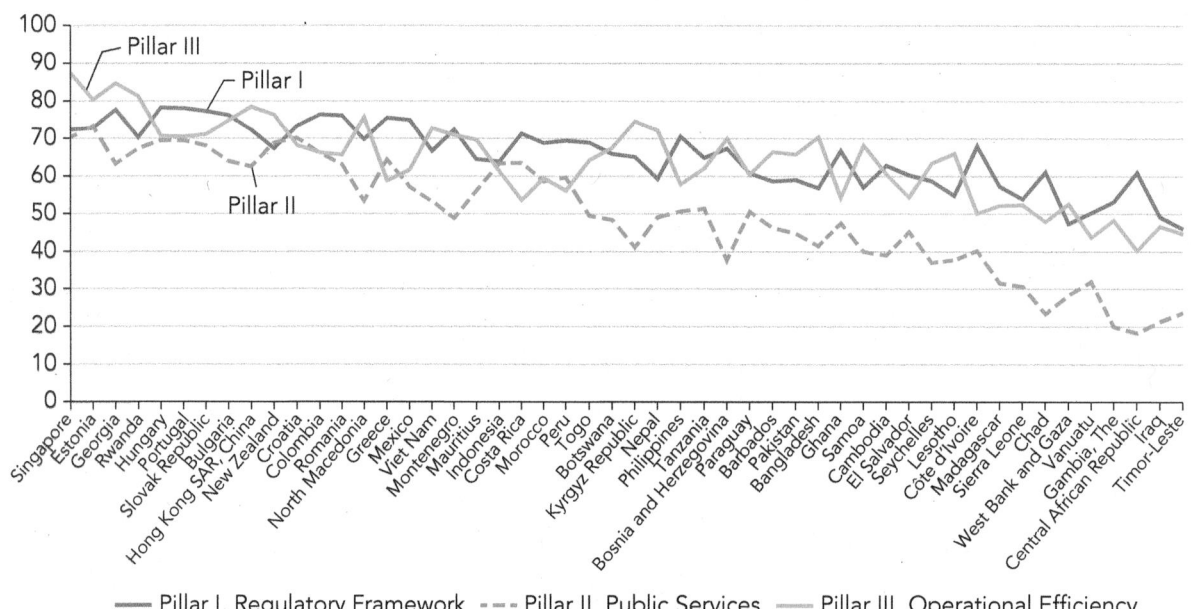

Pillar III

Pillar I

Pillar II

— Pillar I, Regulatory Framework ---- Pillar II, Public Services — Pillar III, Operational Efficiency

Source: B-READY 2024 data.
Note: The sample comprises 50 economies.

How do the pillar scores vary across regions and income levels?

A regional analysis of topic scores provides insights into the composition and distribution of good practices across regions. However, certain limitations are inherent to the data set used in the B-READY 2024 report. Although the 50 economies included in this report were selected to represent all regions and income levels, the sample may not be entirely representative of the overall context within a region. Consequently, any comparisons drawn from this analysis should be interpreted with caution, bearing in mind that full representation across all regions will be achieved in subsequent reports (refer to chapter 5).

Most regions achieve higher scores in Pillar I, Regulatory Framework, than in other pillars, with OECD high-income economies leading the way (refer to figure 3.4). OECD high-income economies also top Pillar II, followed by economies in Latin America and the Caribbean and Europe and Central Asia. For Pillar III, the Europe and Central Asia region has the highest score. The Middle East and North Africa region has the lowest performance across all three pillars.

Pillars II and III exhibit a higher dispersion of the scores within regions than Pillar I, where scores tend to be closer to the regional medians. Sub-Saharan

Africa exhibits the most significant disparities in Pillar II. In terms of Operational Efficiency scores (Pillar III), the East Asia and Pacific region presents a notable contrast, ranging from Vanuatu's 43.94 points to Singapore's 87.33 points.

The data on pillar scores by economy income level show that the higher the income, the better economies tend to perform, on average. High-income economies produce the highest scores across all three pillars, followed by those at the upper-middle-, lower-middle-, and low-income levels. The differences in Regulatory Framework scores among all income levels are small compared with those for Public Services, where low-income economies obtain just over half the average score of high-income economies—an average of 34.47 points and 63.67 points, respectively.

In Pillars II and III, the dispersion of scores among low-income economies is higher than that for other income levels because some low-income economies have been able to achieve higher scores—in some cases, comparable to those of higher-income economies. For example, the Central African Republic's score is 18.35 points for Pillar II and 40.36 points for Pillar III, whereas Rwanda's score is 67.37 points for Pillar II and 81.31 points for Pillar III.

Certain economies from the lower-middle-income level as well as low-income level located in diverse regions such as Sub-Saharan Africa (including Sierra Leone and The Gambia), East Asia and Pacific (including Vanuatu and Timor-Leste), and the Middle East and North Africa (including Iraq and West Bank and Gaza) register the lowest scores on Pillar I. For the Regulatory Framework pillar, the scores tend to be weak for some fragile and conflict-affected economies, such as Timor-Leste (46.21 points), West Bank and Gaza (47.54 points), and Iraq (49.39 points), but there are also examples of economies that perform moderately well, such as the Central African Republic (61.11 points) and Chad (61.22 points). For example, as shown in appendix A (topic scores) in Regulatory Framework, Chad performs strongly in Dispute Resolution on Pillar I (83.44 points) because it adheres to the legal framework developed by OHADA in the fields of arbitration and mediation. Specifically, the OHADA Uniform Act on Arbitration allows courts to provide the arbitral tribunal with the necessary support and precludes parties from using suggestions and statements made during mediation in other types of proceedings, among other good practices.

In Pillar II, Rwanda scores 67.37 points, making it the highest-performing Sub-Saharan Africa economy in providing businesses with public services and the only low-income economy in the first quintile of this pillar. The next Sub-Saharan Africa economy is Mauritius, with a score of 56.28 points in the second quintile of the pillar. Among the lowest-performing economies in Pillar II are fragile and conflict-affected economies assessed by B-READY 2024, such as the Central African Republic, Iraq, Chad, Timor-Leste, and West Bank and Gaza.

FIGURE 3.4 B-READY pillar scores, by region and income level

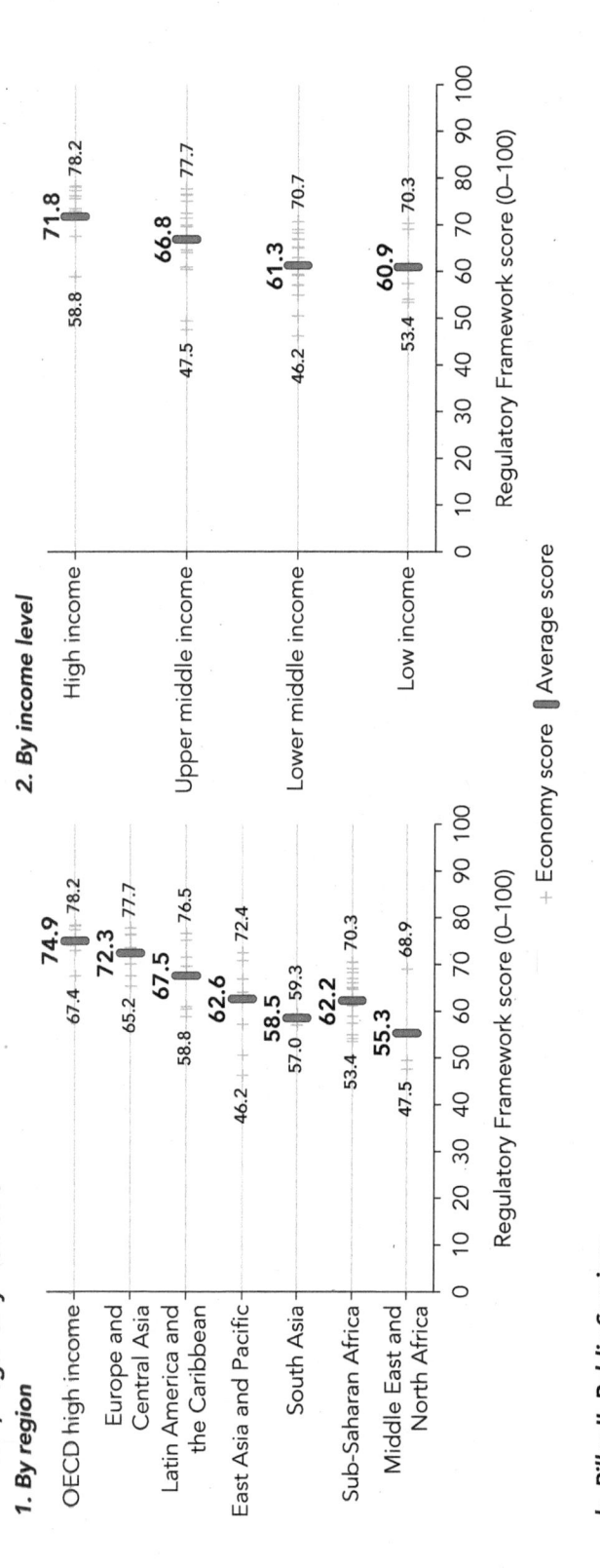

a. Pillar I, Regulatory Framework
1. By region

2. By income level

b. Pillar II, Public Services
1. By region

2. By income level

FIGURE 3.4 B-READY pillar scores, by region and income level (Continued)

c. Pillar III, Operational Efficiency

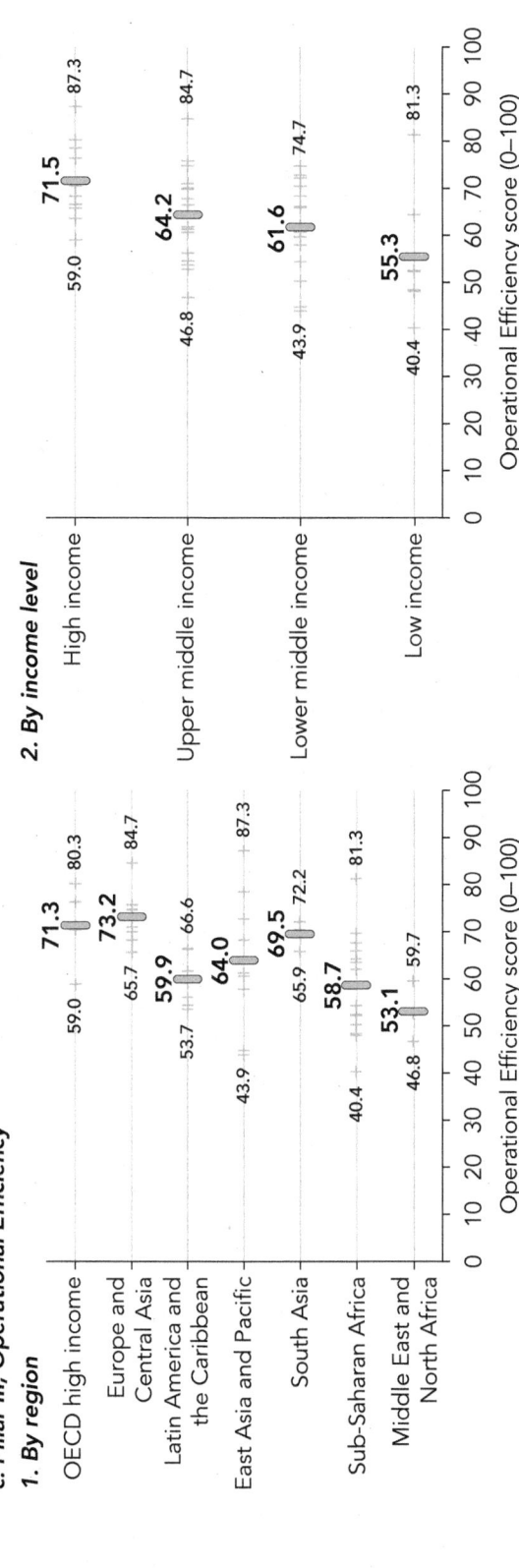

1. By region

2. By income level

+ Economy score | Average score

Source: B-READY 2024 data.

Note: Each cross (+) represents the score of an economy in its region or at its income level. Each vertical colored marker indicates the average score of a region or income group. The minimum and maximum scores within each region or income group are also specified. The East Asia and Pacific region has 9 economies in the sample; Europe and Central Asia, 8; Latin America and the Caribbean, 7; the Middle East and North Africa, 3; the OECD high-income region, 6; South Asia, 3; and Sub-Saharan Africa, 14. The high-income level includes 12 economies; the upper-middle-income level, 16; the lower-middle-income level, 15; and the low-income level, 7. OECD = Organisation for Economic Co-operation and Development.

How does the public services gap vary by economy income, region, and business environment performance?

Economies are better at enacting regulations than providing public services. The B-READY data provide evidence of a "public services gap"—that is, a notable difference between the Regulatory Framework score and the Public Services score—across all regions and income levels. The Public Services score is lower than the Regulatory Framework score for nearly all economies, as evidenced by its position below the 45-degree line in figure 3.5.

The public services gap, while evident across all economies, varies significantly in size across regions and income levels. Across regions, OECD high-income economies exhibit the narrowest gap, with only 5.93 points between the average scores of Pillars I and II (refer to figure 3.6, panel a). The Latin America and the Caribbean, South Asia, and East Asia and Pacific economies follow with considerably larger gaps of 11.89 points, 13.18 points, and 14.13 points, respectively. Europe and Central Asia stands out with a relatively wider gap of 17.05 points, despite performing exceptionally well on average in Pillar I, suggesting that important areas of improvement are needed in the provision of public services. The Middle East and North Africa and Sub-Saharan Africa economies show the widest gaps—19.11 points and 22.16 points, respectively—between Pillars I and II.

The impact of the public services gap is more evident when examining income levels. High-income economies exhibit the narrowest gap between average Pillar I and II scores: 8.13 points (refer to figure 3.6, panel b). Moving toward lower-income levels, the gap widens progressively, ranging from 15.03 points in upper-middle-income economies to 17.75 points in lower-middle-income economies, to 26.46 points in low-income economies. The gap is more pronounced in low-income economies, as well as those affected by fragility and conflict. For example, the gap is 42.76 points in the Central African Republic, 37.72 points in Chad, 27.94 points in Iraq, 22.40 points in Timor-Leste, and 19.12 points in West Bank and Gaza. This disparity highlights the limited nature, or absence, of support mechanisms available to firms operating in low-income settings. Firms and entrepreneurs operating in these settings face greater challenges. Indeed, in some cases economies may not even provide firms with essential public services. Doing so may require stability, which is often a precondition for private sector development.

FIGURE 3.5 **Most economies suffer from a "public services gap": Their scores for Public Services are lower than their scores for Regulatory Frameworks**

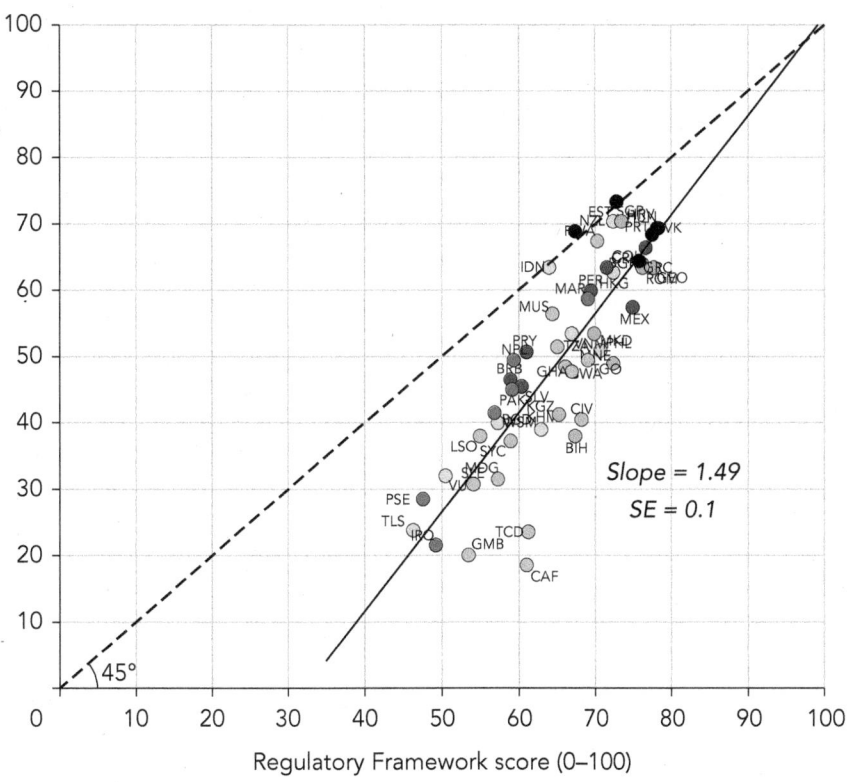

Public Services score (0–100)

Slope = 1.49
SE = 0.1

45°

Regulatory Framework score (0–100)

○ East Asia and Pacific ○ Europe and Central Asia
● Latin America and   ● Middle East and North Africa
  the Caribbean   ● South Asia
● OECD high income   ○ Sub-Saharan Africa

Source: B-READY 2024 data.

Note: The dashed line is set at 45 degrees, and the solid line represents the linear regression of the Public Services pillar score on the Regulatory Framework pillar score. The relationship is significant at the 1 percent level. The dots, representing economies, indicate by color to which regional grouping an economy belongs. The sample comprises 50 economies. The public services gap is represented by the gap as evidenced by the vast majority of economies positioned below the 45-degree line. For economy abbreviations, refer to appendix B and International Organization for Standardization (ISO), https://www.iso.org/obp/ui/#search. OECD = Organisation for Economic Co-operation and Development; SE = standard error.

A significant public services gap also exists across most topics. Business Entry and Business Insolvency have the widest gaps, with 26.38 points and 26.16 points, respectively, suggesting that the process of creative destruction that drives innovation and resource reallocation may be hindered by inadequate provision of public services (refer to figure 3.6, panel c). Financial Services, Business Location, and Dispute Resolution follow closely, with gaps of 25.57 points, 24.55 points, and 23.82 points, respectively. International Trade and Labor show a narrower gap—14.41 points and

8.44 points, respectively. Utility Services and Market Competition have the narrowest gaps—5.00 points and 4.97 points, respectively. By contrast, Taxation is the only area in which Pillar II outperforms Pillar I, on average, by a narrow margin of 1.36 points. This exception suggests that governments may have prioritized facilitation of tax compliance mechanisms, measured in Pillar II, over adequate regulations, measured in Pillar I.

FIGURE 3.6 **The "public services gap" is evident across regions, income levels, and topics**

a. By region

Average pillar score (0–100)

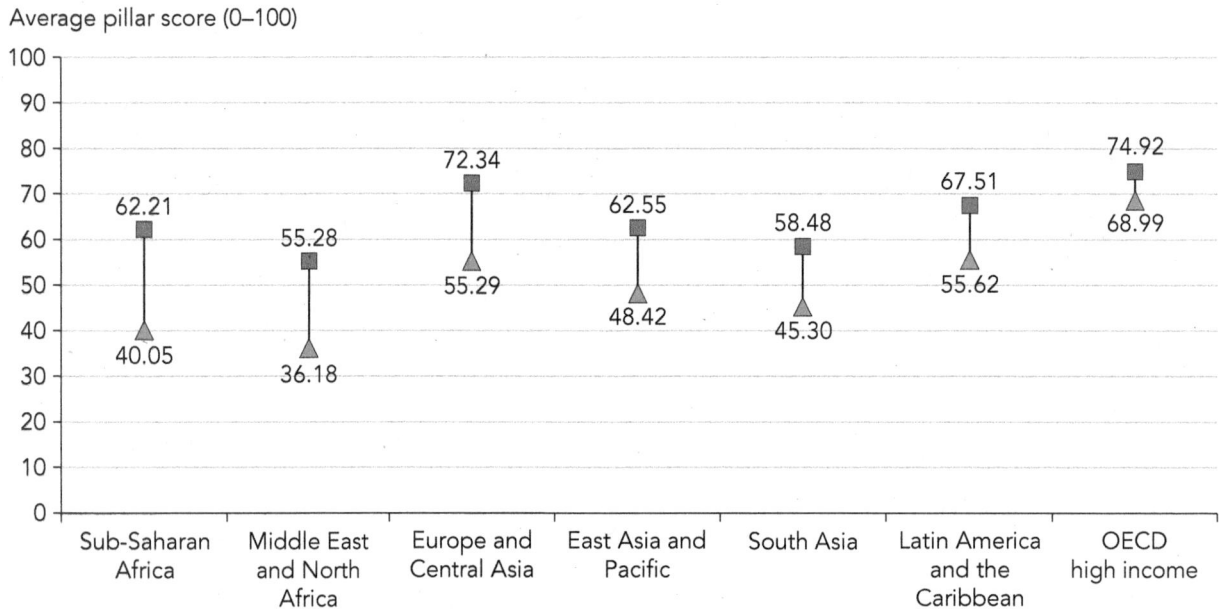

b. By income level

Average pillar score (0–100)

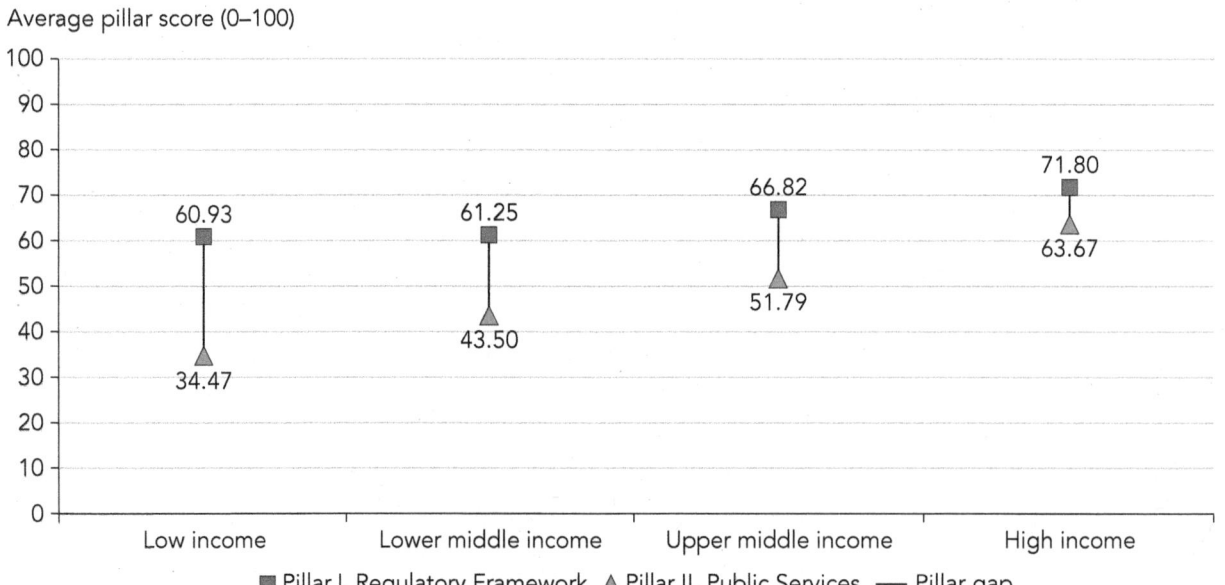

■ Pillar I, Regulatory Framework ▲ Pillar II, Public Services —— Pillar gap

(Continued)

**FIGURE 3.6 The "public services gap" is evident across regions, income levels, and topics
(Continued)**

c. By topic

Average pillar score (0–100)

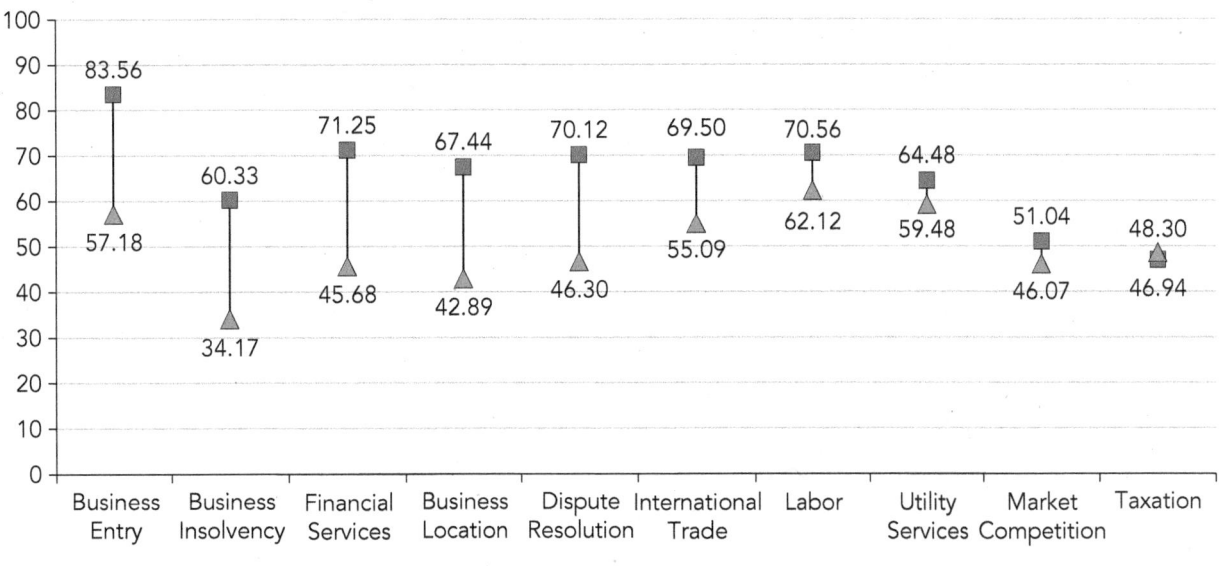

■ Pillar I, Regulatory Framework   ▲ Pillar II, Public Services   — Pillar gap

Source: B-READY 2024 data.
Note: Data in each panel are arranged from the largest to the smallest gap. OECD = Organisation for Economic Co-operation and Development.

The public services gap narrows as the business environment improves. Among the quintiles based on average pillar performance, the last two quintiles have the widest gaps—26.02 points and 19.18 points, respectively. The gap declines progressively toward the higher quintile. The third quintile has a gap of 16.25 points, the second of 9.89 points, and the first of 7.63 points (refer to figure 3.7).

Existing firms can be resilient to poor conditions, but both active and potential firms could thrive if the business environment improves. For most economies, Operational Efficiency scores are higher than the average of the other two pillar scores, Regulatory Framework and Public Services (refer to figure 3.8). These patterns highlight the adaptability of firms in environments marked by deficient public service provision, suggesting they may have developed coping mechanisms to navigate their respective business environments. Although firms exhibit resilience amid challenging conditions, they have the potential to thrive if these conditions improve. Such improvements can also foster market entry for newcomers, essential for cultivating a more dynamic, innovative, and diversified business landscape. It is important, however, to put these findings in context.

The sample of firms providing inputs on their experience in using public services are in the formal sector and exclude very small or recently established firms. Larger and older firms may be less sensitive to weak regulatory and public services environments.

Overall, having sound regulatory frameworks is not enough. Efficient government-provided services that facilitate compliance with regulations and provide institutional support to firms are also important to nurture a thriving business environment. In view of the public services gap, there is ample room to improve the Public Services pillar. Comprehensive reforms across all pillars are ultimately what will drive significant improvements in the business environment and therefore in the B-READY data.

FIGURE 3.7 **The "public services gap" closes remarkably as the business environment improves**

Average pillar score (0–100)

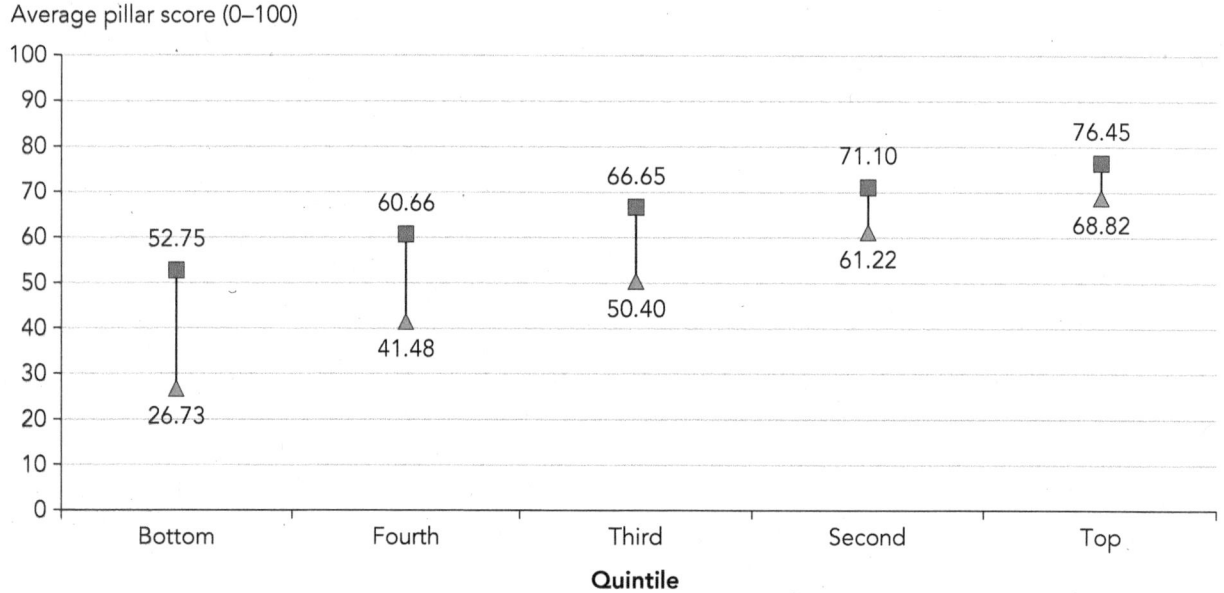

Source: B-READY 2024 data.
Note: The economies in each quintile are determined by the respective scores of the Regulatory Framework and Public Services pillars. Refer to chapter 2 for more details on economy quintiles.

FIGURE 3.8 **For most economies, scores on the Operational Efficiency pillar are higher than the average scores on the Regulatory Framework pillar and the Public Services pillar**

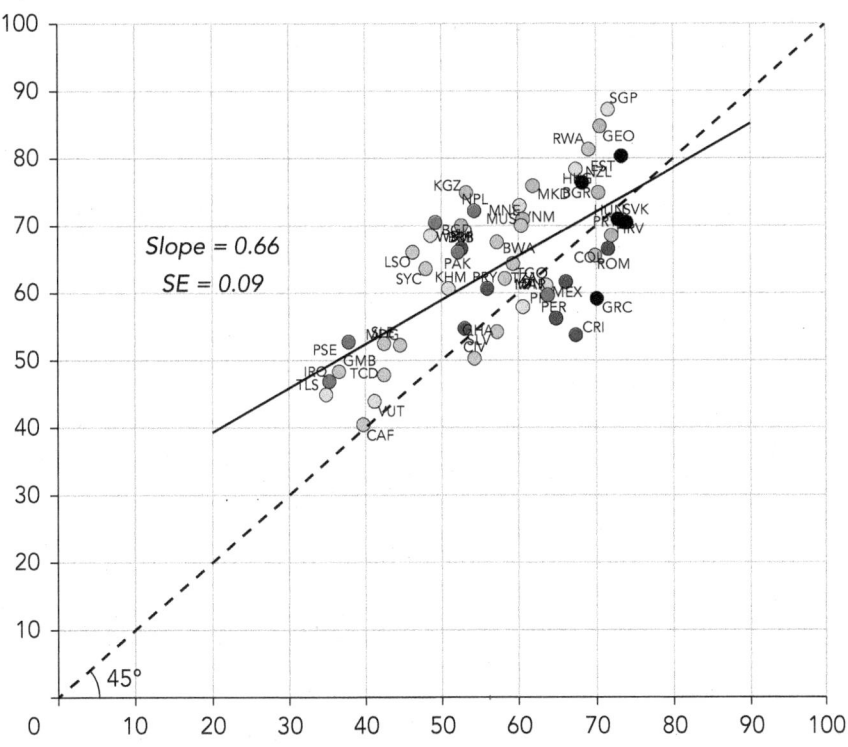

Operational Efficiency score (0–100)

Slope = 0.66
SE = 0.09

45°

Average score, Regulatory Framework and Public Services (0–100)

○ East Asia and Pacific ◐ Europe and Central Asia
● Latin America and the Caribbean ● Middle East and North Africa
● South Asia
● OECD high income ○ Sub-Saharan Africa

Source: B-READY 2024 data.
Note: The dashed line is set at 45 degrees, and the solid line represents the linear regression of the Operational Efficiency score on the average of the Regulatory Framework score and the Public Services score. The relationship is significant at the 1 percent level. The dots, representing economies, indicate by color to which regional grouping an economy belongs. The sample comprises 50 economies. For economy abbreviations, refer to appendix B and International Organization for Standardization (ISO), https://www.iso.org/obp/ui/#search. OECD = Organisation for Economic Co-operation and Development; SE = standard error.

Notes

1. Beneficial ownership refers to the practice in which an individual or entity enjoys the benefits of ownership of a property or asset even though the legal title or ownership may be held by another party.
2. ILO Declaration on Fundamental Principles and Rights at Work, International Labour Organization (ILO), https://www.ilo.org/ilo-declaration-fundamental -principles-and-rights-work.

References

Al-Sadiq, A. J. 2021. "The Role of e-Government in Promoting Foreign Direct Investment Inflows." IMF Working Paper No. 2021/008, International Monetary Fund, Washington, DC.

Bruhn, M., and D. McKenzie. 2014. "Entry Regulation and the Formalization of Microenterprises in Developing Countries." *World Bank Research Observer* 29 (2): 186–201.

Klapper, L., A. Lewin, and J. M. Quesada Delgado. 2011. "The Impact of the Business Environment on the Business Creation Process." Chapter 5 in *Entrepreneurship and Economic Development* (Studies in Development Economics and Policy), edited by W. Naudé. London: Palgrave Macmillan.

Loayza, N. V., and L. Servén. 2010. *Business Regulation and Economic Performance.* Washington, DC: World Bank.

World Bank. 2016. *World Development Report 2016: Digital Dividends.* Washington, DC: World Bank.

World Bank. 2023. *Business Ready: Methodology Handbook.* Washington, DC: World Bank. https://thedocs.worldbank.org/en/doc /357a611e3406288528cb1e05b3c7dfda-0540012023/original/B-READY -Methodology-Handbook.pdf.

B-READY TOPIC RESULTS

Overview of B-READY topics

The selection of B-READY topics is guided by this project's threefold purpose of advocating for policy reform, informing specific policy advice, and providing data for development policy research. The 10 topics were selected using three criteria. The first is relevance; each topic has undergone extensive economic research that demonstrates its impact on and close relationship with private sector development. The second is value added; each topic fills an existing data gap. And the third is complementarity; each topic complements the others, using the life cycle of a firm as the common thread. For the 10 topics, B-READY includes data on three critical cross-cutting themes increasingly important for modern economies: digital adoption, environmental sustainability, and gender.

B-READY does not measure the full range of factors, policies, and institutions that affect the quality of an economy's business environment (such as productivity, informality, or equity) or its national competitiveness. These outcomes are dependent on complex variables encompassing not only the full business environment but also all other aspects of public policy. As such, they are beyond the scope of this project. Furthermore, B-READY does not cover other aspects of the business environment that are well covered by other indicators, including macroeconomic conditions (covered by, among other things, the World Bank's Global Economic Prospects[1]); government corruption

---

A reproducibility package is available for this book in the Reproducible Research Repository at https://reproducibility.worldbank.org/index.php/catalog/187.

and accountability (the World Bank's Worldwide Governance Indicators[2]); human capital (the World Bank's Human Capital Index[3]); and conflict, crime, and violence (United Nations Office on Drugs and Crime[4]).

The *B-READY: Methodology Handbook* documents the project's scope, advantages, and limitations, and presents in thorough detail the methodology used to derive, analyze, and score the topics, including motivation, indicators, questionnaires, and scoring guidelines per topic (World Bank 2023).

 ## TOPIC 1. Business Entry

Once a firm is registered, it benefits from several advantages not available otherwise, such as access to legal services and financial options that facilitate business expansion, leading to more employment opportunities and better access to advanced technology (Capasso and Jappelli 2013; Cirera, Comin, and Cruz 2022). The firm's employees also enjoy social security protection (Medina and Schneider 2018) and better management practices (Islam and Amin 2022). Consequently, formal companies are in a better position to grow and employ workers, as well as to be more productive, profitable, and resilient (Boly 2018; McKenzie and Sakho 2010; Medvedev and Oviedo Silva 2015; Rand and Torm 2012). By contrast, informal enterprises—often operating in less favorable environments with limited infrastructure and a less skilled workforce—face significant challenges in achieving sustainable growth (Loayza 2018).

The overall economy also benefits from the registration of companies. Where formal entrepreneurship is high, job creation, productivity, and economic growth tend to be high, as well (Fritsch and Noseleit 2013; La Porta and Shleifer 2014; Loayza 2016). The success of formal enterprises translates into higher volumes of gross domestic product (GDP) and growth rates at the macro level (La Porta and Shleifer 2008). Through tax revenue, formal businesses also bolster government finances in support of social and economic policy goals. As formality grows in the business sector, governments will have a larger tax base that ultimately will enable the provision of essential public services such as infrastructure, education, and health care (Fajnzylber, Maloney, and Montes-Rojas 2011; McKenzie and Sakho 2010).

A business-friendly environment is one of the factors encouraging a company's decision to register and reap the benefits of formalization.

By contrast, cumbersome regulations for business start-ups are associated with high levels of corruption and informality (Klapper and Love 2016). Entry restrictions can create obstacles to setting up a business and can diminish entrepreneurial activity.[5] Creating the right business environment to facilitate a safe, efficient registration process is key to promoting the formal registration of firms. The implementation of inexpensive, time-saving schemes to incorporate a business is associated with more firms undertaking new business activities (Klapper, Lewin, and Quesada Delgado 2011). Regulations must ensure that the start-up process is not only simple but secure. For example, the introduction of safety checks when filing company incorporation documents or requirements to present information on beneficial ownership promotes a safe environment for business start-ups and prevents the misuse of companies for illegal activities (OECD and IDB 2021; UNCITRAL 2019; World Bank 2020). Public services play a key role in ensuring that compliance is adequate and not onerous. For example, introduction of digital technology and transparency of information can encourage businesses to register by reducing compliance costs (ILO 2021).

What does the Business Entry topic cover?

Business Entry measures three areas corresponding to B-READY's three pillars: (I) the quality of regulations for business entry; (II) the quality of digital public services and the transparency of information for business entry; and (III) the operational efficiency of business entry (refer to table 4.1).

Under the first pillar, the topic measures Information and Procedural Standards, as well as Restrictions on Registering a Business. For example, under Information and Procedural Standards, the topic assesses whether legislation provides for company information filing requirements. Under Restrictions on Registering a Business, the topic looks at whether legislation imposes entry barriers on domestic or foreign firms, such as paid-in minimum capital requirements or investor licenses.

Under the second pillar, the topic assesses the quality of Digital Services—which processes can be completed online without the need to visit the business registry in person; the Interoperability of Services—for example, whether incorporation agencies share information among themselves; and the Transparency of Online Information—for example, what type of company information is available electronically to the public.

Under the third pillar, the topic analyzes the time and cost it takes in practice to incorporate a domestic firm and a foreign firm (operational efficiency).

TABLE 4.1 **Business Entry**

Pillar I, Quality of Regulations for Business Entry		Rescaled points
1.1	**Information and Procedural Standards**	**50.00**
1.1.1	Company Information Filing Requirements	15.00
1.1.2	Beneficial Ownership Filing Requirements	15.00
1.1.3	Availability of Simplified Registration	10.00
1.1.4	Risk-Based Assessment for Operating Business and Environmental Licenses	10.00
1.2	**Restrictions on Registering a Business**	**50.00**
1.2.1	Domestic Firms	25.00
1.2.2	Foreign Firms	25.00
Total		**100.00**
Pillar II, Digital Public Services and Transparency of Information for Business Entry		Rescaled points
2.1	**Digital Services**	**40.00**
2.1.1	Business Start-Up Process	20.00
2.1.2	Storage of Company and Beneficial Ownership Information	10.00
2.1.3	Identity Verification	10.00
2.2	**Interoperability of Services**	**20.00**
2.2.1	Exchange of Company Information	10.00
2.2.2	Unique Business Identification	10.00
2.3	**Transparency of Online Information**	**40.00**
2.3.1	Business Start-Up (includes gender and environment)	20.00
2.3.2	Availability of General Company Information	10.00
2.3.3	General and Sex-Disaggregated Statistics on Newly Registered Firms	10.00
Total		**100.00**
Pillar III, Operational Efficiency of Business Entry		Rescaled points
3.1	**Domestic Firms**	**50.00**
3.1.1	Total Time to Register a New Domestic Firm	25.00
3.1.2	Total Cost to Register a New Domestic Firm	25.00
3.2	**Foreign Firms**	**50.00**
3.2.1	Total Time to Register a New Foreign Firm	25.00
3.2.2	Total Cost to Register a New Foreign Firm	25.00
Total		**100.00**

Source: B-READY project.

 TOPIC 2. Business Location

Choosing the right location is key to the success of businesses, even in the digital age. The significance of securing the proper physical space greatly influences access to customers, transportation, labor, and materials, as well as a firm's adherence to tax, regulatory, and environmental obligations (Carlson 2000).

Whether a firm is leasing or buying property, a solid regulatory framework and public services related to acquiring a location significantly affect the business environment and may foster private sector development in an economy. Research shows that strong, secured property rights encourage investment. An assessment of how well property rights are managed provides a good indication of how likely the economy is to grow (Field 2007). Effective land administration reduces information asymmetry, enhances market efficiency, and ensures transparency of property ownership. Promoting good governance in the land administration system encourages the enactment of publicly accessible laws on ownership and leasing, secure land tenure, and safeguards and service standards to avoid the risk of land disputes and corruption (Wehrmann 2008; Zakout, Wehrmann, and Törhönen 2006). Integrating the land registry with the cadastral system facilitates the maintenance of reliable, up-to-date land use records and is of vital importance for land management.

Obtaining a new business location requires acquiring secure titles for property transfers (the sale or purchase of property) or new construction. Building permits and licenses enhance public safety and the accumulation of capital as property values increase. Clear, accessible environmental regulations can address concerns without burdening firms with unnecessary compliance. A sound, robust environmental framework for construction projects plays a vital role in achieving sustainable construction by identifying and addressing potential environmental impacts in advance. The adoption of good regulatory practices for building regulations and environmental permits enhances safety mechanisms, green building regulations, and gender diversity in building-related professions. Transparency of information for building and environmental permits minimizes information gaps between public services providers and users, fostering accountability through easy access to regulations, fees, and payment tracking.

What does the Business Location topic cover?

The Business Location topic evaluates regulatory quality, governance quality, and the transparency and operational efficiency of services for property transfer, building permits, and environmental permits. The topic spans three pillars: (I) the quality of regulations for business location; (II) the quality of public services and transparency of information for business location; and (III) the operational efficiency of establishing a business location (refer to table 4.2).

The first pillar explores the quality of regulations for an immovable property lease, property ownership, urban planning, and environmental licenses. For example, an effective regulatory framework incorporating good practices contributes to efficient, secured property transactions, effective land dispute mechanisms, and a defined set of building regulation standards and environmental clearances.

TABLE 4.2 **Business Location**

Pillar I, Quality of Regulations for Business Location		Rescaled points
1.1	**Property Transfer and Land Administration**	**40.00**
1.1.1	Property Transfer Standards	15.00
1.1.2	Land Dispute Mechanisms	15.00
1.1.3	Land Administration System	10.00
1.2	**Building, Zoning, and Land Use**	**40.00**
1.2.1	Building Standards	15.00
1.2.2	Building Energy Standards	15.00
1.2.3	Zoning and Land Use Regulations	10.00
1.3	**Restrictions on Owning and Leasing Property**	**10.00**
1.3.1	Domestic Firms–Ownership	2.50
1.3.2	Domestic Firms–Leasehold	2.50
1.3.3	Foreign Firms–Ownership	2.50
1.3.4	Foreign Firms–Leasehold	2.50
1.4	**Environmental Permits**	**10.00**
1.4.1	Environmental Permits for Construction	5.00
1.4.2	Dispute Mechanisms for Construction-Related Environmental Permits	5.00
Total		**100.00**
Pillar II, Quality of Public Services and Transparency of Information for Business Location		Rescaled points
2.1	**Availability and Reliability of Digital Services**	**40.00**
2.1.1	Property Transfer–Digital Public Services	8.00
2.1.2	Property Transfer–Digital Land Management and Identification System	8.00
2.1.3	Property Transfer–Coverage of the Land Registry and Mapping Agency	8.00
2.1.4	Building Permits–Digital Public Services	8.00
2.1.5	Environmental Permits–Digital Public Services	8.00
2.2	**Interoperability of Services**	**20.00**
2.2.1	Interoperability of Services for Property Transfer	10.00
2.2.2	Interoperability of Services for Building Permits	10.00
2.3	**Transparency of Information**	**40.00**
2.3.1	Immovable Property (includes gender)	20.00
2.3.2	Building, Zoning and Land Use	15.00
2.3.3	Environmental Permits	5.00
Total		**100.00**
Pillar III, Operational Efficiency of Establishing a Business Location		Rescaled points
3.1	**Property Transfer and Land Administration**	**40.00**
3.1.1	Major Constraints on Access to Land*	13.33
3.1.2	Time to Obtain a Property Transfer	13.33
3.1.3	Cost to Obtain a Property Transfer	13.33
3.2	**Construction Permits**	**40.00**
3.2.1	Time to Obtain Construction-Related Permits*	13.33
3.2.2	Time to Obtain a Building Permit	13.33
3.2.3	Cost to Obtain a Building Permit	13.33
3.3	**Environmental Permit**	**20.00**
3.3.1	Time to Obtain an Environmental Permit	10.00
3.3.2	Cost to Obtain an Environmental Permit	10.00
Total		**100.00**

Source: B-READY project.

Note: An asterisk (*) indicates a subcategory containing data collected through the World Bank Enterprise Surveys, https://www.enterprisesurveys.org/en/enterprisesurveys.

The second pillar captures the quality of public services and transparency of information, such as having online services for building permits, electronic storage of cadastral information, and data exchange across property administration institutions, and evaluating the extent of transparency across agencies for environmental licenses.

The third pillar measures the operational efficiency of obtaining a business location: the time and cost to obtain a building permit, an environmental permit, and a property transfer. The topic also evaluates data on property ownership broken down by gender, with the aim of improving policies and practices to narrow the gender gap.

 TOPIC 3. Utility Services

Utility services play a vital role in economic and social development by providing the essential inputs that every business needs to function. Electricity, water, and internet services support business operations and are essential factors of production. Entrepreneurs may face substantial burdens in operating their businesses when utility services are unreliable, inefficient, or costly. Disruptions in electricity supply impair firm productivity, revenue, and economic growth (Allcott, Collard-Wexler, and O'Connell 2016). One-third of firms globally identify an unreliable electricity supply as a major constraint on their operations.[6] Similarly, an inadequate water supply arising from aging infrastructure, poor water quality, and changes in water pressure can lead to lower firm productivity, deterioration of machinery, and reduced profits (World Bank 2017). Overall, losses stemming from power and water outages have been estimated at US$82 billion annually for firms in developing economies (Rentschler et al. 2019). Internet connectivity is also indispensable for digital adoption by firms. In many economies, particularly developing ones, the number of high-speed internet subscriptions remains limited. As of 2022, just over 17 percent of the population globally had access to fixed broadband subscriptions (WIPO 2023), and the share was only 1.6 percent in the least developed economies.[7] Unreliable networks and the high cost of establishing a broadband connection may prevent firms from adopting and upgrading digital technology in their business operations (Chen 2019).

Good regulatory frameworks are fundamental to improving sector performance and consumer outcomes, such as quality and affordability in the provision of utility services (OECD 2021). Established performance standards, coupled with a system of incentives, compel utility companies to ensure an adequate supply of electricity, water, and internet services (Foster and Rana 2020). Fostering accountability across the supply chain, professional certifications reduce information asymmetry (Leland 1979), inspections boost compliance with safety standards (Boyne, Day, and Walker 2002), and transparent liability regimes facilitate effective risk management (Wilson, Klass, and Bergan 2009).

An efficient regulatory framework can pave the way for the effective performance of infrastructure services. Adequate monitoring of the quality of service supply, the safety and transparency of connections, and the interoperability of utility services is fundamental to enhancing public accountability and ensuring efficient provision of high-quality electricity, water, and internet services (Foster and Rana 2020). Simultaneously, the regulatory and administrative framework should aim to reduce the administrative burden and compliance costs imposed on businesses. Therefore, facilitating timely access to resources at a reasonable cost and in an environmentally sustainable manner is vital for promoting investment and economic growth (World Bank 2017).

What does the Utility Services topic cover?

The Utility Services topic covers the three key utilities supporting firm operations—electricity, water, and internet—and spans three pillars: (I) the quality of regulations for utility services; (II) the quality of governance and transparency of utility services; and (III) the operational efficiency of utility service provision (refer to table 4.3). The indicators assess commercial electricity, water, and high-speed broadband internet connections.

The first pillar covers the quality of regulations for efficient deployment of utility connections and quality of supply. It assesses regulatory monitoring, utility infrastructure sharing, and the operational efficiency of digital connectivity, as well as mechanisms for service quality assurance, among other components. This pillar also looks at the environmental sustainability of the provision and use of electricity, water, and internet services, as well as sustainable wastewater practices, such as discharge limits and wastewater reuse requirements.

The second pillar evaluates the quality of monitoring of the reliability and sustainability of service supply and safety of connections. Aspects examined include the availability of key performance indicators on the reliability and environmental sustainability of utility services, as well as monitoring of the safety of utility connections in practice. The second pillar also measures the transparency surrounding service outages, tariffs, connection requirements, and complaint mechanisms, as well as the existence of customer surveys. Finally, the pillar measures aspects of interoperability at the utility level, as well as the existence of electronic applications and electronic payments (e-payments).

The third pillar examines the operational efficiency of utility service provision—specifically, the time and cost associated with obtaining a connection and the ongoing service expenses, as well as the reliability of the service supply.

TABLE 4.3 **Utility Services**

Pillar I, Quality of Regulations on Utility Services		Rescaled points
1.1	**Electricity**	**33.33**
1.1.1	Regulatory Monitoring of Tariffs and Service Quality	8.33
1.1.2	Utility Infrastructure Sharing and Quality Assurance Mechanisms	8.33
1.1.3	Safety of Utility Connections	8.33
1.1.4	Environmental Sustainability	8.33
1.2	**Water**	**33.33**
1.2.1	Regulatory Monitoring of Tariffs and Service Quality	8.33
1.2.2	Utility Infrastructure Sharing and Quality Assurance Mechanisms	8.33
1.2.3	Safety of Utility Connections	8.33
1.2.4	Environmental Sustainability	8.33
1.3	**Internet**	**33.33**
1.3.1	Regulatory Monitoring of Tariffs and Service Quality	8.33
1.3.2	Utility Infrastructure Sharing and Quality Assurance Mechanisms	13.33
1.3.3	Safety of Utility Connections	8.33
1.3.4	Environmental Sustainability	3.33
Total		**100.00**
Pillar II, Quality of the Governance and Transparency of Utility Services		Rescaled points
2.1	**Electricity**	**33.33**
2.1.1	Digital Services and Interoperability	8.33
2.1.2	Availability of Information and Transparency	8.33
2.1.3	Monitoring of Service Supply (includes gender and environment)	8.33
2.1.4	Enforcement of Safety Regulations and Consumer Protection Mechanisms	8.33
2.2	**Water**	**33.33**
2.2.1	Digital Services and Interoperability	8.33
2.2.2	Availability of Information and Transparency	8.33
2.2.3	Monitoring of Service Supply (includes gender and environment)	8.33
2.2.4	Enforcement of Safety Regulations and Consumer Protection Mechanisms	8.33
2.3	**Internet**	**33.33**
2.3.1	Digital Services and Interoperability	8.33
2.3.2	Availability of Information and Transparency	8.33
2.3.3	Monitoring of Service Supply (includes gender and environment)	8.33
2.3.4	Enforcement of Safety Regulations and Consumer Protection Mechanisms	8.33
Total		**100.00**
Pillar III, Operational Efficiency of Utility Service Provision		Rescaled points
3.1	**Electricity**	**33.33**
3.1.1	Time to Obtain a Connection*	16.67
3.1.2	Reliability of Supply*	16.67
3.2	**Water**	**33.33**
3.2.1	Time to Obtain a Connection*	16.67
3.2.2	Reliability of Supply*	16.67
3.3	**Internet**	**33.33**
3.3.1	Time to Obtain a Connection*	16.67
3.3.2	Reliability of Supply*	16.67
Total		**100.00**

Source: B-READY project.

Note: An asterisk (*) indicates a subcategory containing data collected through the World Bank Enterprise Surveys, https://www
.enterprisesurveys.org/en/enterprisesurveys.

 **TOPIC 4. Labor**

Labor is the most important source of income for most people (World Bank 2012) and a key driver of poverty reduction (Azevedo et al. 2013), allowing individuals and families to meet their needs and improve their living standards. Labor is also a fundamental factor of production, which drives economic growth. A labor market that provides firms with opportunities and workers with protections can improve employment dynamics and productivity. Conversely, labor market imperfections can impede job quality and job creation (World Bank 2012).

Labor regulations and labor market institutions must strive to achieve a fair balance between the need to protect workers' rights and labor market flexibility that fosters a conducive environment for the creation of productive employment opportunities (Kuddo 2018). Regulations and public services related to labor are fundamental drivers of private sector development because they affect firms' decisions to expand by hiring labor, and whether to do so formally or informally (Almeida and Carneiro 2011). If labor regulations make hiring costs too high and rules too cumbersome, firms may choose to use more capital than labor or to hire informally. Some workers may lose when firms make such choices, and workers employed in the informal sector can be prevented from entering the formal workforce (Chaudhary and Sharma 2022; Loayza 2016; Ulyssea 2020).

A lack of worker protection can lower standards of living—generating an unhealthy, unmotivated workforce that could lead to poor firm productivity. Discrimination in access to employment and persistent gaps in income may discourage workers from entering the labor market or participating in it to their full potential. Sound, balanced labor regulations are needed for firms and workers to benefit from a dynamic, innovative labor market that does not come at the expense of income security or basic workers' rights (World Bank 2012).

What does the Labor topic cover?

The Labor topic measures good practices in employment regulations and public services from the perspective of both firms and employees across three pillars: (I) the quality of labor regulations; (II) the adequacy of public services for labor; and (III) the operational efficiency of labor regulations and public services (refer to table 4.4).

The first pillar examines the quality of de jure features needed for the functioning of the labor market and to stipulate obligations and relevant safeguards related to workers' conditions and employment restrictions and costs, such as the provision of a minimum wage, equal remuneration for work of equal value, and health and safety.

TABLE 4.4 **Labor**

Pillar I, Quality of Labor Regulations		Rescaled points
1.1	**Workers' Conditions**	**50.00**
1.1.1	Labor Rights	16.67
1.1.2	Minimum Wage Attributes	16.67
1.1.3	Termination of Employment	16.67
1.2	**Employment Restrictions and Costs**	**50.00**
1.2.1	Terms of Employment	16.67
1.2.2	Minimum Wage Rate	16.67
1.2.3	Termination of Employment	16.67
Total		**100.00**
Pillar II, Adequacy of Public Services for Labor		**Rescaled points**
2.1	**Social Protection**	**50.00**
2.1.1	Unemployment Insurance	16.67
2.1.2	Health Care Coverage	16.67
2.1.3	Retirement Pension	16.67
2.2	**Employment Services**	**50.00**
2.2.1	Employment Centers and Training	16.67
2.2.2	Labor Dispute Resolution Mechanisms	16.67
2.2.3	Labor Inspectorates	16.67
Total		**100.00**
Pillar III, Operational Efficiency of Labor Regulations and Public Services in Practice		**Rescaled points**
3.1	**Employment Restrictions and Costs**	**50.00**
3.1.1	Social Contribution*	16.67
3.1.2	Obstacles to Hiring*	16.67
3.1.3	Dismissal Time and Cost*	16.67
3.2	**Employment Services**	**50.00**
3.2.1	On-the-Job Training*	16.67
3.2.2	Prevalence and Operational Efficiency of Labor Disputes*	16.67
3.2.3	Health and Safety Inspection*	16.67
Total		**100.00**

Source: B-READY project.
Note: An asterisk (*) indicates a subcategory containing data collected through the World Bank Enterprise Surveys, https://www.enterprisesurveys.org/en/enterprisesurveys.

The second pillar looks at the existence of critical public services that can help enforce, facilitate, and complement quality labor regulations, such as unemployment protection, health care coverage, and retirement pension for workers, as well as employment centers, labor inspectorates, and dispute resolution mechanisms.

The third pillar provides insights into nonwage labor costs, employment restrictions and costs, training, and the prevalence of labor disputes and efficiency in resolving them from the firm's perspective.

TOPIC 5. Financial Services

The financial sector plays an essential role in allocating capital in an economy. Well-developed financial systems, which offer a wide range of financial services and products, promote economic growth primarily by improving resource allocation and promoting technological innovation (Levine 2005). Well-functioning financial systems can help increase resilience to shocks and can encourage formalization of businesses. In addition, they play an important role in income distribution as they shape the economic opportunities available to individuals. By providing the poor segments of society with access to finance, the financial sector can help reduce poverty and income inequality (Beck, Demirgüç-Kunt, and Levine 2007).

Better-functioning financial systems are vital because they can stimulate the formation of new firms by funding new ventures and can promote the expansion of existing firms by easing external financing constraints. Efficient, timely access to finance and payment services can help firms ride out periods of low or volatile cash flow; can promote firm growth, innovation, and job growth; can enable firms to expand their customer base; and can influence their decision to be environmentally conscious (Amin and Viganola 2021; Ayyagari et al. 2021; Mare, de Nicola, and Miguel 2021; Qi and Ongena 2019; Rahaman 2011; Wellalage and Fernandez 2019; Wellalage and Locke 2020).

Despite being essential for firms' operations and expansion and positively associated with firms' innovation, access to finance remains a major constraint for firms worldwide[8] and is also one of the main policy challenges. Access to financial services depends not only on the availability of financial infrastructures, markets, and intermediaries, but also on the underlying laws and regulations pertaining to financial systems and institutions. The presence of robust regulatory frameworks based on good practices is important for maintaining the integrity and stability of financial systems, protecting consumers and investors, and ensuring that the financial sector continues to allocate funds efficiently for productive uses. Effective regulations can also boost the trust and confidence of users of financial services and can determine the likelihood of firms being able to afford and obtain financial services.

What does the Financial Services topic cover?

The Financial Services topic spans three pillars: (I) the quality of regulations for financial services; (II) the accessibility of information in credit infrastructure; and (III) the operational efficiency of receiving financial services (refer to table 4.5).

TABLE 4.5 **Financial Services**

Pillar I, Quality of Regulations for Financial Services		Rescaled points
1.1	**Commercial Lending**	**20.00**
1.1.1	Customer Due Diligence (CDD) and Risk Factors	10.00
1.1.2	Record Keeping of Customer Information	5.00
1.1.3	Availability of Enhanced and Simplified CDD Measures	5.00
1.2	**Secured Transactions**	**40.00**
1.2.1	Integrated Legal Framework for Secured Transactions	10.00
1.2.2	Types of Movable Assets, Debts and Obligations that Can Be Secured	20.00
1.2.3	Priority/Enforcement of Security Interests	10.00
1.3	**e-Payments**	**40.00**
1.3.1	Risk Management	10.00
1.3.2	Consumer Protection	20.00
1.3.3	Interoperability of Payment Systems and Promotion of Competition	10.00
Total		**100.00**
Pillar II, Accessibility of Information in Credit Infrastructure		Rescaled points
2.1	**Operation of Credit Bureaus and Registries**	**50.00**
2.1.1	Data Coverage	16.67
2.1.2	Types of Data Collected and Shared	16.67
2.1.3	Additional Services and Borrower's Access to Information	16.67
2.2	**Operation of Collateral Registries**	**50.00**
2.2.1	Existence of a Centralized and Publicly Available Registry	16.67
2.2.2	Notice-Based Registry Updates	16.67
2.2.3	Autonomy of Secured Creditors to Access and Update the Registry	16.67
Total		**100.00**
Pillar III, Operational Efficiency of Receiving Financial Services		Rescaled points
3.1	**Loans**	**50.00**
3.1.1	Obtaining a Loan*	40.00
3.1.2	Operational Efficiency of Security Interest and Credit Data Update	10.00
3.2	**e-Payments**	**50.00**
3.2.1	Cost of e-Payments*	20.00
3.2.2	Time to Receive e-Payments*	10.00
3.2.3	Usage Level of e-Payments*	20.00
Total		**100.00**

Source: B-READY project.
Note: An asterisk (*) indicates a subcategory containing data collected through the World Bank Enterprise Surveys, https://www
.enterprisesurveys.org/en/enterprisesurveys. e-Payments = electronic payments.

The first pillar assesses the quality of regulatory practices for commercial
lending, secured transactions, and e-payments. For example, under
Commercial Lending, the pillar looks at regulations pertaining to customer
due diligence (CDD), the existence of simplified and enhanced CDD

measures, and recordkeeping. Under Secured Transactions, the pillar assesses the regulations for an integrated legal framework, the types of movable assets that may be used as nonpossessory security interests, and the priority of such security interests and enforcement mechanisms. Under e-Payments, it examines regulations for risk management, consumer protection, and interoperability conditions and the promotion of competition.

The second pillar assesses the quality of de facto and some de jure elements associated with the accessibility of information in credit infrastructure. It looks at credit bureaus and registries, as well as collateral registries. It also includes data on the level of usage of credit reports and collateral registry services by commercial banks while reviewing corporate loan applications.

The third pillar covers de facto elements and measures the ease of obtaining a loan, the ease of registering a security interest, the timeliness with which credit information is shared, and the ease of making and receiving e-payments (operational efficiency).

 ## TOPIC 6. International Trade

International trade, one of the key drivers of economic growth, is vital for promoting private sector development. It affects the private sector through various channels, including greater competition, domestic firm specialization, resource reallocation (Melitz 2003), and productivity growth (Sampson 2016). International trade supports economic growth by providing access to bigger markets and less expensive, higher-quality inputs (Goldberg et al. 2010); promoting technology transfer (Madsen 2007), leading to larger, more productive firms; and bringing about a more diverse, competitive, and resilient private sector overall.

Full realization of the benefits of international trade requires a conducive business environment that reduces trade barriers and lowers the compliance and transaction costs for firms. Adequate regulations and public services, as well as efficient procedures, enable both small and large firms to participate in international trade and access global markets (Fontagné, Orefice, and Piermartini 2020). A regulatory framework that establishes a fair, transparent, and predictable trading environment gives firms a level playing field, thereby helping to facilitate trade, ensure compliance, attract investments, and improve competitiveness (Handley 2014). Public services that facilitate trade processes help the private sector to maximize the benefits and minimize the burdens arising from the regulatory framework. As such, improving the quality of digital and physical infrastructure strengthens the transparency, accountability, and efficiency of clearance processes (Donaubauer et al. 2018; UNECE 2021), while enhancing risk management (UNCTAD n.d.), fostering coordinated border management (OSCE/UNECE 2012; WCO 2020), and establishing trusted trader programs (ITC 2020), thereby enabling the efficient allocation of public resources and reducing costs for firms.

Efficient procedures and costs are integral to international trade. The operational, transaction, and compliance costs associated with exporting and importing can become burdensome for firms that trade internationally (Hummels and Schaur 2013; Volpe Martincus, Carballo, and Graziano 2015). Factors such as lengthy customs clearance procedures, lack of coordination among border agencies, inadequate trade infrastructure, and limited logistics services increase the time and costs to comply with export and import requirements (WTO 2021). Thus, an enabling environment makes it easier and more cost-effective for firms to engage in international trade, thereby reducing delays and lowering compliance and transaction costs.

What does the International Trade topic cover?

The International Trade topic encompasses three pillars: (I) the quality of regulations for international trade; (II) the quality of public services for the facilitation of international trade; and (III) the operational efficiency of importing goods, exporting goods, and engaging in digital trade (refer to table 4.6).

The first pillar measures the quality of regulations in international trade on the creation of a fair, transparent, and secure environment for international trade in goods and services and for digital trade. For example, this pillar measures the implementation of international standards, regulations governing regulatory decisions and appeals, practices supporting digital and sustainable trade, and the nature and extent of international trade cooperation, as well as restrictions on international trade in goods, services, and digital trade.

The second pillar measures de facto aspects of the quality of public services for the facilitation of international trade, including digital and physical infrastructure, and border management. It assesses the availability of electronic systems, the relevant trade infrastructure, the transparency and availability of information, risk management, coordinated border management, and trusted trader programs.

The third pillar evaluates the operational efficiency of importing and exporting goods and engaging in digital trade. It gauges the time, cost, and ease of complying with trade requirements, and the share of firms exporting digitally ordered goods, as well as the perceived major obstacles related to business transportation, customs, and trade regulations.

TABLE 4.6 **International Trade**

Pillar I, Quality of Regulations for International Trade		Rescaled points
1.1	**Practices Supporting International Trade**	**50.00**
1.1.1	International Trade in Goods and Services	16.67
1.1.2	Digital and Sustainable Trade (includes gender and environment)	16.67
1.1.3	International Trade Cooperation	16.67
1.2	**Regulatory Restrictions on International Trade**	**50.00**
1.2.1	International Trade in Goods (includes gender)	20.00
1.2.2	International Trade in Services	20.00
1.2.3	Digital Trade	10.00
Total		**100.00**
Pillar II, Quality of Public Services for the Facilitation of International Trade		Rescaled points
2.1	**Digital and Physical Infrastructure**	**50.00**
2.1.1	Electronic Systems and Interoperability of Services	16.67
2.1.2	Transparency and Availability of Information	16.67
2.1.3	Trade Infrastructure	16.67
2.2	**Border Management**	**50.00**
2.2.1	Risk Management	20.00
2.2.2	Coordinated Border Management	20.00
2.2.3	Trusted Trader Programs	10.00
Total		**100.00**
Pillar III, Operational Efficiency of Exporting Goods, Importing Goods, and Engaging in Digital Trade		Rescaled points
3.1	**Compliance with Export Requirements**	**40.00**
3.1.1	Total Time to Comply with Export Requirements*	20.00
3.1.2	Total Cost to Comply with Export Requirements*	20.00
3.2	**Compliance with Import Requirements**	**40.00**
3.2.1	Total Time to Comply with Import Requirements*	20.00
3.2.2	Total Cost to Comply with Import Requirements*	20.00
3.3	**Participation in Cross-Border Digital Trade**	**10.00**
3.3.1	Share of Trading Firms Exporting Digitally Ordered Goods*	10.00
3.4	**Perceived Major Obstacles: Business Transportation, Customs, and Trade Regulations**	**10.00**
3.4.1	Share of Firms Identifying Customs and Trade Regulations as Major or Severe Constraints*	5.00
3.4.2	Share of Firms Identifying Business Transportation as Major or Severe Constraints*	5.00
Total		**100.00**

Source: B-READY project.
Note: An asterisk (*) indicates a subcategory containing data collected through the World Bank Enterprise Surveys, https://www.enterprisesurveys.org/en/enterprisesurveys.

TOPIC 7. Taxation

Taxation is an important tool employed by governments worldwide to generate revenue and reallocate resources to various social sectors, thereby fostering economic development and addressing public needs. A sound fiscal environment can nurture the private sector by providing infrastructure, human capital, law enforcement, and other public services (Besley and Persson 2019). Conversely, complexity in tax regulation, inefficiency in the tax administration system, and high costs of compliance are associated with more corruption, less investment, and lower firm entry (Dabla-Norris et al. 2017).

Effective tax policies should strike a balance between generating revenue and minimizing the burden on companies. Efficient tax administration systems, easy access to information, the use of systems to pay taxes electronically, and transparency enhance firm productivity and economic growth (Dabla-Norris et al. 2017). Reducing the likelihood of audits for low-risk taxpayers also encourages greater compliance, while the presence of impartial, accessible, and efficient tax dispute resolution mechanisms protects taxpayers' rights (Koos 2014).

Excessive taxation may foster tax evasion (Clotfelter 1983). Meanwhile, cumbersome regulations may discourage formalization (Coolidge and Ilic 2009) because they pose additional compliance costs for firms (Alm et al. 2010). Complex tax codes disproportionately burden small and medium enterprises because of their limited resources for navigating complexity and uncertainty, prompting the need for governments to enact measures that restrict discretion and ensure taxpayer certainty.

In the area of environmental taxation, fiscal instruments empower consumers and businesses to choose the most cost-effective solutions to promote sustainability, thereby fostering innovation and investment in low-carbon emission technologies (Aldy and Stavins 2011).

What does the Taxation topic cover?

The Taxation topic captures a variety of aspects of the fiscal system relevant to private sector development. It spans three pillars: (I) the quality of regulations on taxation; (II) the quality of public services provided by the tax administration; and (III) the operational efficiency of the tax system (refer to table 4.7).

TABLE 4.7 **Taxation**

Pillar I, Quality of Regulations on Taxation		Rescaled points
1.1	**Clarity and Transparency**	**40.00**
1.1.1	Clarity of Tax Regulations	20.00
1.1.2	Transparency of Changes in Tax Regulations	20.00
1.2	**Administrative Procedures**	**40.00**
1.2.1	Simplified Tax Record Keeping and Reporting	10.00
1.2.2	General Tax Registration	10.00
1.2.3	VAT Registration	10.00
1.2.4	VAT Refund	10.00
1.3	**Environmental Taxes**	**20.00**
1.3.1	Existence of Environmental Fiscal Instruments	4.00
1.3.2	Availability of Public Consultations	8.00
1.3.3	Transition Periods	8.00
Total		**100.00**
Pillar II, Public Services Provided by the Tax Administration		Rescaled points
2.1	**Digital Services for Taxpayers**	**25.00**
2.1.1	Online Service Taxpayer Portal	6.25
2.1.2	Electronic Filing of Taxes	6.25
2.1.3	Pre-Filled Tax Declarations	6.25
2.1.4	Electronic Payment of Taxes	6.25
2.2	**Data Management and System Integration in Tax Administration**	**25.00**
2.2.1	Tax Registration	6.25
2.2.2	Taxpayer Database and Tax Identification Number (TIN)	6.25
2.2.3	Tax Deregistration	6.25
2.2.4	Data Exchange and Usage (includes gender)	6.25
2.3	**Transparency**	**25.00**
2.3.1	Annual Performance and Gender Diversity in Tax Administration	12.50
2.3.2	Public Accountability	12.50
2.4	**Tax Audits and Related Disputes**	**25.00**
2.4.1	Tax Audits	12.50
2.4.2	Dispute of Tax Audit Results	12.50
Total		**100.00**
Pillar III, Operational Efficiency of Tax System in Practice		Rescaled points
3.1	**Time and Functionality of Processes**	**50.00**
3.1.1	Time to File and Pay Taxes*	10.00
3.1.2	Use of Electronic System to File and Pay Taxes*	10.00
3.1.3	Duration of a Generic Tax Audit*	10.00
3.1.4	Duration of a Tax Dispute*	10.00
3.1.5	Use of a VAT Refund*	10.00
3.2	**Financial Burden on Firms**	**50.00**
3.2.1	Effective Tax Rate (ETR) for Profit Taxes*	25.00
3.2.2	Effective Tax Rate (ETR) for Employment Taxes and Social Contributions*	25.00
Total		**100.00**

Source: B-READY project.

Note: An asterisk (*) indicates a subcategory containing data collected through the World Bank Enterprise Surveys, https://www.enterprisesurveys.org/en/enterprisesurveys. VAT = value added tax.

The first pillar measures the quality (clarity and transparency) of tax regulations, such as accessibility of tax guides, the existence of binding rulings, transparency in the introduction of new regulations, and the tax administration's feedback and public consultation practices. It also examines good practices in administrative procedures, focusing on the availability of tax registration information, the existence of value added tax (VAT) thresholds, and the availability of and restrictions on VAT cash refunds, alongside simplified recordkeeping and filing processes. This pillar also focuses on environmental fiscal instruments such as carbon taxes, energy taxes, emissions trading systems, feebates, and fossil fuel subsidies. It assesses governance measures and strategies for transitioning to a lower-carbon future, such as incorporating explicit adjustment mechanisms for environmental tax rates into legislation and clearly communicating the transition period for implementing new environmental instruments.

The second pillar captures the quality of four main areas: Digital Services for Taxpayers, Data Management and System Integration in Tax Administration, Transparency, and Tax Audits and Related Disputes. For example, it covers online public services provided to taxpayers, interoperability between tax administration and other government institutions, transparency and accountability of tax administration, types of audits, and mechanisms for resolving a tax dispute.

The third pillar measures the time and functionality (operational efficiency) of processes such as the use of electronic systems to file and pay taxes, the duration of a generic tax audit and disputes, and obtaining a VAT refund in practice. The pillar also evaluates the financial burden on firms by measuring the effective tax rate for profit taxes and employment taxes and social contributions.

 TOPIC 8. Dispute Resolution

Commercial disputes inevitably occur in developed and developing economies alike. When these disputes cannot be resolved properly, adverse economic outcomes can arise for the private sector, ranging from reduced entrepreneurial activity and lower investment to macroeconomic volatility (Esposito, Lanau, and Pompe 2014). A well-functioning dispute resolution system is therefore essential for a healthy business environment.

Private sector growth requires time- and cost-effective mechanisms for resolving disputes. A number of studies have found correlations between judicial efficiency and facilitation of entrepreneurial activity (Garcia-Posada and Mora-Sanguinetti 2015; Ippoliti, Melcarne, and Ramello 2015). Evidence also suggests that under a more effective court system businesses are likely to have greater access to finance and borrow more (Moro, Maresch, and Ferrando 2018). Importantly, expeditious judiciaries are associated with higher levels of domestic and foreign investment (Koutroumpis and Ravasan 2020). When investors faced with nonperformance of an obligation know that their claim will be considered in a timely manner, they may have more incentives to increase their investment (Chemin 2009; Dejuan-Bitria and Mora-Sanguinetti 2021). Enhancing the efficiency of the judiciary may also strengthen competition and foster innovation (OECD 2013).

Private sector development also benefits from dispute resolution mechanisms that are trustworthy. When confidence in the court system is low, firms may become more constrained in their operations and refuse to expand their businesses or look for alternative trade partners (World Bank 2004). To attract more investors, economies should ensure not only the effectiveness of judiciaries but also their strength and reliability (Staats and Biglaiser 2011; World Bank 2019). Limited enforceability of contracts is associated with the suboptimal distribution of resources, the use of inefficient technologies, and greater macroeconomic volatility (Adama 2020; Amaral and Quintin 2010; Cooley, Marimon, and Quadrini 2004; Dumav, Fuchs, and Lee 2022). Because poor commercial dispute resolution may deprive firms of timely and full payments, liquidity and insolvency issues can follow, as can subsequent bankruptcies and unemployment (Esposito, Lanau, and Pompe 2014).

What does the Dispute Resolution topic cover?

The Dispute Resolution topic focuses on settlement of commercial cases through court litigation and alternative dispute resolution (ADR) mechanisms, such as arbitration and mediation. It spans three pillars: (I) the quality of regulations for dispute resolution; (II) the quality of public services for dispute resolution; and (III) ease of resolving a commercial dispute (refer to table 4.8).

The first pillar studies the quality of laws and regulations that govern court litigation, arbitration, and mediation. Specifically, it looks at good practices that streamline court processes, ensure judicial integrity, improve access to justice, support arbitration, and promote mediation.

The second pillar examines the quality of key public services that make dispute resolution mechanisms more efficient and attractive. At the court level, it considers good practices that strengthen the institutional framework, favor digital adoption, and increase transparency. At the ADR level, the pillar captures the extent of arbitration and mediation services, the availability of necessary incentives, and the degree of digitalization and transparency.

TABLE 4.8 **Dispute Resolution**

Pillar I, Quality of Regulations for Dispute Resolution		Rescaled points
1.1	**Court Litigation**	**66.67**
1.1.1	Procedural Certainty (includes environment)	40.00
1.1.2	Judicial Integrity (includes gender)	26.67
1.2	**Alternative Dispute Resolution (ADR)**	**33.33**
1.2.1	Legal Safeguards in Arbitration	16.67
1.2.2	Legal Safeguards in Mediation	16.67
Total		**100.00**
Pillar II, Public Services for Dispute Resolution		**Rescaled points**
2.1	**Court Litigation**	**66.67**
2.1.1	Organizational Structure of Courts	22.22
2.1.2	Digitalization of Court Processes	22.22
2.1.3	Transparency of Courts (includes gender)	22.22
2.2	**Alternative Dispute Resolution (ADR)**	**33.33**
2.2.1	Public Services for Arbitration (includes gender)	16.67
2.2.2	Public Services for Mediation (includes gender)	16.67
Total		**100.00**
Pillar III, Ease of Resolving a Commercial Dispute		**Rescaled points**
3.1	**Court Litigation**	**66.67**
3.1.1	Reliability of Courts*	26.67
3.1.2	Operational Efficiency of Court Processes	40.00
3.2	**Alternative Dispute Resolution (ADR)**	**33.33**
3.2.1	Reliability of ADR	13.33
3.2.2	Operational Efficiency of Arbitration Processes	20.00
Total		**100.00**

Source: B-READY project.
Note: An asterisk (*) indicates a subcategory containing data collected through the World Bank Enterprise Surveys, https://www.enterprisesurveys.org/en/enterprisesurveys.

The third pillar focuses on how the relevant regulatory framework and public services are applied in practical terms. More precisely, it studies the reliability of dispute resolution mechanisms, records the time and cost to settle a claim, and measures the efficiency of procedures related to recognition and enforcement of judgments and arbitral awards.

 TOPIC 9. Market Competition

Market competition spurs economic growth by igniting innovation (He and Tian 2020) and enhancing productivity within industries and firms. The result is a landscape characterized by better products, more and better jobs, and higher incomes (World Bank 2017). Beyond these immediate advantages, a competitive market environment stimulates product innovation and ensures service quality, protects consumers, and compels market operators to offer products and services at competitive costs (Begazo Gomez and Nyman 2016).

A dynamic, competitive market is paramount for achieving sustained growth and maintaining reasonable prices—both needed to aid consumers and foster the expansion of employment opportunities and small businesses—thereby contributing to poverty alleviation (EC 2014; Tang 2006). Product and process innovation drive improvements in the efficiency of firms (Neely and Hii 1998). Innovation determines long-term performance, stability, and the business survival of firms (Ortiz-Villajos and Sotoca 2018; Porter 1992).

Effective regulations and well-functioning public services play pivotal roles in fostering competitive, dynamic markets. They act as deterrents to anticompetitive behavior, promote market entry, ensure a fair level of competition, and mitigate distortions arising from market failures (Tirole 2017). A regulatory framework and public services that encourage market competition, innovation, protection of intellectual property rights, and technology transfer (Audretsch, Lehmann, and Wright 2014), as well as fair bidding for public contracts, yield benefits for both firms and society at large. For example, the diffusion of innovation facilitates high social returns and benefits society (Gilbert 2006). This inclusive approach positively affects markets and consumers alike. Considering these facets, Market Competition benchmarks the quality of key regulations that promote competitive behaviors and innovation from the perspective of the entire private sector.

What does the Market Competition topic cover?

The Market Competition topic spans three pillars: (I) the quality of regulations that promote market competition; (II) the quality of public services that promote market competition; and (III) implementation of key services promoting market competition (refer to table 4.9).

The first pillar measures the quality of regulations that promote market competition, including good practices in antitrust laws, property rights protection, licensing, and technology transfer. Examples include prohibition of anticompetitive agreements, provisions to prevent abuse of dominance, and merger control procedures.

The second pillar measures the quality of public services that promote market competition—that is, the institutional framework of competition authorities and their role in competition policy, as well as the digitalization of intellectual property services and systems. Examples include the availability of an electronic database on locally registered intellectual property rights.

TABLE 4.9 **Market Competition**

Pillar I, Quality of Regulations that Promote Market Competition		Rescaled points
1.1	**Competition**	**33.33**
1.1.1	Antitrust	10.00
1.1.2	Merger Control	10.00
1.1.3	State-Owned Enterprises Framework and Scope of Competition Law	6.67
1.1.4	Enforcement of Competition Regulations	6.67
1.2	**Innovation and Technology Transfer**	**33.33**
1.2.1	Strength of Intellectual Property Rights Protection	8.33
1.2.2	Licensing and Technology Transfer	8.33
1.2.3	Fair Access to Innovation (includes environment)	8.33
1.2.4	University-Industry Collaboration	8.33
1.3	**Bidding for Public Contracts**	**33.33**
1.3.1	Access and Firm's Participation (includes gender)	11.67
1.3.2	Best Value for Money (includes gender and environment)	11.67
1.3.3	Fairness of the Procurement Process	5.00
1.3.4	Transparency of Key Procurement Documents	5.00
Total		**100.00**
Pillar II, Public Services that Promote Market Competition		Rescaled points
2.1	**Competition Authority**	**33.33**
2.1.1	Institutional Framework	16.67
2.1.2	Advocacy and Transparency	16.67
2.2	**Innovation in Firms**	**33.33**
2.2.1	Institutional Framework to Support Innovation	11.11
2.2.2	Digitalization of Intellectual Property Services	11.11
2.2.3	Innovation Systems (includes gender)	11.11
2.3	**E-Procurement**	**33.33**
2.3.1	Digitalization of Procurement Procedures (includes environment)	22.22
2.3.2	Transparency of Key Procurement Documents (includes gender)	11.11
Total		**100.00**
Pillar III, Implementation of Key Services Promoting Market Competition		Rescaled points
3.1	**Competition**	**33.33**
3.1.1	Simplified Merger Review	6.67
3.1.2	Market Dynamism and Competitive Behaviors*	26.67
3.2	**Innovation**	**33.33**
3.2.1	Proportion of Highly Innovative Firms*	16.67
3.2.2	Use of International Quality Certifications*	16.67
3.3	**Public Procurement**	**33.33**
3.3.1	Time to Award Public Contracts	8.33
3.3.2	Time to Receive a Payment from a Government Contract*	8.33
3.3.3	Firms' Perceptions on the Ease of Bidding*	8.33
3.3.4	Gender Gap in Government Suppliers*	8.33
Total		**100.00**

Source: B-READY project.

Note: An asterisk (*) indicates a subcategory containing data collected through the World Bank Enterprise Surveys, https://www.enterprisesurveys.org/en/enterprisesurveys. E-Procurement = electronic procurement.

The third pillar measures the operational efficiency in implementing key services promoting market competition. It reflects how the two pillars on regulations and public services contribute in practice to promoting market competition. Examples include the time required to award a public contract through a bidding process and the time required to pay government contractors and late payment penalties.

 ## TOPIC 10. Business Insolvency

An efficient insolvency system enhances the creation of new firms, increases the size of the private sector, encourages greater entrepreneurial activity, and promotes economic stability and growth (Cirmizi, Klapper, and Uttamchandani 2012). It allows the effective exit of nonviable companies (so that entrepreneurs can reinvent themselves) by spurring the reallocation of productivity-enhancing capital and promoting firm creation and access to finance. It also ensures the survival of economically viable businesses by reorganizing their financial structure. All this encourages greater entrepreneurial activity and job creation (Menezes 2014).

The stability of the financial system also depends on an efficient insolvency framework. Only when nonviable firms can be swiftly liquidated and viable firms restructured in a sustainable way will investors be willing to make commitments for lending. Indeed, lack of efficient bankruptcy procedures results in lower aggregate productivity as lenders risk allocating funds to less productive firms, thus endangering the financial system (González-Torres and Rodano 2020).

What does the Business Insolvency topic cover?

The Business Insolvency topic measures key features of insolvency in three pillars: (I) the quality of regulations for judicial insolvency proceedings; (II) the quality of institutional and operational infrastructure for judicial insolvency proceedings; and (III) the operational efficiency of resolving judicial insolvency proceedings (refer to table 4.10).

The first pillar assesses the quality of regulations pertaining to liquidation and reorganization proceedings, covering the de jure features of a regulatory framework necessary for structured debt resolution proceedings. It is based on international good practices. These practices provide objectives and principles that should be reflected in an economy's insolvency legal regime in areas such as precommencement and commencement of insolvency proceedings, treatment and protection of a debtor's assets during liquidation and reorganization, and rules governing insolvency administrators.[9] In addition, the pillar assesses the rights of or safeguards for creditors because they play a key role in insolvency proceedings by maximizing the value of a creditor's assets and therefore increasing debt recovery. Specialized proceedings for micro and small enterprises are evaluated. The pillar also examines cross-border insolvency regulations within the insolvency legal framework aimed at facilitating the coordination and cooperation of economies in transnational insolvency cases.

The second pillar measures the quality of institutional and operational infrastructure for insolvency processes, assessing de facto aspects of insolvency resolution mechanisms and the infrastructure required to implement the legal framework for in-court liquidation and reorganization proceedings. This includes an assessment of the digitalization and specialization of bankruptcy courts or bankruptcy judges and court automation features, the availability of information on the number and length of liquidation and reorganization proceedings, and the existence of a public registry of insolvency administrators.

The third pillar measures the time and cost required for a standardized company to resolve in-court liquidation and reorganization proceedings (operational efficiency). The objective of this set of indicators is to identify the bureaucratic hurdles when resolving insolvency disputes and promote efficient debt resolution mechanisms.

TABLE 4.10 Business Insolvency

Pillar I, Quality of Regulations for Judicial Insolvency Proceedings		Rescaled points
1.1	**Legal and Procedural Standards in Insolvency Proceedings**	**30.00**
1.1.1	Pre-Commencement and Commencement Standards in Liquidation and Reorganization	15.00
1.1.2	Post-Commencement Standards in Liquidation and Reorganization	15.00
1.2	**Debtor's Assets and Creditor's Participation in Insolvency Proceedings**	**50.00**
1.2.1	Treatment and Protection of Debtor's Assets during Liquidation and Reorganization (includes environment)	20.00
1.2.2	Creditor's Rights in Liquidation and Reorganization (includes environment)	20.00
1.2.3	Selection and Dismissal of the Insolvency Administrator	10.00
1.3	**Specialized Insolvency Proceedings and International Insolvency**	**20.00**
1.3.1	Specialized Insolvency Proceedings for Micro and Small Enterprises (MSEs)	10.00
1.3.2	Cross-Border Insolvency	10.00
Total		**100.00**

(Continued)

TABLE 4.10 **Business Insolvency** *(Continued)*

Pillar II, Quality of Institutional and Operational Infrastructure for Judicial Insolvency Proceedings		Rescaled points
2.1	**Digital Services (e-Courts) in Insolvency Proceedings**	**40.00**
2.1.1	Electronic Services in Liquidation and Reorganization	20.00
2.1.2	Electronic Case Management Systems in Liquidation and Reorganization	20.00
2.2	**Interoperability in Insolvency Proceedings**	**20.00**
2.2.1	Digital Services Connectivity with External Systems in Liquidation and Reorganization	10.00
2.2.2	Interconnection between e-Case Management System and e-Filing Systems in Liquidation and Reorganization	10.00
2.3	**Public Information on Insolvency Proceedings and Registry of Insolvency Practitioners**	**20.00**
2.3.1	Public Information on the Number and Length of Liquidation and Reorganization, and Insolvency Judgments	10.00
2.3.2	Availability of a Public Registry of Insolvency Practitioners	10.00
2.4	**Public Officials and Insolvency Administrator**	**20.00**
2.4.1	Specialization of Courts with Jurisdiction on Reorganization and Liquidation Proceedings	10.00
2.4.2	Insolvency Administrator's Expertise in Practice	10.00
Total		**100.00**
Pillar III, Operational Efficiency of Resolving Judicial Insolvency Proceedings		Rescaled points
3.1	**Liquidation Proceedings**	**50.00**
3.1.1	Time to Resolve a Liquidation Proceeding	25.00
3.1.2	Cost to Resolve a Liquidation Proceeding	25.00
3.2	**Reorganization Proceedings**	**50.00**
3.2.1	Time to Resolve a Reorganization Proceeding	25.00
3.2.2	Cost to Resolve a Reorganization Proceeding	25.00
Total		**100.00**

Source: B-READY project.
Note: e-Case = electronic case; e-Court = electronic court; e-Filing = electronic filing.

What do the topic scores tell us?

There is room for improvement across all topics for most economies, suggesting the need for comprehensive reforms. Across all B-READY topics within any economy the scores vary. This variation indicates that an economy can have a strong performance in one topic, which can coexist with a weaker performance in another. Similarly, within each topic, across all economies, scores vary considerably between pillars. This suggests significant diversity across economies in adopting and implementing good practices in regulatory frameworks and public services, highlighting opportunities for comprehensive reforms across all topics. On a scale of 0 to 100, the average score of all 10 topics is 59.73 points. The topics with the highest average scores are Business Entry (69.96 points), followed by Utility Services (65.13 points) and Labor (64.99 points)—refer to table 4.11 and figure 4.1. The topic with the lowest average score is Market Competition (48.04 points), followed by Business Insolvency (49.99 points) and Taxation (53.50 points).

TABLE 4.11 **Summary statistics, B-READY topic scores**

Topic	Minimum	Maximum	Median	Mean	SD
Business Entry	40.99	96.58	72.23	69.96	16.52
Business Location	33.42	83.01	61.85	61.32	12.06
Utility Services	35.04	86.42	65.34	65.13	11.52
Labor	49.22	83.46	65.21	64.99	8.41
Financial Services	24.82	86.03	62.10	61.49	13.40
International Trade	34.82	90.77	64.16	63.67	14.35
Taxation	23.28	71.74	55.65	53.50	10.62
Dispute Resolution	36.47	82.87	61.54	59.26	12.91
Market Competition	16.69	68.55	51.42	48.04	14.12
Business Insolvency	0.00	89.69	49.61	49.99	19.61

Source: B-READY 2024 data.
Note: Scores for each B-READY topic range from 0 to 100. SD = standard deviation.

The topics with the highest median score are Business Entry (72.23 points), followed by Utility Services (65.34 points) and Labor (65.21 points). When the median is higher than the average—for example, in Market Competition, where the median is 51.42 points and the average is 48.04 points—that suggests that there are some economies whose performance is much weaker than that of most economies in the same topic. In Market Competition, the performance of some economies is weaker because their antitrust laws, merger control regulations, and intellectual property rights protection, among other aspects, are far from good regulatory practice.

The maximum observed score across all topics is 96.58 points in Business Entry (Greece), followed by International Trade (Hong Kong SAR, China, with 90.77 points) and Business Insolvency (Singapore with 89.69 points). Business Insolvency is the only topic in which the minimum is 0.00, indicating that one economy has no practice in judicial reorganization and judicial liquidation as measured by the topic (Timor-Leste). The second-lowest minimum is in Market Competition (Timor-Leste with 16.69 points), followed by Taxation (the Central African Republic with 23.28 points). The topics with the highest difference between the maximum and minimum values are Business Insolvency (89.69 points), followed by Financial Services (61.21 points) and International Trade (55.95 points). This finding suggests wide diversity across economies in adopting best practices in regulations and public services and undertaking their practical implementation. The narrowest range is in Labor (34.24 points).

FIGURE 4.1 The distribution of scores shows scope for improvement across all topics

Topic score (0–100)

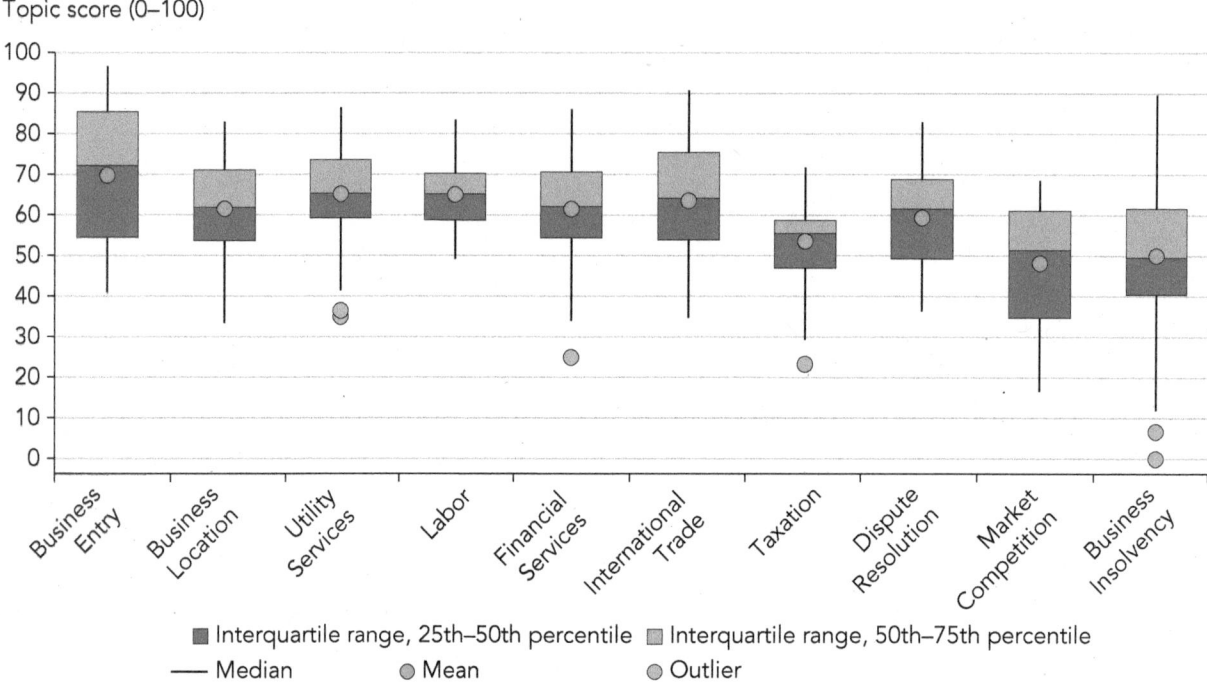

Source: B-READY 2024 data.
Note: The figure displays the distribution of B-READY topic scores across the 50 sampled economies. It presents the median (horizontal black line dividing the light blue and dark blue boxes), mean (orange dots), the interquartile range (25th–75th percentiles, light blue and dark blue boxes), and standard whiskers. Points outside the whiskers represent outliers for each topic (green dots).

In almost all topics, scores are higher in the Regulatory Framework pillar (Pillar I) than in the Public Services and Operational Efficiency pillars (Pillars II and III, respectively), suggesting that the adoption of quality regulations is more common than the provision of good-practice public services and their efficient implementation (refer to figure 4.2). However, Business Location, Utility Services, and Taxation see a different trend, with their highest scores in Pillar III. This finding suggests that firms in these areas can withstand adverse conditions in the regulatory framework and public services. For example, firms can still operate businesses without having full access to an online service taxpayer portal or to simplified recordkeeping and filing. Business Entry has the highest score of 83.56 points in the Regulatory Framework pillar across all topics, followed by Financial Services (71.25 points) and Labor (70.56 points). Conversely, Taxation (46.94 points), Market Competition (51.04 points), and Business Insolvency (60.33 points) have the lowest scores under the Regulatory Framework pillar.

In the Public Services pillar, Labor achieves the highest score (62.12 points), followed by Utility Services (59.48 points) and Business Entry (57.18 points). This finding suggests that public services in the areas of Labor, Utility Services, and Business Entry perform better or are more accessible than in other areas. The lowest scores in Pillar II were recorded by Business Insolvency (34.17 points), Business Location (42.89 points), and Financial Services (45.68 points). This finding points to significant challenges in these areas, suggesting that public services related to Business Insolvency, Business Location, and Financial Services are less effective or less accessible, potentially impairing the overall business environment.

All topics get higher scores in the Operational Efficiency pillar than in the Public Services pillar. This suggests that existing firms demonstrate resilience even in contexts where public services provision is not sufficient. The three highest-scoring topics in Pillar III are Business Location (73.61 points), Utility Services (71.43 points), and Business Entry (69.14 points). The lowest scores are in Market Competition (47.00 points), Business Insolvency (55.49 points), and Dispute Resolution (61.35 points).

FIGURE 4.2 Firms are resilient to the "public services gap" across topics

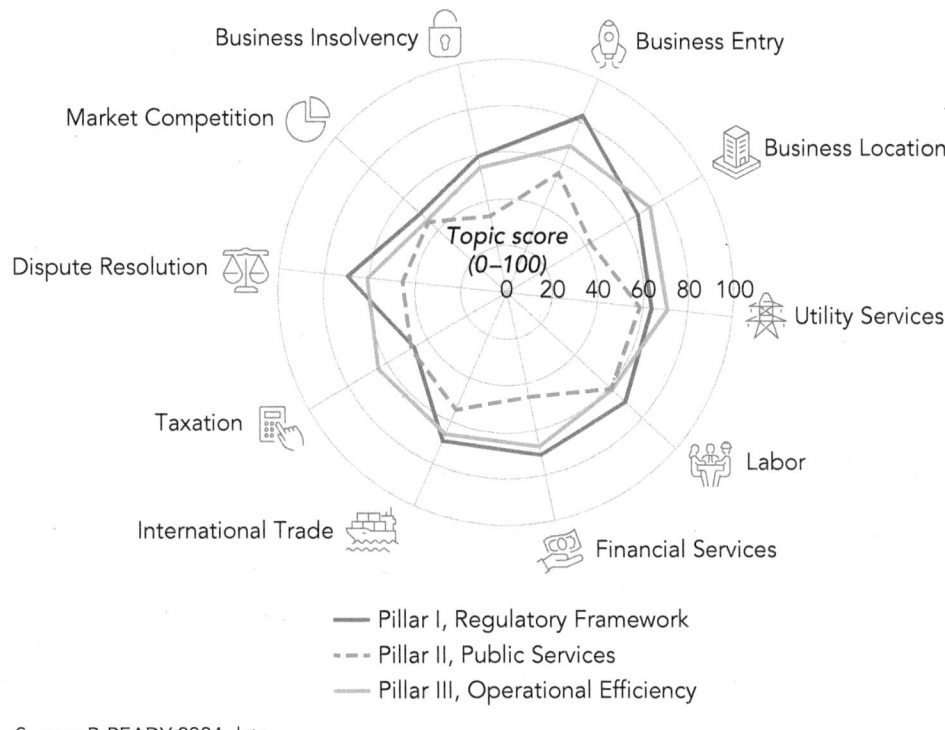

Source: B-READY 2024 data.
Note: The sample comprises 50 economies.

How do the topic scores relate to one another?

There is a positive and statistically significant correlation across all topics, indicating that economies with a favorable business environment in one area also tend to have a good business environment in the other areas (refer to figure 4.3). Conversely, if an economy performs poorly in one area, it is likely that it does not perform well in the other areas. This trend could also be explained by the interconnectedness of the topics. For example, improvements in Market Competition may have positive spillover effects on Business Entry and Labor by making the economy more dynamic. Similarly, improving the online systems for electronic filing and payment of taxes can facilitate both taxation and international trade. Embracing a comprehensive reform agenda spanning all topics is essential for driving significant improvements in the business landscape.

FIGURE 4.3 Economies with a favorable business environment in one topic tend to perform well in others

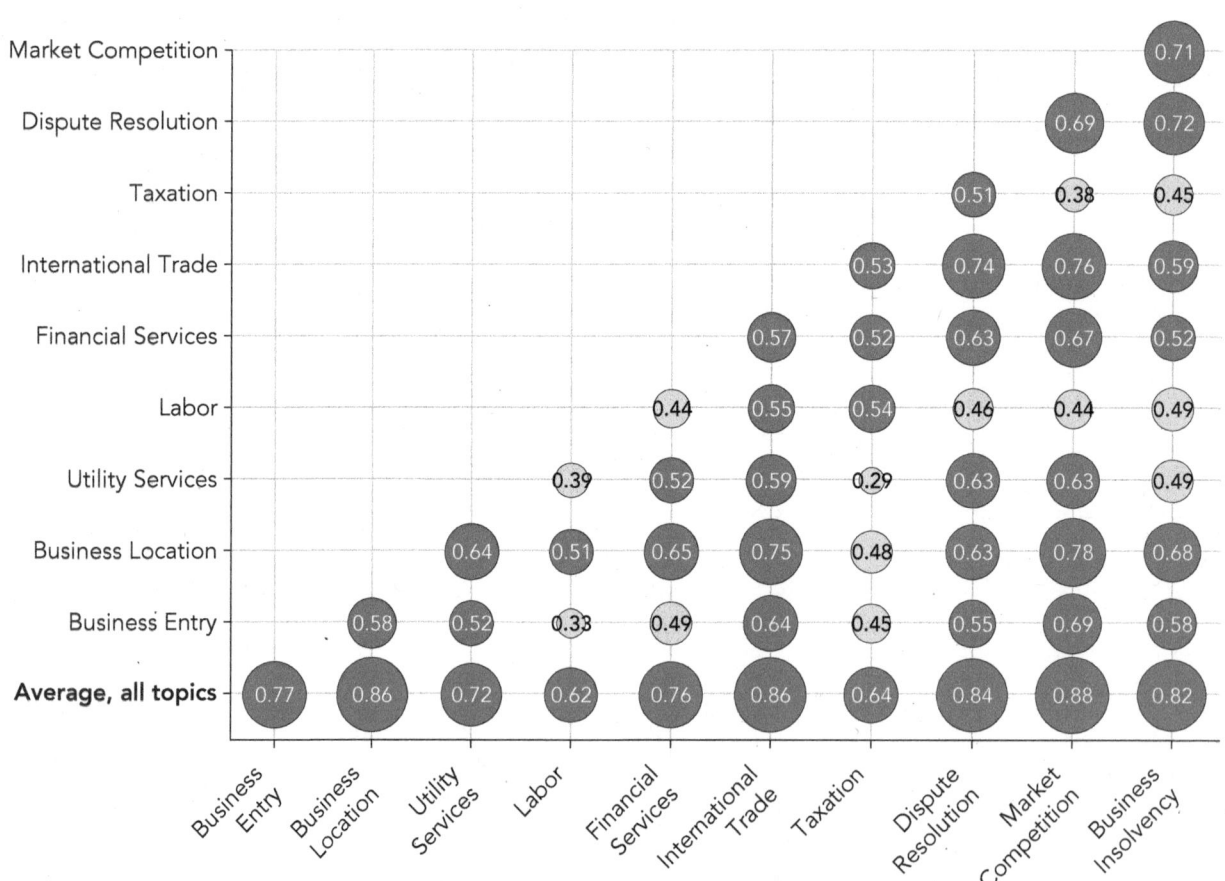

Correlation of topic pairs: ● Above 0.5 ○ Below 0.5

Source: B-READY 2024 data.
Note: Data are based on the B-READY topic scores across the 50 sampled economies. The blue bubbles indicate a correlation of topic pairs above 0.5, while yellow bubbles indicate a correlation below 0.5. The size of the bubble indicates the relative size of the correlation. All correlations are positive and statistically significant at the 1 percent level.

The strength of the correlation depends on the specific pair of topics considered. The topics most correlated with the other ones include Market Competition, Business Location, and International Trade. This close correlation is indicated by their pairwise correlation with the scores of other topics, as well as by their correlation with the average of all topic scores (0.88, 0.86, and 0.86, respectively). Labor and Taxation are the topics least correlated with others and with the average topic scores (0.62 and 0.64, respectively).

Among the most highly correlated topic pairs, the relationship between Business Location and Market Competition (0.78) stands out, indicating that economies that protect fair and efficient allocation of resources between competing firms are also more likely to have regulations and services that reduce the market distortion of land and property rights. Similarly, a strong positive association can be observed between Market Competition and International Trade (0.76), suggesting that economies that foster a level playing field for domestic firms are also more likely to bolster trade. Another notable correlation is between Dispute Resolution and Business Insolvency (0.72), suggesting a likely complementarity arising from the characteristics of the judiciary institutions benchmarked within these topics.

Conversely, a possible explanation of the weakest association of Labor and Taxation with the average topic score is that regulations and public services in the areas of Labor and Taxation stem from broader policy considerations—for example, of workers' rights—that go beyond the business environment itself. The presence of these and other indirect effects could explain the associations with the average topic score.

Figure 4.4 depicts the full distribution of each topic score, offering a comparison with the average topic score for the same economy. The figure shows that most economies have a higher Business Entry score than their average topic score, and all but two have a lower Market Competition score than their average topic score. This finding suggests that, globally, economies have achieved more progress toward best practices in aspects related to business incorporation than in good practices in antitrust laws. The slopes of the regression lines demonstrate that a stronger performance, on average, across the 10 topic scores is associated with a significantly larger than one-to-one increase in Business Entry, Market Competition, and Business Insolvency, and a significantly lower than one-to-one increase in Taxation and Labor. The R-squared values, which measure dispersion around the regression line, show a similar pattern. The average topic score displays a weak relationship with Taxation and Labor scores, with R-squared coefficients of 0.41 and 0.39, respectively, and strong relationships with Market Competition (0.78), Business Location (0.74), and International Trade (0.74). However, because of the limited number of economies analyzed, the conclusions presented in this section should be interpreted with caution. The results are subject to refinement in subsequent editions of the report (refer to chapter 5).

FIGURE 4.4 Relationship between topic scores and the average score of all topics

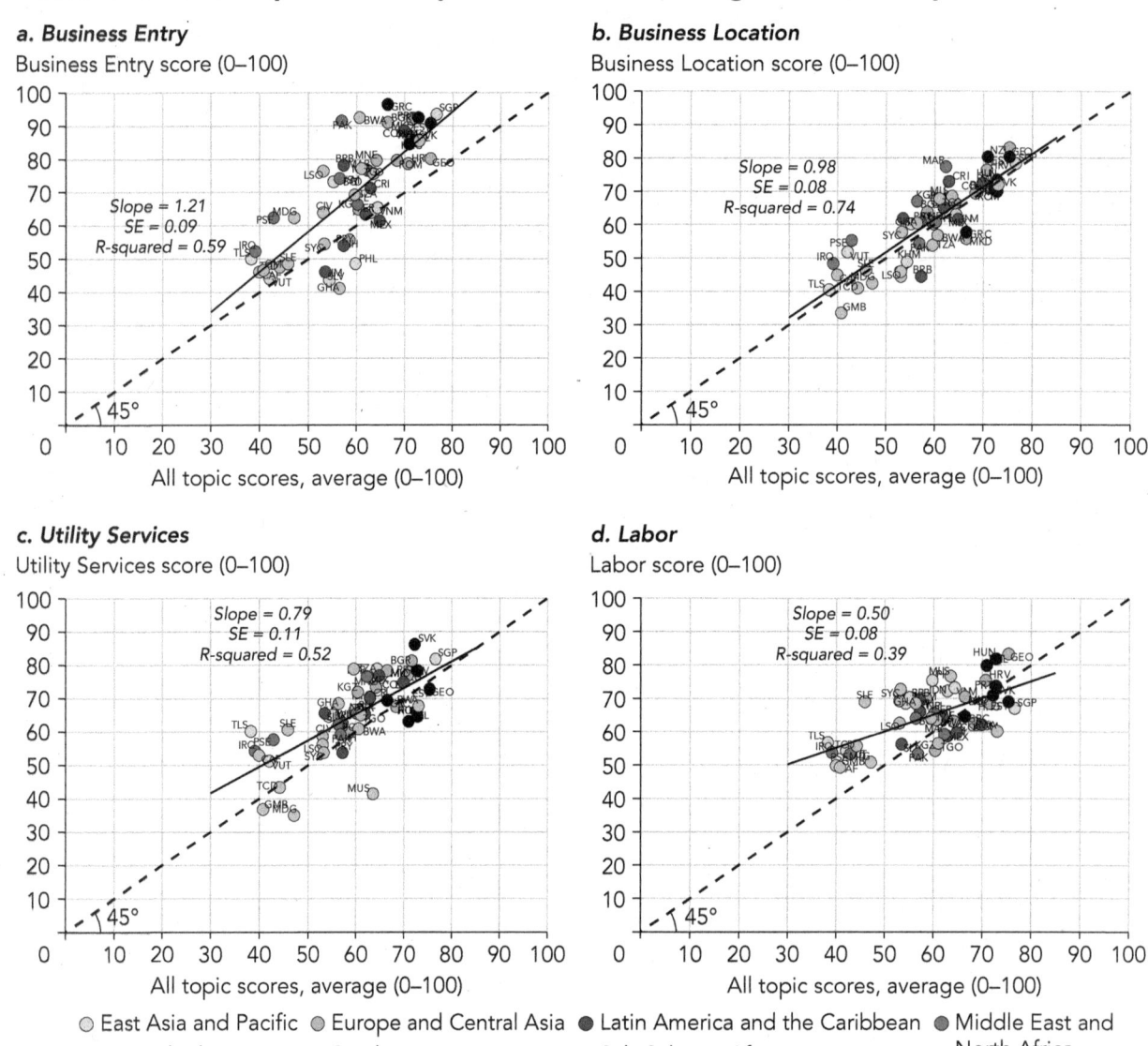

a. Business Entry

b. Business Location

c. Utility Services

d. Labor

○ East Asia and Pacific ◐ Europe and Central Asia ● Latin America and the Caribbean ● Middle East and North Africa
● OECD high income ◑ South Asia ○ Sub-Saharan Africa

(Continued)

FIGURE 4.4 Relationship between topic scores and the average score of all topics *(Continued)*

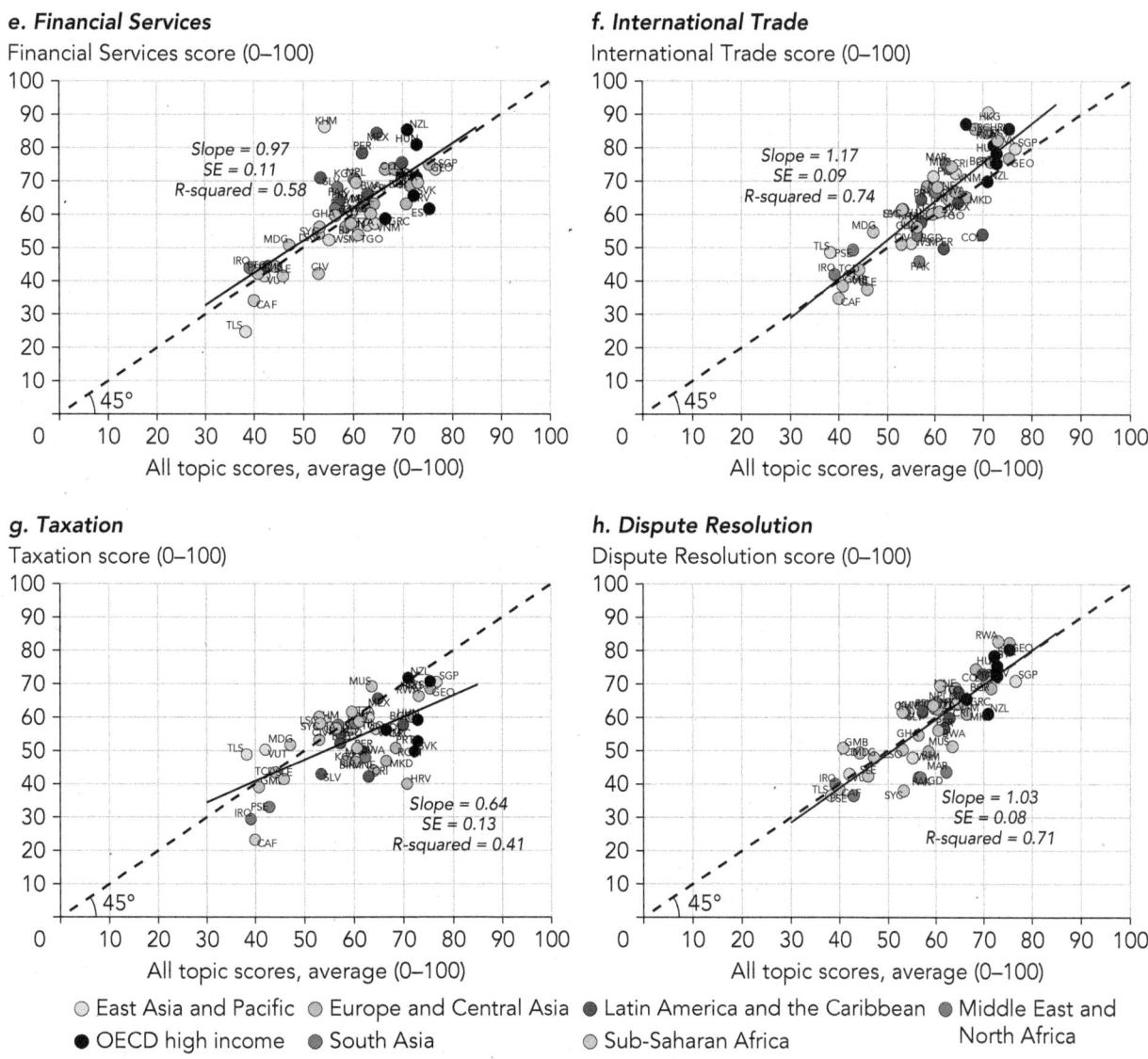

e. Financial Services

Financial Services score (0–100)

Slope = 0.97
SE = 0.11
R-squared = 0.58

All topic scores, average (0–100)

f. International Trade

International Trade score (0–100)

Slope = 1.17
SE = 0.09
R-squared = 0.74

All topic scores, average (0–100)

g. Taxation

Taxation score (0–100)

Slope = 0.64
SE = 0.13
R-squared = 0.41

All topic scores, average (0–100)

h. Dispute Resolution

Dispute Resolution score (0–100)

Slope = 1.03
SE = 0.08
R-squared = 0.71

All topic scores, average (0–100)

- ○ East Asia and Pacific ○ Europe and Central Asia ● Latin America and the Caribbean ● Middle East and North Africa
- ● OECD high income ● South Asia ○ Sub-Saharan Africa

(Continued)

FIGURE 4.4 Relationship between topic scores and the average score of all topics *(Continued)*

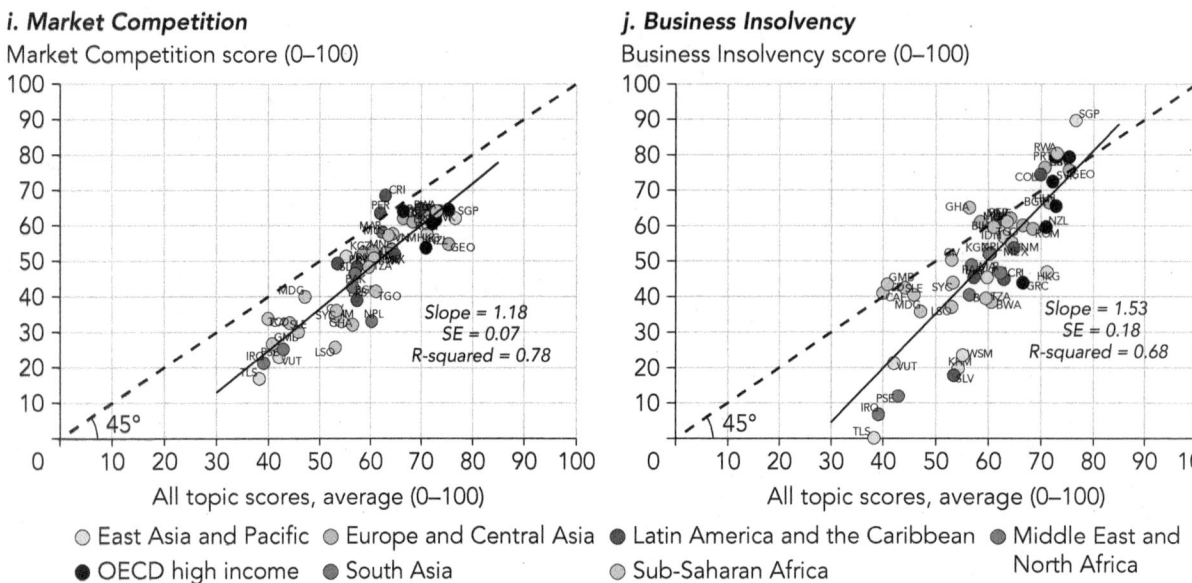

Source: B-READY 2024 data.
Note: The dashed line is set at 45 degrees, and the solid line represents the linear regression of the topic score and the average score of all 10 topics. The associations between the average of all topics scores and the B-READY topic scores are significant at the 1 percent level. The sample comprises 50 economies. For economy abbreviations, refer to appendix B and International Organization for Standardization (ISO), https://www.iso.org/obp/ui/#search. OECD = Organisation for Economic Co-operation and Development; SE = standard error.

How do the topic scores vary across regions and income levels?

A regional analysis of topic scores provides valuable insights into the composition and distribution of good practices across regions. Comparisons drawn from this analysis should, however, be interpreted with caution, bearing in mind that, although the 50 economies included in this report were selected to represent all regions and income levels, full representation within regions will be achieved in subsequent editions of this report (refer to chapter 5).

High-income economies that are members of the Organisation for Economic Co-operation and Development (OECD) attain the highest average scores across all B-READY topics except Financial Services and Utility Services (refer to figure 4.5). The Europe and Central Asia region has the second-highest average score across 7 of the 10 B-READY topics, while Latin America and the Caribbean has the third-highest average in 4 of the 10 topic scores. The highest topic scores are not confined to specific regions, however. For example, Cambodia; Hong Kong SAR, China; and Singapore, all from East Asia and Pacific, lead the Financial Services, International Trade, and Business Insolvency topics, respectively. Costa Rica, in Latin America and the Caribbean, achieves the highest score in Market Competition, while Rwanda, in Sub-Saharan Africa, takes the lead in Dispute Resolution. In Europe and Central Asia, Georgia stands out for having the highest score in Labor.

FIGURE 4.5 B-READY topic scores, by region

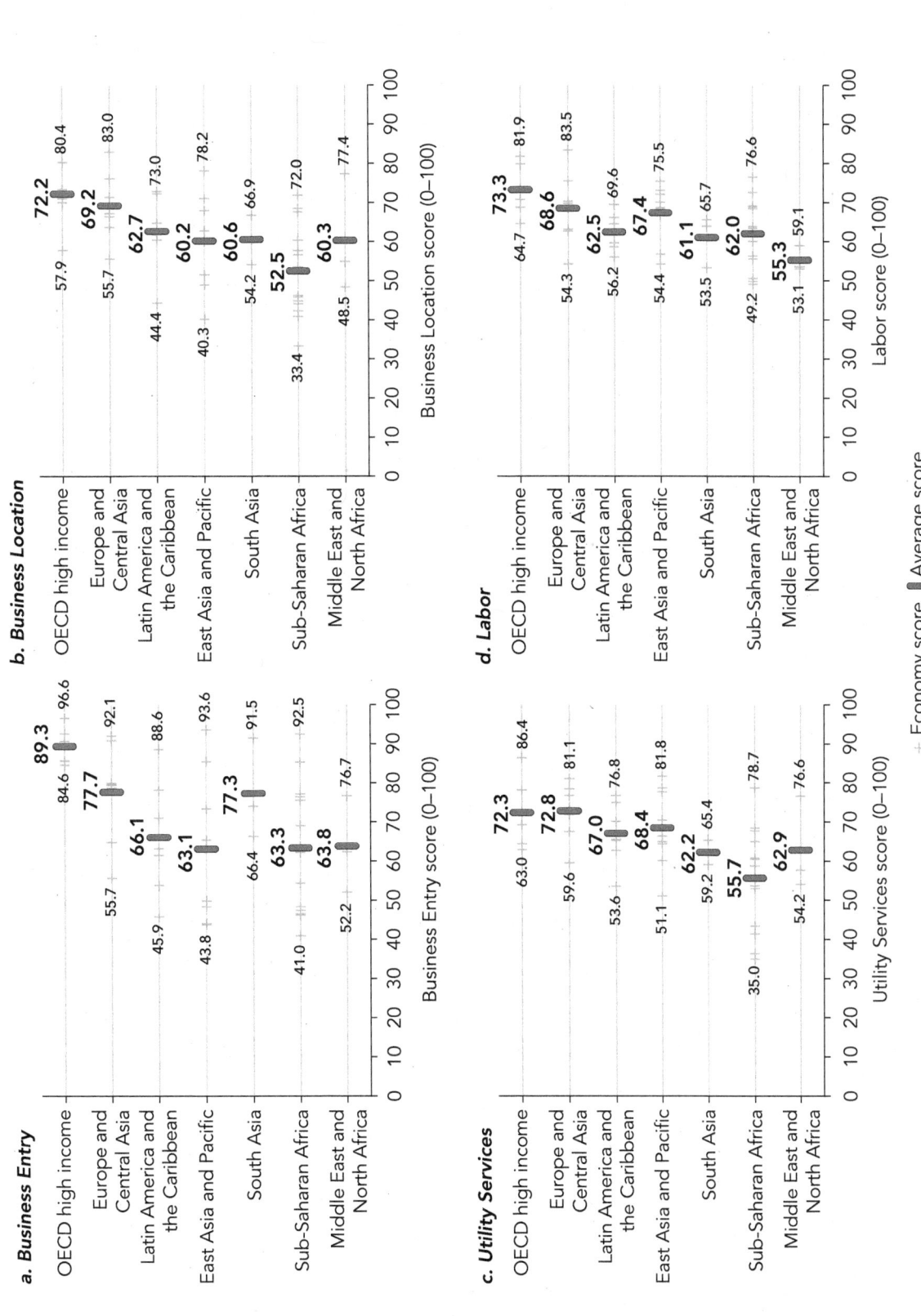

a. Business Entry

OECD high income **89.3** (84.6–96.6)
Europe and Central Asia **77.7** (55.7–92.1)
Latin America and the Caribbean **66.1** (45.9–88.6)
East Asia and Pacific **63.1** (43.8–93.6)
South Asia **77.3** (66.4–91.5)
Sub-Saharan Africa **63.3** (41.0–92.5)
Middle East and North Africa **63.8** (52.2–76.7)

Business Entry score (0–100)

b. Business Location

OECD high income **72.2** (57.9–80.4)
Europe and Central Asia **69.2** (55.7–83.0)
Latin America and the Caribbean **62.7** (44.4–73.0)
East Asia and Pacific **60.2** (40.3–78.2)
South Asia **60.6** (54.2–66.9)
Sub-Saharan Africa **52.5** (33.4–72.0)
Middle East and North Africa **60.3** (48.5–77.4)

Business Location score (0–100)

c. Utility Services

OECD high income **72.3** (63.0–86.4)
Europe and Central Asia **72.8** (59.6–81.1)
Latin America and the Caribbean **67.0** (53.6–76.8)
East Asia and Pacific **68.4** (51.1–81.8)
South Asia **62.2** (59.2–65.4)
Sub-Saharan Africa **55.7** (35.0–78.7)
Middle East and North Africa **62.9** (54.2–76.6)

Utility Services score (0–100)

d. Labor

OECD high income **73.3** (64.7–81.9)
Europe and Central Asia **68.6** (54.3–83.5)
Latin America and the Caribbean **62.5** (56.2–69.6)
East Asia and Pacific **67.4** (54.4–75.5)
South Asia **61.1** (53.5–65.7)
Sub-Saharan Africa **62.0** (49.2–76.6)
Middle East and North Africa **55.3** (53.1–59.1)

Labor score (0–100)

+ Economy score | Average score

(Continued)

FIGURE 4.5 **B-READY topic scores, by region (Continued)**

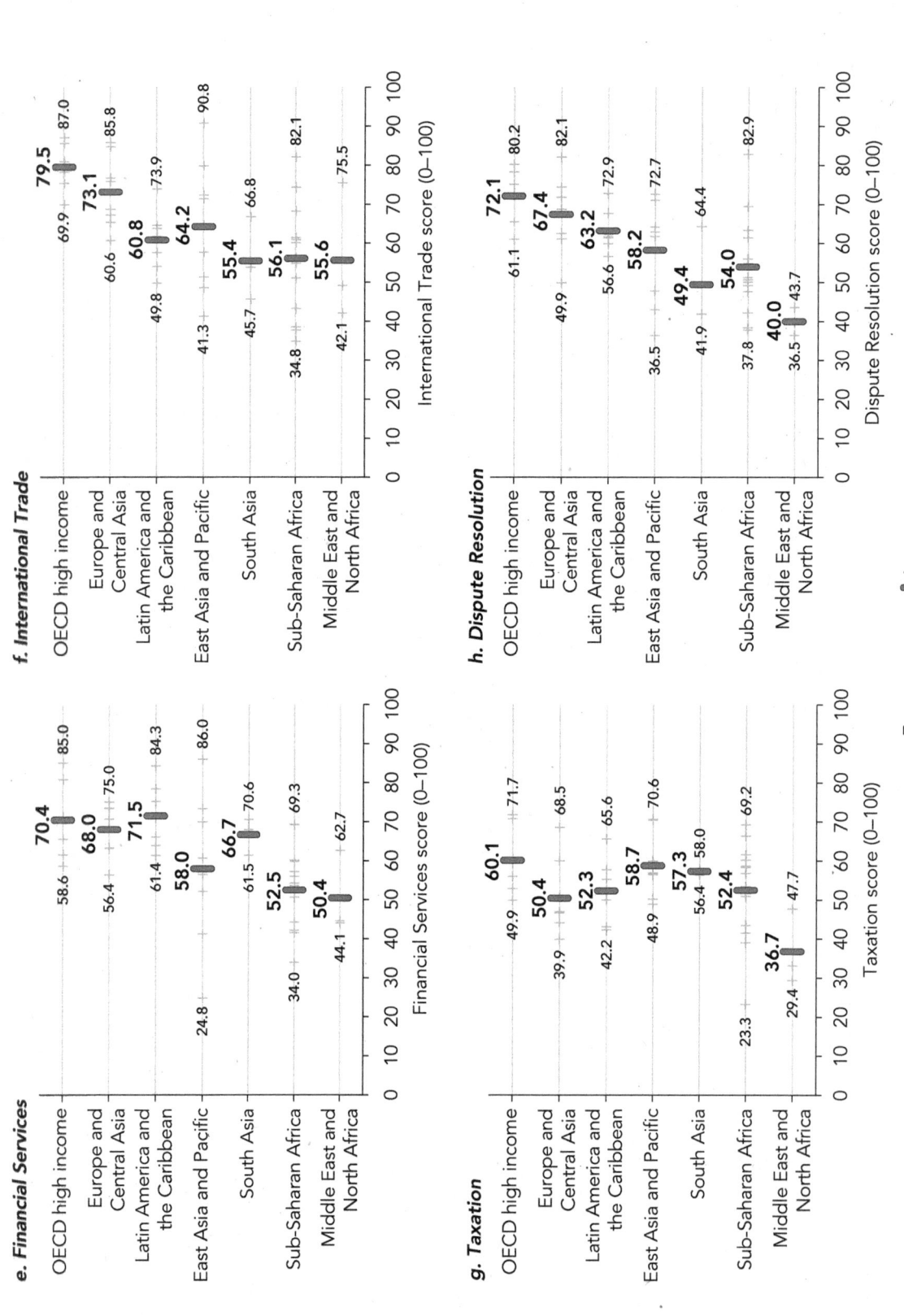

e. Financial Services

f. International Trade

g. Taxation

h. Dispute Resolution

+ Economy score   ▮ Average score

(Continued)

FIGURE 4.5 **B-READY topic scores, by region (Continued)**

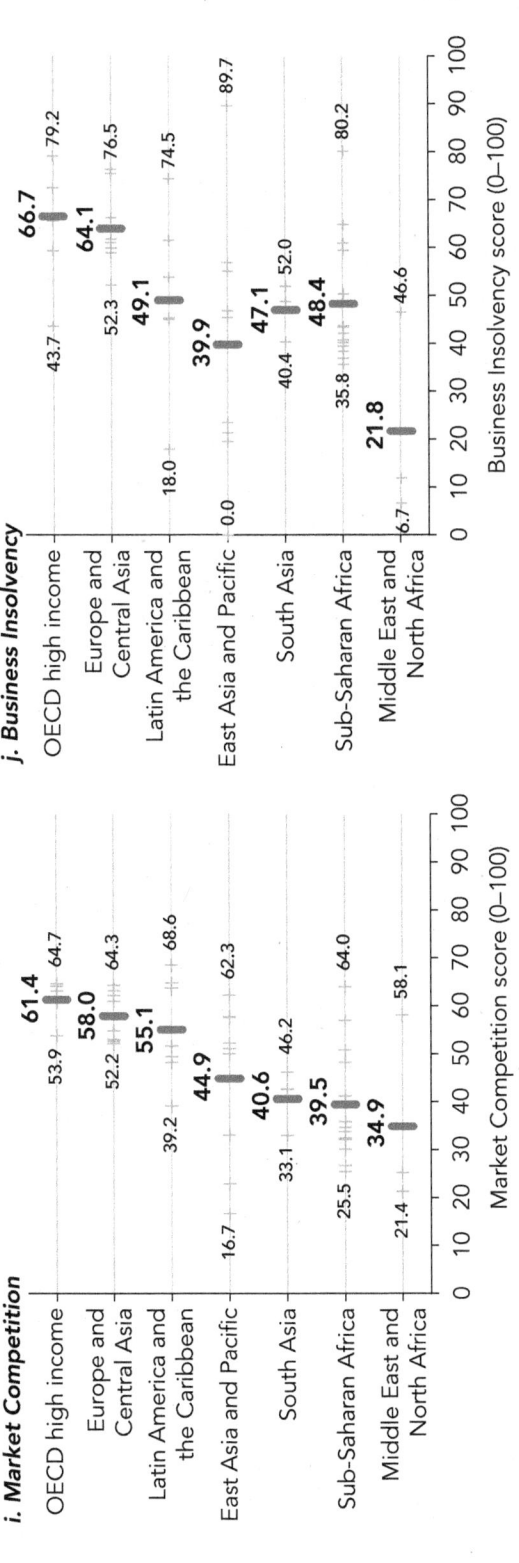

i. Market Competition

j. Business Insolvency

+ Economy score | Average score

Source: B-READY 2024 data.

Note: Each cross (+) represents the score of an economy in its region. Each vertical blue marker indicates the average score of a region. The minimum and maximum scores within each region are also specified. The East Asia and Pacific region has 9 economies in the sample; Europe and Central Asia, 8; Latin America and the Caribbean, 7; the Middle East and North Africa, 3; the OECD high-income region, 6; South Asia, 3; and Sub-Saharan Africa, 14. OECD = Organisation for Economic Co-operation and Development.

Sampled economies in the East Asia and Pacific, Sub-Saharan Africa, and Middle East and North Africa regions tend to have weaker performance and bigger gaps in performance within them than other regions. For example, in Business Insolvency, East Asia and Pacific economies display considerable differences in scores, with Cambodia scoring 19.63 points, Indonesia 56.96 points, and Singapore 89.69 points. Similarly, in Business Location, Sub-Saharan African economies show considerable dispersion in scores with, for example, The Gambia scoring 33.42 points, Tanzania 53.62 points, and Rwanda 72.01 points. This suggests that good practices can be adopted and implemented in any context, and economies can learn from one another in their efforts to improve the business environment.

High-income economies tend to achieve, on average, higher scores across all B-READY topics, followed by those at the upper-middle-income, lower-middle-income, and low-income levels. This pattern, however, changes when looking at individual topics such as Taxation, Dispute Resolution, and Business Insolvency (refer to figure 4.6). In Taxation, lower-middle-income economies perform better, on average, than upper-middle-income economies, with average scores of 55.05 points and 51.41 points, respectively. In addition, lower-middle-income economies are relatively more consistent (with a minimum score of 46.59 points and a maximum score of 61.57 points), whereas upper-middle-income economies display greater variability (with a minimum score of 29.40 points and a maximum score of 69.22 points). Among low-income economies, Rwanda stands out particularly in Dispute Resolution and Business Insolvency, where it contributes to raising the average of its income level by achieving topic scores of 82.87 points and 80.20 points, respectively.

Economies that perform well in one of the three B-READY pillars have a relatively balanced contribution by all topics. Figure 4.7 illustrates this by showing the points, by segments, contributed by each topic to the pillar score of the 50 sampled economies, with each topic contributing a maximum of 10 points. For example, in Pillar I, Hungary is situated at the highest end of the distribution. The topics contributing the most to its Regulatory Framework score are Financial Services (9.9 points) and Dispute Resolution (8.7 points), while Market Competition (6.8 points) and Taxation (4.1 points) are the topics that contribute the least. Timor-Leste is among the economies positioned in the lower end of the score distribution. In Timor-Leste, Business Entry contributes the most to its Pillar I score (8.6 points), followed by Labor (6.9 points) and Business Insolvency (0.0 points).

FIGURE 4.6 **B-READY topic scores, by economy income level**

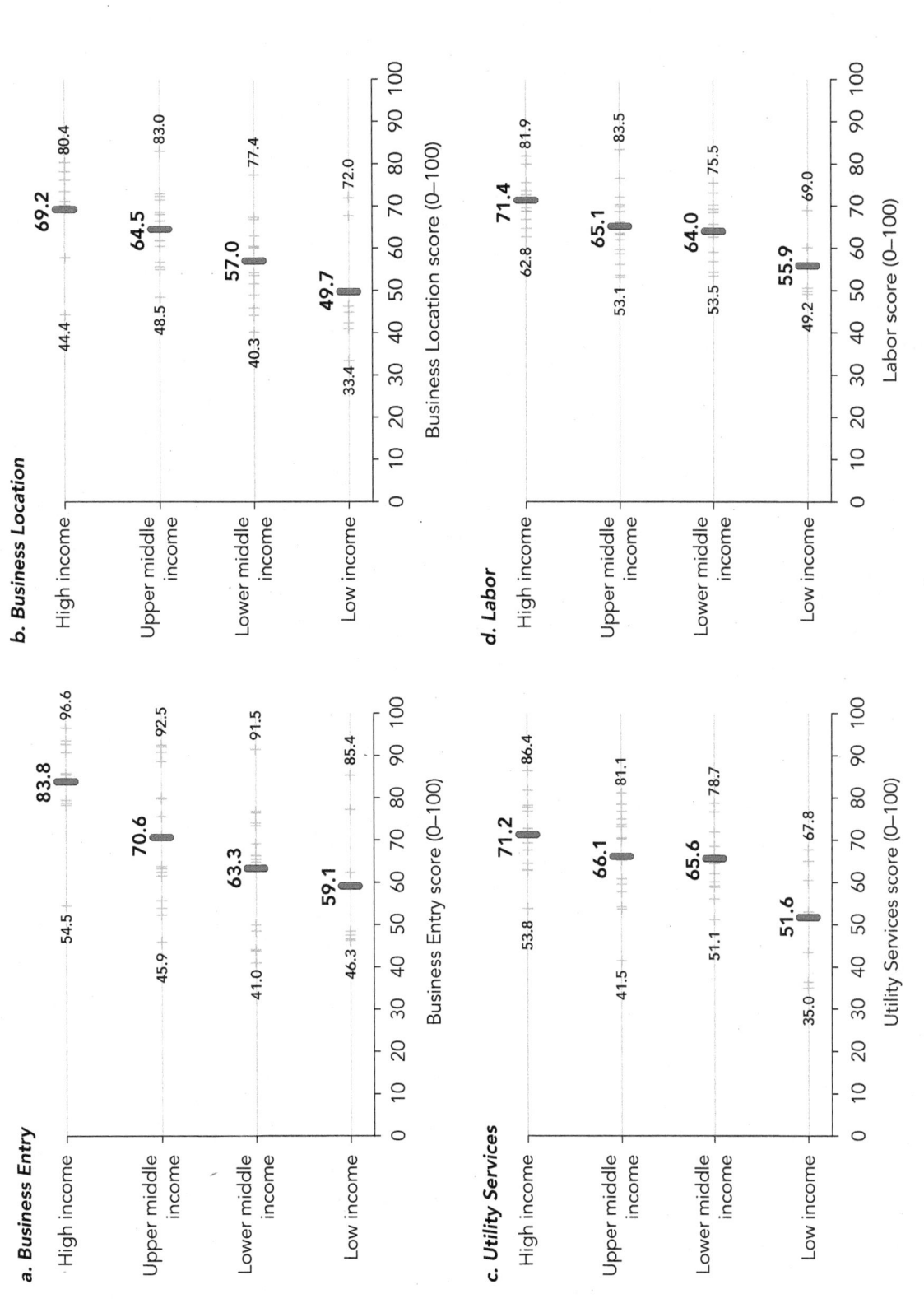

a. Business Entry

b. Business Location

c. Utility Services

d. Labor

+ Economy score ● Average score

(Continued)

FIGURE 4.6 **B-READY** topic scores, by economy income level (*Continued*)

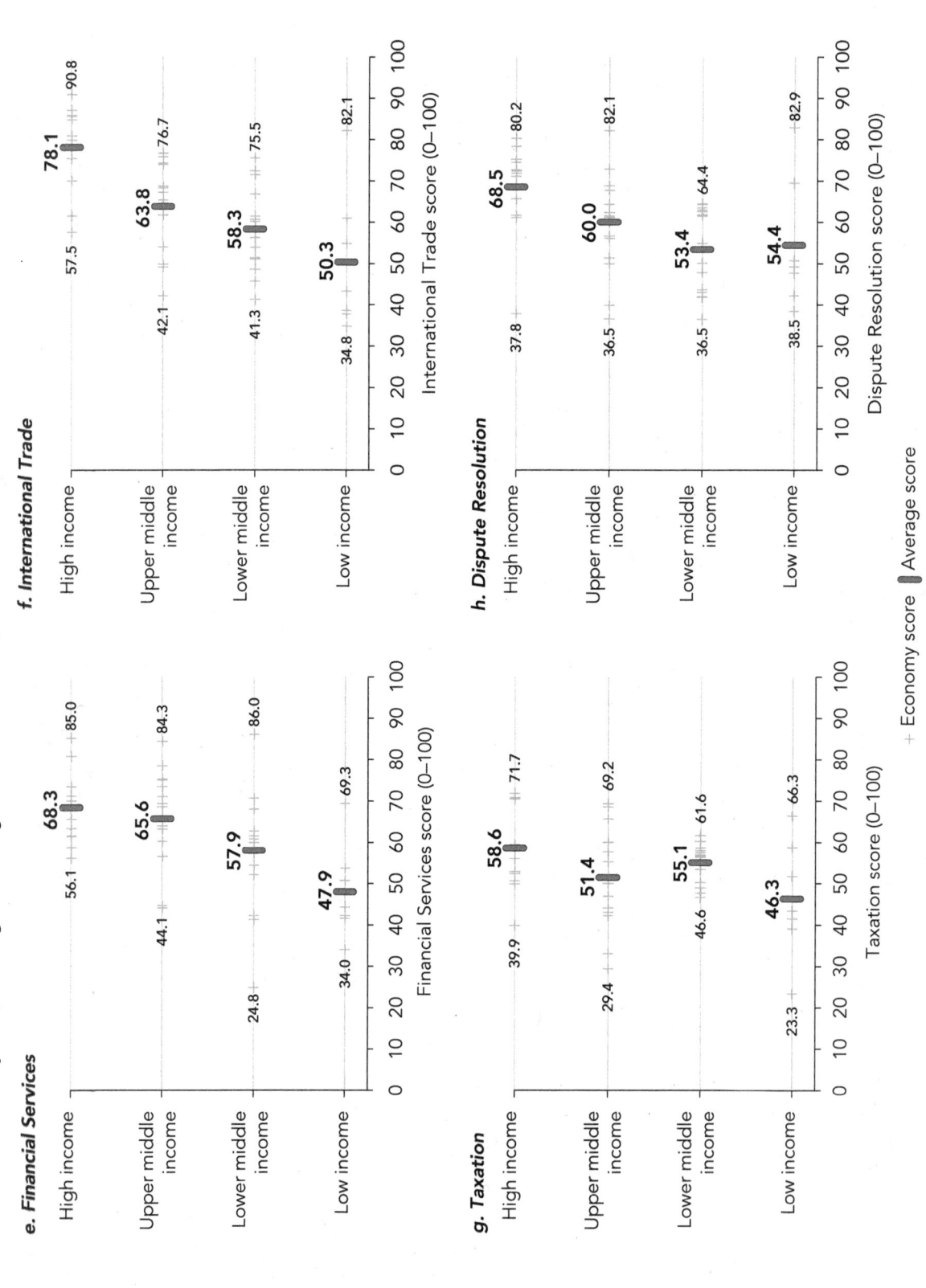

e. *Financial Services*

f. *International Trade*

g. *Taxation*

h. *Dispute Resolution*

+ Economy score ▮ Average score

(Continued)

FIGURE 4.6 B-READY topic scores, by economy income level (Continued)

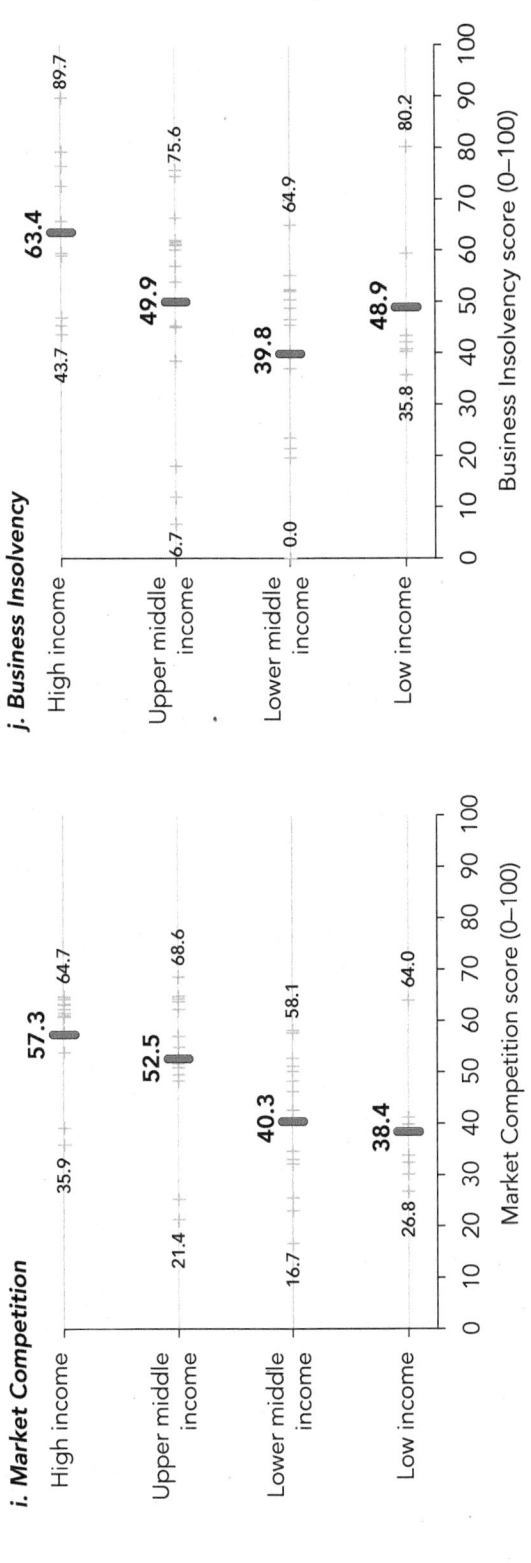

i. Market Competition

j. Business Insolvency

Market Competition score (0–100)

Business Insolvency score (0–100)

+ Economy score | Average score

Source: B-READY 2024 data.

Note: Each cross (+) represents the score of an economy at its income level. Each vertical blue marker indicates the average score of an income level. The minimum and maximum scores within each income level are also specified. The high-income level includes 12 economies; the upper-middle-income level, 15; and the low-income level, 7.

FIGURE 4.7 Contribution of the topic scores to each of the three B-READY pillar scores, by economy

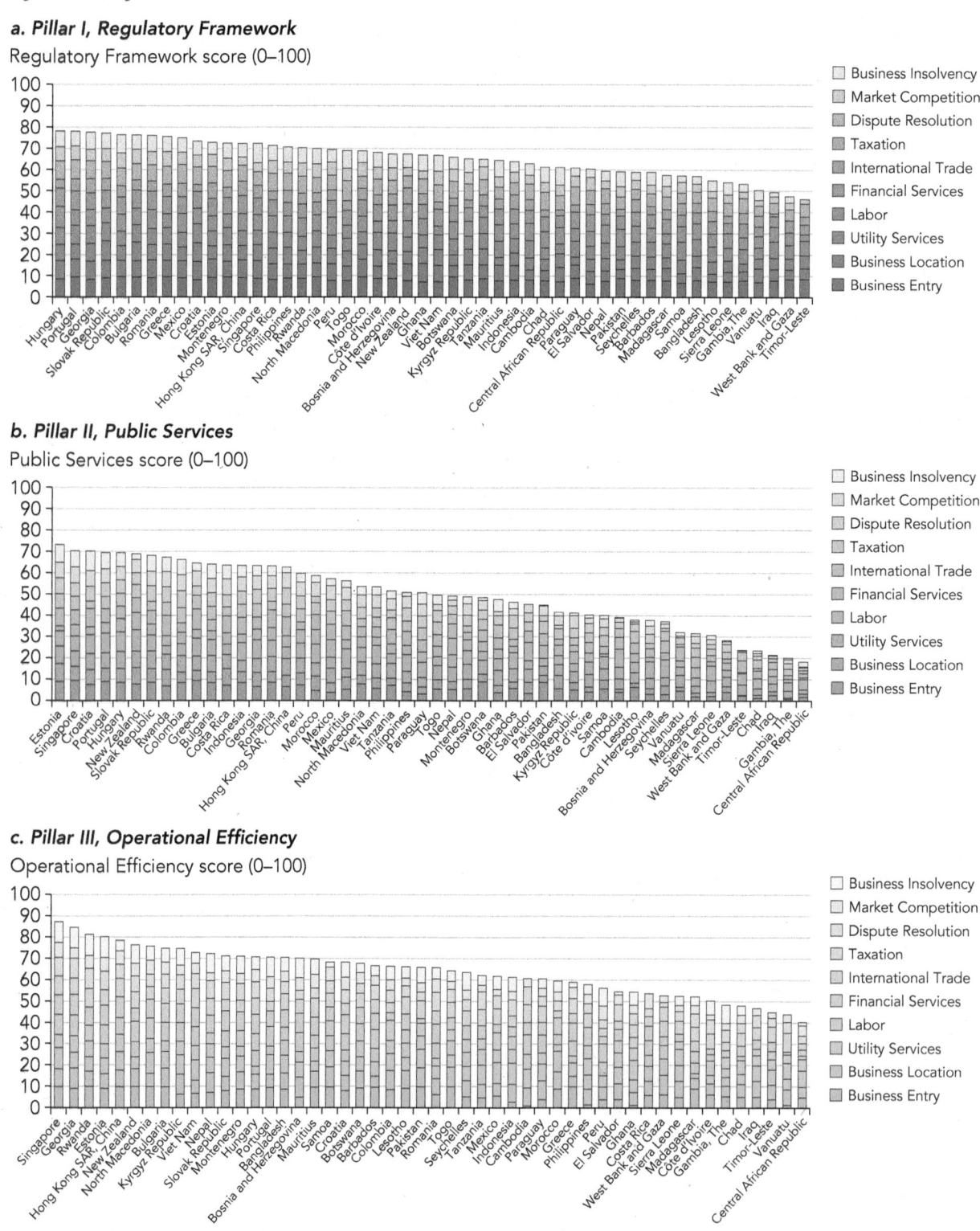

a. Pillar I, Regulatory Framework

Regulatory Framework score (0–100)

b. Pillar II, Public Services

Public Services score (0–100)

c. Pillar III, Operational Efficiency

Operational Efficiency score (0–100)

Source: B-READY 2024 data.
Note: The pillar scores for each topic are rescaled based on the topic's contribution to the pillar score. The length of each bar segment indicates the points contributed by that topic, with each topic contributing a maximum of 10 points. The pillar score is the sum of the rescaled scores for the corresponding pillar across all 10 topics.

Similarly in Pillar II, Singapore is situated at the higher end of the distribution, with each topic contributing between 5.2 points (Financial Services) and 9.4 points (Business Entry) to its Public Services score. Conversely, in economies such as Sierra Leone, positioned in the lower end of the distribution, the majority of topic scores contribute less than 3 points to the Pillar II score, except for its largest contributors Labor (6.9 points) and Utility Services (5.5 points).

In Pillar III, Georgia is situated at the higher end of the distribution, with six topics contributing more than 9 points each to its Operational Efficiency score: Business Entry, Business Location, Financial Services, Dispute Resolution, International Trade, and Business Insolvency. Utility Services (7.3 points) and Market Competition (4.9 points) contribute the least. Vanuatu is positioned at the lower end of the distribution with topic contributions varying from 0 points (Business Insolvency) to 8.8 points (Taxation). Decomposing the B-READY pillar scores by topic can help policy makers identify and address the specific areas in their economies that could benefit from improvements, while learning from the experience of others in the region and at a similar level of development.

What do the data reveal about the cross-cutting themes of digital adoption, environmental sustainability, and gender?

Overview of B-READY cross-cutting themes

The 10 B-READY topics include data on three critical cross-cutting themes that affect business operations and are increasingly important for modern economies: digital adoption, environmental sustainability, and gender. The themes are anchored in specific areas of the business environment, following the life cycle of the firm. They are not meant to serve as stand-alone topics or separate areas but to complement the existing B-READY topics and other projects. For example, the area of gender was designed to complement the World Bank project *Women, Business and the Law* (WBL).[10] The WBL and B-READY teams are continually exploring whether there are gaps in coverage of gender issues in each B-READY topic and jointly determine which project should expand its set of indicators to address these gaps.

On digital adoption, most topics include an assessment of the provision of digital public services within the relevant domain. Likewise, on environmental sustainability, topics include an assessment of environmental licenses and the presence of carbon pricing instruments, among others. On gender, topics include, where relevant, indicators on the collection and availability of anonymized data disaggregated by sex. The cross-cutting indicators are embedded into topics' corresponding pillars, making them an integral part of topic scores. The indicators are also interrelated. For example, the same indicator can be relevant to both digital adoption and environmental sustainability. Examples are indicators on environmental reporting for digital connectivity infrastructure, as measured by Utility Services, and the online availability of environmental requirements for new businesses, as measured by Business Entry. Indicators are also relevant to both gender and digital adoption, such as the online availability of sex-disaggregated analysis of taxpayer information, as measured by Taxation, and of information on publicly funded programs to support women-owned companies, as measured by Business Entry. B-READY does not aim to benchmark overarching digital, environmental, or gender regulation. Instead, it offers data emerging on cross-cutting themes within the specific B-READY topics.

The sections that follow provide more insights into each of the cross-cutting themes by presenting what the cross-cutting theme covers specifically and analyzing selected cross-cutting indicators within B-READY topics.

Digital adoption

Governments and businesses are increasingly embracing digital technologies to improve efficiency, accessibility, and service delivery. The adoption of digital technologies by governments enables more efficient, user-friendly provision of public services and promotes greater transparency and accountability (World Bank 2016). The adoption of digital technologies by businesses fosters productivity, innovation, and the creation of highly skilled jobs (Ramdani, Raja, and Kayumova 2021).

What does the digital adoption cross-cutting theme cover?

B-READY looks at digital adoption, by either governments or businesses, as a cross-cutting theme anchored in specific areas of the business environment. More than 400 variables on digital adoption spanning the three pillars are embedded within all B-READY topics except Labor. Digital adoption by governments is covered by nine topics under Public Services (Pillar II). Digital adoption by businesses is measured by three topics (Utility Services, Financial Services, International Trade) under Regulatory Framework (Pillar I) and by four topics (Utility Services, Financial Services, International Trade, Taxation) under Operational Efficiency (Pillar III).

Digital adoption by governments includes, among other aspects, the availability of digital public services (refer to table 4.12), which can save time and reduce the administrative burden on entrepreneurs.

TABLE 4.12 Digital public services measured by B-READY topics

Topic	Area(s) covered
Business Entry	• Online company registration
Business Location	• Online platform for issuing building authorizations • Online platform to register the transfer of property ownership
Utility Services	• Online application for new commercial electricity connections • Online application for new commercial water connections • Online application for new commercial internet connections
Financial Services	• Online system for registrations, amendments, renewals, cancellations, and searches of security interests
International Trade	• Electronic single window for trade
Taxation	• Online service taxpayer portal
Dispute Resolution	• Online filing of initial complaint, together with all its attachments
Market Competition	• Online notification of a transaction subject to merger control regulation • Online platform allowing intellectual property holders to manage their rights • Electronic public procurement portal
Business Insolvency	• Electronic auctions conducted at the relevant court

Source: B-READY project.

Economies differ in their level of digital public services adoption across all topics. Whereas most sampled economies (46 of 50) have an online services portal, only a small subset of economies (7 of 50) conduct electronic auctions at the relevant court, as measured by the Business Insolvency topic.

The adoption of digital public services tends to be positively associated with income level. On average, high-income economies perform better than low-income ones. Estonia; Hong Kong SAR, China; New Zealand; and Singapore are the most advanced on the availability of online public services within the high-income group. Yet the diversity across economies within income levels is wide, suggesting that strong digitalization of public services can be achieved even at lower income levels. For example, Rwanda features online public services across all nine topics.[11]

OECD high-income economies in the sample of 50 economies exhibit the highest concentration of digital public services, but no economy provides all measured public services online. Adoption of digital public services is weaker, on average, in the sampled economies in the Middle East and North Africa.

B-READY data also provide insights into digital adoption by businesses, as measured in Regulatory Framework (Pillar I) and Operational Efficiency (Pillar III). Pillar I captures the regulatory framework enabling businesses to adopt digital technologies. For example, Utility Services and Financial Services measure requirements for cybersecurity in Regulatory Framework (Pillar I). In all, 29 of the 50 sampled economies have regulatory provisions on cybersecurity safeguards, including minimum cybersecurity protections or standards and modus operandi for an incident response to a major cyberattack or a compromise of service availability. In all, 39 of the 50 economies have provisions in the regulatory framework for e-payments that list requirements for cybersecurity and provisions for e-payments requiring the development of contingency plans and business continuity procedures in the event of technology failures for both bank and nonbank payment service providers.

Pillar III captures use of digital technologies by businesses via the World Bank Enterprise Surveys. For example, the use of electronic systems to file and pay taxes by firms is widespread across the 50 sampled economies. In about 30 economies, over 70 percent of firms use electronic systems to file and pay taxes.

There is a significant gap between high-income and low-income economies in the use of e-payments by firms. The average score on usage level for receiving e-payments at the high-income level is 80.92 points, but in low-income economies it is only 13.57 points.[12] Low-income economies, on average, score even lower on the usage level for making e-payments (6.71 points) than high-income economies (75.50 points).

Environmental sustainability

Sustainability is integral to achieving the goals of eradicating poverty and promoting shared prosperity on a livable planet.[13] These goals emphasize the importance of ensuring that economic growth and development are environmentally sustainable. This entails adopting policies and practices that balance economic progress with the preservation of natural resources, the reduction of greenhouse gas emissions, and the promotion of social equity.

Regulation is a crucial tool for governments to achieve environmental goals, but an enabling regulatory framework is essential for businesses to navigate the trade-offs between improved environmental performance and compliance costs. Although environmentally sustainable practices may initially incur compliance costs for businesses, they offer longer-term cost savings and welfare benefits for individual firms, the private sector, and society at large (OECD 2017).

What does the environmental sustainability cross-cutting theme cover?

The B-READY project presents indicators that reflect environmental regulatory provisions affecting business operations within specific areas of the business environment. Environmental sustainability areas are covered in 8 of the 10 B-READY topics, comprising more than 100 data points (refer to table 4.13). Although most questions are included in Regulatory Framework (Pillar I), four topics include questions that relate to the public sector covered under Public Services (Pillar II). The Business Location topic also includes environmental sustainability indicators within Operational Efficiency (Pillar III), focusing on compliance costs for businesses. The B-READY project does not aim to benchmark comprehensive environmental regulations such as laws on pollution, biodiversity, or deforestation.

Eighty percent of economies provide for a risk-based assessment for issuing environmental operating licenses (measured in the Business Entry topic), and 27 of 50 economies allow any party to bring an environmental dispute against a business entity in court, even if that party has not suffered actual harm (measured in the Dispute Resolution topic).

TABLE 4.13 Environmental sustainability indicators measured by B-READY topics

Topic	Area(s) covered
Business Entry	• Risk management for environmental clearances required before the start of business operations • Online availability of environmental-related requirements
Business Location	• Environmental licensing requirements, including time to obtain an environmental permit • Building energy efficiency standards
Utility Services	• Energy and water use efficiency standards to account for solutions promoting energy savings and reducing water loss • Wastewater treatment requirements • Key Performance Indicators
International Trade	• Tariffs on environmental goods • Cross-border carbon pricing instruments • Ratification of relevant international standards
Taxation	• Fiscal instruments to discourage or cap activities harmful to the environment
Dispute Resolution	• Good regulatory practices in environmental disputes
Market Competition	• Sustainable procurement • Intellectual property in environmental sustainability policies
Business Insolvency	• Environmental obligations in bankruptcy, including treatment of claims related to the environment

Source: B-READY project.

Environmental permitting is a critical aspect of construction project planning and management. According to the Business Location data, 47 of 50 economies have national environmental regulations for the construction process and obligations to conduct an environmental impact assessment. High-income economies do not appear to be efficient in providing public services: companies have to wait 471 days, on average, to obtain environmental permits in these economies, or three times more than the average of 159 days in low- and lower-middle-income economies. However, their lower performance in this area is partially offset by having a strong regulatory framework in the area of environmental permits. Building energy standards are essential tools for promoting energy efficiency and reducing greenhouse gas emissions in the building sector. However, only 10 economies have incentives to promote green building standards. Rwanda is the only low-income economy to offer such incentives.

The Utility Services topic assesses best practices in delivering essential services such as electricity, water, and digital connectivity in an environmentally sustainable manner. Enhancing water quality, increasing water use efficiency, and ensuring safe water reuse are crucial for sustainable development. However, only about half of the economies have implemented environmental standards and requirements for an efficient water supply to promote water conservation. Wastewater treatment requirements are also critical. Six economies still do not have any mandates for treating wastewater before it is discharged into water bodies or onto land.

Power generation is a major source of air pollution. It is encouraging that most economies have implemented environmental standards for electricity generation. Moreover, 22 economies have financial incentives for businesses to adopt energy-saving practices, and 16 economies have put in place nonfinancial incentives. Taxation is among the topics in which environmental good practices are not widely implemented. Only 12 economies have adopted instruments that put a price on carbon or other greenhouse gases. Environmental taxes serve to reduce carbon output, curb fuel consumption, facilitate innovation, and move toward environmentally friendly technologies while raising revenue.

There is room for improvement in International Trade, as well. Tariffs on the importation of environmental goods[14] remain high, particularly in low-income economies. Tariffs on environmental goods in high-income and upper-middle-income economies average 6.2 percent, whereas tariffs in low-income and lower-middle-income economies are twice as high, averaging 12.8 percent. Of the 50 economies covered, 10 economies from all income levels have eliminated tariffs on environmental goods.

Finally, substantial improvements are needed in the area of Business Insolvency, where only 2 economies give priority to environmental claims, and 3 economies have exceptions to an automatic stay of proceedings based on refrain from environmental damage.

Gender

Women are underrepresented in firm ownership and senior management roles, and they tend to be concentrated in lower-ranking positions. Specifically, only 33 percent of formal firms have female participation in ownership; only 14.7 percent of formal firms have women in top manager positions (World Bank Group 2024).[15]

Gender equality in business is associated with better financial outcomes, including higher equity returns and lower loan defaults (IFC 2023). Gender equality is smart economics (Loayza and Trumbic 2022). The World Bank Group Gender 2024–2030 strategy focuses on promoting gender equality to achieve sustainable and inclusive growth (World Bank Group 2024). It includes the use of gender indicators to guide policy reforms and enhance women's involvement in business. As noted, the B-READY project complements the World Bank's WBL project. However, although WBL focuses exclusively on women's economic opportunities, B-READY considers gender through the lens of private sector development by introducing new gender dimensions not covered by other gender-focused products. These dimensions focus on the collection and availability of anonymized data disaggregated by sex not analyzed by WBL, as well as on measuring the implementation and targeting of programs and gender-sensitive regulations in economies in areas related to B-READY topics.

What does the gender cross-cutting theme cover?

About 40 variables on gender span all three pillars and eight B-READY topics. Gender is measured in Regulatory Framework (Pillar I) by International Trade, Dispute Resolution, and Market Competition, and in Public Services (Pillar II) by Business Entry, Business Location, Taxation, Dispute Resolution, and Market Competition. Utility Services covers gender indicators under Pillar III, Operational Efficiency (refer to table 4.14).

TABLE 4.14 Gender indicators covered by B-READY topics

Topic	Area(s) covered
Business Entry	• Existence and accessibility of publicly funded programs to support women-owned small and medium enterprises • Sex-disaggregated data on the ownership and staff composition of limited liability corporations
Business Location	• Sex-disaggregated data on land ownership by the land registry
Utility Services	• Sex-disaggregated data on customer service at internet/water/electricity utility
International Trade	• Gender-specific provisions in trade agreements • Additional restrictions on female service providers and other discrimination measures
Taxation	• Availability of sex-disaggregated data and their analysis • Gender composition of the staff in tax administration
Dispute Resolution	• Equal rights for men and women in commercial litigation • Production of key statistics on the representation of women in the judiciary • Transparency of arbitration and mediation/conciliation
Market Competition	• Promotion of gender equality in public procurement • Incorporation of gender clauses in standard bidding documents and incentives to consider gender in tenders • Publication of open data on tenders and contracts disaggregated by sex • Availability of business accelerators and incubators that target women entrepreneurs and women-founded businesses

Source: B-READY project.

For most economies, improving the availability of sex-disaggregated data to quantify the existing gender gaps in several B-READY areas remains a work in progress. For example, in 12 percent of economies, tax authorities collect sex-disaggregated data on taxpayers. These economies are predominantly high-income and upper-middle-income, yet such data are rarely analyzed and made publicly available. Also in the area of Taxation, 22 percent of economies publish information on the gender composition of the senior executives in the tax authority, including in high-income economies such as Singapore and low-income economies such as Rwanda. The economies measured in this report lag in areas such as collecting sex-disaggregated data on land ownership, as well as in Dispute Resolution, specifically collecting and publishing sex-disaggregated data on judges, mediators, and arbitrators. Only 4 economies (Colombia, Mexico, Portugal, and Singapore) of 50 collect sex-disaggregated data on judges, and only 2 other economies (Singapore and Hong Kong SAR, China) publish statistics on the number of arbitrators disaggregated by sex. None of the sampled economies publishes sex-disaggregated data on mediators.

In terms of gender-targeted programs for women entrepreneurs, approximately 50 percent of the sampled economies have incubators or accelerators specifically aimed at women entrepreneurs—that is, organizations that help and mentor women entrepreneurs to develop their business ideas. Moreover, about 34 percent of economies have publicly available information about publicly funded programs to support women-owned businesses, facilitating easy access for these entrepreneurs across various income levels and regions, including in high-income economies such as Singapore (Women Entrepreneurship Incubator) and Colombia (Programa Mujer Emprendedora y Productiva) and in middle-income economies such as El Salvador (Programa Nacional de Empresarialidad Femenina) and Viet Nam (Vườn ươm khởi nghiệp).

As for specific gender-sensitive provisions that promote the inclusion of women-owned businesses, significant progress remains to be made in areas measured by B-READY. In Market Competition in the area of public procurement, only 2 economies of 50 (Greece and Togo) have implemented gender-specific provisions that require firms participating in tenders to demonstrate adherence to the principle of gender nondiscrimination. Greater efforts are needed to implement legal provisions requiring firms participating in public tenders to conduct a gender analysis in their needs assessment. Moreover, legal provisions need to be established to exclude firms with a history of violating gender equality obligations or with a poor record on gender equality issues. None of the sampled economies includes such gender provisions for firms participating in tenders. In the area of International Trade, B-READY assesses whether economies have ratified and implemented enforceable provisions that establish minimum commitments to gender equality and women's participation in economic and development activities within preferential trade agreements. Overall, 44 percent of economies have ratified and implemented provisions for gender equality, and 40 percent have done so for women's participation. There are still notable gaps in the gender areas measured by B-READY across the 50 economies sampled for this report.

Finally, the project's indicators on gender originally included areas not described in this report because the quality of data was poor or the expert knowledge on the evaluated matters was insufficient. These domains primarily pertained to Financial Services, focusing on the availability of women-targeted financial and nonfinancial products offered by commercial banks, training bank staff on unconscious gender bias, and initiatives to enhance the representation of women in senior executive or management positions in the banking sector. Similarly, under the Business Location topic, indicators were related to incentives for increasing female participation in sectors such as construction, environmental permitting, and property transfer.

However, the team received very few responses from its experts on these areas and decided that because of the low quality of the data it would drop these indicators. These instances illustrate that during this rollout phase, indicators are being evaluated, and the quality of data as well as the expertise of respondents are determining factors in the decision to retain or drop certain gender indicators.

As the project incorporates additional economies in subsequent editions, additional insights from gender-related data will be forthcoming, offering a clearer perspective on regional and income-level trends.

Notes

1. https://www.worldbank.org/en/publication/global-economic-prospects.
2. https://www.worldbank.org/en/publication/worldwide-governance-indicators.
3. https://www.worldbank.org/en/publication/human-capital.
4. https://www.unodc.org/unodc/en/data-and-analysis/statistics/index.html.
5. Product Market Regulation Indicator, Organisation for Economic Co-operation and Development, https://www.oecd.org/economy/reform/indicators-of -product-market-regulation/.
6. World Bank Enterprise Surveys (database), https://www.enterprisesurveys.org/en /enterprisesurveys.
7. International Telecommunication Union (ITU), World Telecommunication/ICT Indicators Database, 2022, https://www.itu.int/pub/D-IND-WTID-2022.
8. World Bank Enterprise Surveys, "Biggest Obstacle," https://www .enterprisesurveys.org/en/data/exploretopics/biggest-obstacle.
9. Good practices are based on the World Bank's Principles for Effective Insolvency and Creditor and Debtor Regimes (https://documents.worldbank.org/en /publication/documents-reports/documentdetail/391341619072648570 /principles-for-effective-insolvency-and-creditor-and-debtor-regimes) and the United Nations Commission on International Trade Law (UNCITRAL) Legislative Guide on Insolvency Law (https://uncitral.un.org/en/texts/insolvency /legislativeguides/insolvency_law).
10. https://wbl.worldbank.org/en/wbl.
11. There are two exceptions. In Market Competition, Rwanda does not have an online platform allowing intellectual property holders to manage their rights. In Utility Services, Rwanda does not have an online application for new commercial water connections.
12. The indicators used to calculate the average score on the use of e-payments by firms are (1) percentage of monthly sales received electronically and (2) percentage of monthly payments conducted electronically.
13. https://www.worldbank.org/en/who-we-are#:~:text=Our%20mission%20is%20 to%20end,threatened%20by%20multiple%2C%20intertwined%20crises.
14. The analysis pertains to the top five most traded environmental products by total trade value at the global level between 2015 and 2019 (UN COMTRADE) within the Asia-Pacific Economic Cooperation (APEC) list of environmental goods at the HS subheading level (six-digit). These products

are HS 854140 (Electrical apparatus); HS 901380 (Optical appliances and instruments); HS 847989 (Machines and mechanical appliances); HS 903289 (Regulating or controlling instruments and apparatus); and HS 903180 (Instruments, appliances and machines for measuring or checking, not elsewhere specified in chapter 90).
15. World Bank Enterprise Surveys, 2024 data, https://www.enterprisesurveys.org /en/enterprisesurveys.

References

Adama, A. 2020. "Financial Contracting and Misreporting with Limited Enforcement, Firm Financing and Growth." *Cogent Economics and Finance* 8 (1): 1–24.

Aldy, J. E., and R. Stavins. 2011. "The Promise and Problems of Pricing Carbon: Theory and Experience." NBER Working Paper 17569, National Bureau of Economic Research, Cambridge, MA.

Allcott, H., A. Collard-Wexler, and S. O'Connell. 2016. "How Do Electricity Shortages Affect Industry? Evidence from India." *American Economic Review* 106 (3): 587–624.

Alm, J., T. Cherry, M. Jones, and M. McKee. 2010. "Taxpayer Information Assistance Services and Tax Compliance Behavior." *Journal of Economic Psychology* 31: 577–86.

Almeida, R., and P. Carneiro. 2011. "Enforcement of Labor Regulation and Informality." *American Economic Journal: Applied Economics* 4 (3): 64–89.

Amaral, P. S., and E. Quintin. 2010. "Limited Enforcement, Financial Intermediation, and Economic Development: A Quantitative Assessment." *International Economic Review* 51 (3): 785–811.

Amin, M., and D. Viganola. 2021. "Does Better Access to Finance Help Firms Deal with the COVID-19 Pandemic? Evidence from Firm-Level Survey Data." Policy Research Working Paper 9697, World Bank, Washington, DC.

Audretsch, D., E. Lehmann, and M. Wright. 2014. "Technology Transfer in a Global Economy." *Journal of Technology Transfer* 39 (3): 301–12.

Ayyagari, M., P. Pedro Juarros, M. S. Martinez Peria, and S. Singh. 2021. "Access to Finance and Job Growth: Firm-Level Evidence across Developing Countries." *Review of Finance* 25 (5): 1473–96.

Azevedo, João Pedro, Gabriela Inchauste, Sergio Olivieri, Jaime Saavedra, and Hernan Winkler. 2013. "Is Labor Income Responsible for Poverty Reduction? A Decomposition Approach." Policy Research Working Paper 6414, World Bank, Washington, DC.

Beck, T., A. Demirgüç-Kunt, and R. Levine. 2007. "Finance, Inequality and the Poor." *Journal of Economic Growth* 12: 27–49.

Begazo Gomez, T. P., and S. Nyman. 2016. "Competition and Poverty." View Point Note No. 350, World Bank, Washington, DC.

Besley, T., and T. Persson. 2019. "Democratic Values and Institutions." *American Economic Review: Insights* 1 (1): 59–76.

Boly, A. 2018. "On the Short- and Medium-Term Effects of Formalisation: Panel Evidence from Viet Nam." *Journal of Development Studies* 54 (4): 641–56.

Boyne, G., P. Day, and R. Walker. 2002. "The Evaluation of Public Service Inspection: A Theoretical Framework." *Urban Studies* 39 (7): 1197–1212.

Capasso, S., and T. Jappelli. 2013. "Financial Development and the Underground Economy." *Journal of Development Economies* 101 (C): 167–78.

Carlson, V. 2000. "Studying Firm Locations: Survey Responses vs. Econometric Models." *Journal of Regional Analysis and Policy* 30 (1): 1–22.

Chaudhary, S., and S. Sharma. 2022. "The Impact of Lifting Firing Restrictions on Firms: Evidence from a State Level Labor Law Amendment." World Bank, Washington, DC.

Chemin, M. 2009. "The Impact of the Judiciary on Entrepreneurship: Evaluation of Pakistan's Access to Justice Programme." *Journal of Public Economics* 93 (1–2): 114–25.

Chen, R. 2019. "Policy and Regulatory Issues with Digital Businesses." Policy Research Working Paper 8948, World Bank, Washington, DC.

Cirera, X., D. Comin, and M. Cruz. 2022. *Bridging the Technological Divide: Technology Adoption by Firms in Developing Countries.* Washington, DC: World Bank.

Cirmizi, E., L. Klapper, and M. Uttamchandani. 2012. "The Challenges of Bankruptcy Reform." *World Bank Research Observer* 27 (2): 185–203.

Clotfelter, C. T. 1983. "Tax Evasion and Tax Rates: An Analysis of Individual Returns." *Review of Economics and Statistics* 65 (3): 363–73.

Cooley, T., R. Marimon, and V. Quadrini. 2004. "Aggregate Consequences of Limited Contract Enforceability." *Journal of Political Economy* 112 (4): 817–47.

Coolidge, J., and D. Ilic. 2009. "Tax Compliance Perceptions and Formalization of Small Businesses in South Africa." Policy Research Working Paper 4992, World Bank, Washington, DC.

Dabla-Norris, E., F. Misch, D. Cleary, and M. Khwaja. 2017. "Tax Administration and Firm Performance: New Data and Evidence for Emerging Market and Developing Economies." IMF Working Paper WP 2017/095, International Monetary Fund, Washington, DC.

Dejuan-Bitria, D., and J. S. Mora-Sanguinetti. 2021. "Which Legal Procedure Affects Business Investment Most, and Which Companies Are Most Sensitive? Evidence from Microdata." *Economic Modelling* 94 (C): 201–20.

Donaubauer, J., A. Glas, B. Meyer, and P. Nunnenkamp. 2018. "Disentangling the Impact of Infrastructure on Trade Using a New Index of Infrastructure." *Review of World Economics* 154 (4): 745–84.

Dumav, M., W. Fuchs, and J. Lee. 2022. "Self-Enforcing Contracts with Persistence." *Journal of Monetary Economics* 128: 72–87.

EC (European Commission). 2014. *Evaluation of SMEs' Access to Public Procurement Markets in the EU: Final Report.* Directorate General for Enterprise and Industry. Brussels: European Union.

Esposito, G., S. Lanau, and S. Pompe. 2014. "Judicial System Reform in Italy–A Key to Growth." IMF Working Paper WP/14/32, International Monetary Fund, Washington, DC.

Fajnzylber, P., W. Maloney, and G. Montes-Rojas. 2011. "Does Formality Improve Micro-Firm Performance? Evidence from the Brazilian SIMPLES Program." *Journal of Development Economics* 94 (2): 262–76.

Field, E. 2007. "Entitled to Work: Urban Property Rights and Labor Supply in Peru." *Quarterly Journal of Economics* 122 (4): 1561–1602.

Fontagné, L., G. Orefice, and R. Piermartini. 2020. "Making Small Firms Happy? The Heterogeneous Effect of Trade Facilitation Measures." *Review of International Economics* 28 (2020): 565–98.

Foster, V., and A. Rana. 2020. *Rethinking Power Sector Reform in the Developing World.* Sustainable Infrastructure Series. Washington, DC: World Bank.

Fritsch, M., and F. Noseleit. 2013. "Investigating the Anatomy of the Employment Effect of New Business Formation." *Cambridge Journal of Economics* 37 (2): 349–77.

Garcia-Posada, M., and J. Mora-Sanguinetti. 2015. "Entrepreneurship and Enforcement Institutions: Disaggregated Evidence for Spain." *European Journal of Law and Economics* 40 (1): 49–74.

Gilbert, R. J. 2006. "Competition and Innovation." *Journal of Industrial Organization Education* 1 (1): 8.

Goldberg, P. K., A. K. Khandelwal, N. Pavcnik, and P. Topalova. 2010. "Imported Intermediate Inputs and Domestic Product Growth: Evidence from India." *Quarterly Journal of Economics* 125 (4): 1727–67.

González-Torres, G., and G. Rodano. 2020. "Court Efficiency and Aggregate Productivity: The Credit Channel." Bank of Italy Working Paper No. 1287, Bank of Italy, Rome.

Handley, K. 2014. "Exporting under Trade Policy Uncertainty: Theory and Evidence." *Journal of International Economics* 94 (1): 50–66.

He, J., and X. Tian. 2020. "Institutions and Innovation: A Review of Recent Literature." *Annual Review of Financial Economics* 12: 377–98.

Hummels, D. L., and G. Schaur. 2013. "Time as a Trade Barrier." *American Economic Review* 103 (7): 2935–59.

IFC (International Finance Corporation). 2023. "IFC Banking on Women, Business Case Update #5: Lower NPLs for Women-Owned SMEs." IFC, Washington, DC.

ILO (International Labour Organization). 2021. *Small Goes Digital: How Digitalization Can Bring about Productive Growth for Micro and Small Enterprises.* Geneva: ILO.

Ippoliti, R., A. Melcarne, and G. B. Ramello. 2015. "Judicial Efficiency and Entrepreneurs' Expectations on the Reliability of European Legal Systems." *European Journal of Law and Economics* 40 (1): 75–94.

Islam, A., and M. Amin. 2022. "The Gender Labor Productivity Gap across Informal Firms." Policy Research Working Paper 10011, World Bank, Washington, DC.

ITC (International Trade Centre). 2020. "Getting Down to Business: Making the Most of the WTO Trade Facilitation Agreement." ITC, Geneva.

Klapper, L., A. Lewin, and J. M. Quesada Delgado. 2011. "The Impact of the Business Environment on the Business Creation Process." Chapter 5 in *Entrepreneurship and Economic Development* (Studies in Development Economics and Policy), edited by W. Naudé. London: Palgrave Macmillan.

Klapper, L., and I. Love. 2016. "The Impact of Business Environment Reforms on New Firm Registration." *World Bank Economic Review* 30 (2): 332–56.

Koos, E. 2014. "Tax Dispute Resolution Mechanisms in Developed and Developing Countries: An Analysis of Factors that Affect Dispute Mechanism Design and Functionality." Harvard Law School, Cambridge, MA.

Koutroumpis, P., and F. R. Ravasan. 2020. "Do Court Delays Distort Capital Formation?" Working Paper No. 2020-4, Oxford Martin Working Paper Series on Economic and Technological Change, University of Oxford, Oxford, UK.

Kuddo, A. 2018. "Labor Regulations throughout the World: An Overview." Jobs Working Paper Issue No. 16, World Bank, Washington, DC.

La Porta, R., and A. Shleifer. 2008. "The Unofficial Economy and Economic Development." *Brookings Papers on Economic Activity*, Fall 2008, 275–352.

La Porta, R., and A. Shleifer. 2014. "Informality and Development." *Journal of Economic Perspectives* 28 (3): 109–26.

Leland, H. E. 1979. "Quacks, Lemons, and Licensing: A Theory of Minimum Quality Standards." *Journal of Political Economy* 87 (6): 1328–46.

Levine, R. 2005. "Finance and Growth: Theory and Evidence." *Handbook of Economic Growth* 1: 865–934.

Loayza, N. V. 2016. "Informality in the Process of Development and Growth." *World Economy* 39 (12): 1856–1916.

Loayza, N. V. 2018. "Informality: Why Is It So Widespread and How Can It Be Reduced?" Research and Policy Brief No. 20, World Bank, Washington, DC.

Loayza, N. V., and T. Trumbic. 2022. "Gender Equality Is Smart Economics. Yet, Its Progress Remains Slow." *Let's Talk Development* (blog), March 1, 2022. https://blogs.worldbank.org/en/developmenttalk/gender-equality-smart-economics-yet-its-progress-remains-slow.

Madsen, J. B. 2007. "Technology Spillover through Trade and TFP Convergence: 135 Years of Evidence for the OECD Countries." *Journal of International Economics* 72 (2): 464–80.

Mare, D. S., F. de Nicola, and F. Miguel. 2021. "Financial Structure and Firm Innovation: Evidence from around the World." Policy Research Working Paper 9670, World Bank, Washington, DC.

McKenzie, D., and Y. Sakho. 2010. "Does It Pay Firms to Register for Taxes? The Impact of Formality on Firm Profitability." *Journal of Development Economics* 91 (1): 15–24.

Medina, L., and F. Schneider. 2018. "Shadow Economies around the World: What Did We Learn over the Last 20 Years?" IMF Working Paper 18/17, International Monetary Fund, Washington, DC.

Medvedev, D., and A. M. Oviedo Silva. 2015. "Informality and Profitability: Evidence from a New Firm Survey in Ecuador." *Journal of Development Studies* 52 (3): 1–25.

Melitz, M. J. 2003. "The Impact of Trade on Intra-Industry Reallocations and Aggregate Industry Productivity." *Econometrica* 71 (6): 1695–1725.

Menezes, A. 2014. "Debt Resolution and Business Exit: Insolvency Reform for Credit, Entrepreneurship, and Growth." World Bank Group Knowledge Note, World Bank, Washington, DC.

Moro, A., D. Maresch, and A. Ferrando. 2018. "Creditor Protection, Judicial Enforcement and Credit Access." *European Journal of Finance* 24 (3): 250–81.

Neely, A., and J. Hii. 1998. "Innovation and Business Performance: A Literature Review." Judge Institute of Management Studies, University of Cambridge, Cambridge, UK.

OECD (Organisation for Economic Co-operation and Development). 2013. "What Makes Civil Justice Effective?" OECD Economics Department Policy Note 18, OECD, Paris.

OECD (Organisation for Economic Co-operation and Development). 2017. "Private Sector Engagement to Address Climate Change and Promote Green Growth." Private Sector Peer Learning Policy Brief 4, OECD, Paris.

OECD (Organisation for Economic Co-operation and Development). 2021. *OECD Regulatory Policy Outlook 2021*. Paris: OECD.

OECD (Organisation for Economic Co-operation and Development) and IDB (Inter-American Development Bank). 2021. *Building Effective Beneficial Ownership Frameworks: A Joint Global Forum and IDB Toolkit*. Global Forum on Enhancing Government Effectiveness and Transparency, OECD and IDB.

Ortiz-Villajos, J. M., and S. Sotoca. 2018. "Innovation and Business Survival: A Long-Term Approach." *Research Policy* 47 (8): 1418–36.

OSCE/UNECE (Organization for Security and Co-operation in Europe/United Nations Economic Commission for Europe). 2012. *Handbook of Best Practices at Border Crossings–A Trade and Transport Facilitation Perspective*. Vienna: OSCE.

Porter, M. 1992. "Capital Choices: Changing the Way America Invests in Industry." *Journal of Applied Corporate Finance* 5 (2): 4–16.

Qi, S., and S. Ongena. 2019. "Fuel the Engine: Bank Credit and Firm Innovation." *Journal of Financial Services Research* 57: 115–47.

Rahaman, M. M. 2011. "Access to Financing and Firm Growth." *Journal of Banking and Finance* 35 (3): 709–23.

Ramdani, B., S. Raja, and M. Kayumova. 2021. "Digital Innovation in SMEs: A Systematic Review, Synthesis and Research Agenda." *Information Technology for Development* 28 (1): 1–24.

Rand, J., and N. Torm. 2012. "The Benefits of Formalization: Evidence from Vietnamese Manufacturing SMEs." *World Development* 40 (5): 983–98.

Rentschler, J., M. Kornejew, S. Hallegatte, and J. Braese. 2019. "Underutilized Potential: The Business Costs of Unreliable Infrastructure in Developing Countries." Policy Research Working Paper 8899, World Bank, Washington, DC.

Sampson, T. 2016. "Dynamic Selection: An Idea Flows Theory of Entry, Trade, and Growth." *Quarterly Journal of Economics* 131 (1): 315–80.

Staats, J. L., and G. Biglaiser. 2011. "The Effects of Judicial Strength and Rule of Law on Portfolio Investment in the Developing World." *Social Science Quarterly* 92 (3): 609–30.

Tang, J. 2006. "Competition and Innovation Behavior." *Research Policy* 35 (1): 68–82.

Tirole, J. 2017. *Economics for the Common Good.* Princeton, NJ: Princeton University Press.

Ulyssea, G. 2020. "Informality: Causes and Consequences for Development." *Annual Review of Economics* 2 (1): 525–46.

UNCITRAL (United Nations Commission on International Trade Law). 2019. *UNCITRAL Legislative Guide on Key Principles of a Business Registry.* Vienna: UNCITRAL.

UNCTAD (United Nations Conference on Trade and Development). No date. "Getting Down to Business: Making the Most of the WTO Trade Facilitation Agreement." https://unctad.org/publication/getting-down-business-making -most-wto-trade-facilitation-agreement.

UNECE (United Nations Economic Commission for Europe). 2021. "Recommendation No. 38: Trade Information Portals (ECE/TRADE/465)." UNECE, Geneva.

Volpe Martincus, C., J. Carballo, and A. Graziano. 2015. "Customs." *Journal of International Economics* 96 (1): 119–37.

WCO (World Customs Organization). 2020. *Coordinated Border Management Compendium.* Brussels: WCO.

Wehrmann, B. 2008. *Land Conflicts: A Practical Guide to Dealing with Land Disputes.* Eschborn, Germany: Deutche GTZ (Gesellschaft für Technische Zusammenarbeit).

Wellalage, N. H., and V. Fernandez. 2019. "Innovation and SME Finance: Evidence from Developing Countries." *International Review of Financial Analysis* 66: 101370.

Wellalage, N. H., and S. Locke. 2020. "Formal Credit and Innovation: Is There a Uniform Relationship across Types of Innovation?" *International Review of Economics and Finance* 70: 1–15.

Wilson, E. J., A. B. Klass, and S. Bergan. 2009. "Assessing a Liability Regime for Carbon Capture and Storage." *Energy Procedia* 1 (1): 4575–82.

WIPO (World Intellectual Property Organization). 2023. *Global Innovation Index 2023: Innovation in the Face of Uncertainty.* Geneva: WIPO.

World Bank. 2004. *World Development Report 2005: A Better Investment Climate for Everyone.* Washington, DC: World Bank.

World Bank. 2012. *World Development Report 2013: Jobs.* Washington, DC: World Bank.

World Bank. 2016. *World Development Report 2016: Digital Dividends.* Washington, DC: World Bank.

World Bank. 2017. *A Step Ahead: Competition Policy for Shared Prosperity and Inclusive Growth.* Washington, DC: World Bank.

World Bank. 2019. "Retention and Expansion of Foreign Direct Investment: Political Risk and Policy Responses: Summary of Research Findings and Policy Implications." Working paper, World Bank, Washington, DC. https://openknowledge.worldbank.org/bitstream/handle/10986/33082/Political-Risk -and-Policy-Responses.pdf?sequence=1&isAllowed=y.

World Bank. 2020. *Enhancing Government Effectiveness and Transparency: The Fight against Corruption.* Kuala Lumpur: World Bank.

World Bank. 2023. *Business Ready: Methodology Handbook.* Washington, DC: World Bank. https://thedocs.worldbank.org/en/doc/357a611e3406288528 cb1e05b3c7dfda-0540012023/original/B-READY-Methodology-Handbook.pdf.

World Bank Group. 2024. *World Bank Group Gender Strategy 2024–2030: Accelerate Gender Equality to End Poverty on a Livable Planet.* Washington, DC: World Bank.

WTO (World Trade Organization). 2021. *Adapting to the Digital Trade Era: Challenges and Opportunities,* edited by Maarten Smeets. Geneva: WTO.

Zakout, W., B. Wehrmann, and M.-P. Törhönen. 2006. "Good Governance in Land Administration Principles and Good Practices." Food and Agriculture Organization of the United Nations, Rome.

5

LESSONS LEARNED AND WHAT IS NEXT

Refinements implemented during B-READY 2024

The first three-year cycle of B-READY 2024 is serving as the project's rollout phase, during which time its methodology will be refined from year to year. Throughout this phase, data collection and feedback from experts and users may uncover practical challenges, inconsistencies, or other methodological issues that become evident only after data collection and analysis. The methodology will then be improved to enhance its accuracy, efficiency, and effectiveness.

After completing the first round of data collection in 2024, the B-READY team carefully reviewed the data and implemented some changes to the indicators of the B-READY topics. These changes include, among others, adding new indicators considering their relevance, as well as dropping some categories and subcategories due to low data variation, low informed response rate, interpretation issues, and redundancy of indicators and questions. This chapter describes the main revisions made to individual topics.[1]

Business Location

In Pillar I, the questions related to gender incentives for professional participation were dropped due to a low informed response rate. In Pillar III, two subcategories for Occupancy Permits were also dropped due to a low

---

A reproducibility package is available for this book in the Reproducible Research Repository at https://reproducibility.worldbank.org/index.php/catalog/187.

informed response rate. Meanwhile, two subcategories—Major Constraints on Access to Land, and Time to Obtain a Construction-Related Permit—were added to measure access to land and the time needed to obtain construction permits as a proxy for the operational efficiency of property transfer and building permits for firms. The new data were collected through the Enterprise Surveys.[2]

Utility Services

By means of expert questionnaires and the Enterprise Surveys, the Utility Services topic tested data collection for the time needed to obtain a new utility connection. The data collected by the Enterprise Surveys had a better response rate than those collected through expert questionnaires, which exhibited a low informed response rate and interpretation issues. Therefore, data collection will rely only on data collected through the Enterprise Surveys.

Labor

In Pillar III, two subcategories—Proportion of Vacancies Filled, and Cost to Resolve a Labor Dispute—were removed due to a low informed response rate. In addition, On-the-Job Training was introduced to reflect the importance and readiness of employers to invest in the skills of their workers, thereby increasing the overall productivity of a firm. The new data were collected through the Enterprise Surveys.

Financial Services

The Green Finance subtopic was dropped because of the challenge of identifying relevant experts in the assessed economies and the lack of established international good practices. In addition, the topic no longer includes the gender component from the Customer Due Diligence questionnaire due to a low informed response rate. Cost of Loan was deleted from Pillar III and replaced with perception questions because firms were not able to provide the actual cost of their most recent loan. The new data were collected through the Enterprise Surveys.

International Trade

In Pillar III, one category—Perceived Major Obstacles: Business Transportation, Customs, and Trade Regulations—was added. The new data for this category were collected through the Enterprise Surveys. Second-order subcategories of express shipment programs were eliminated due to the reduced scope and depth of the set of indicators, in addition to a low informed response rate.

Taxation

Due to absence of variation across economies, the topic no longer includes the gender questions on whether women have the same rights as men in tax-related disputes.

Dispute Resolution

In Pillar III, a new indicator on whether courts are perceived by firms as an obstacle to business operations was added to ensure a more solid and comprehensive assessment of the reliability of courts. The new data were collected through the Enterprise Surveys.

Market Competition

Four subcategories were removed from the Market Competition topic. In the Competition questionnaire, the subcategory measuring the impact of the presence of state-owned enterprises in markets was removed due to a low informed response rate. In the Procurement questionnaire, the subcategory targeting gender gap perceptions on the ease of bidding was removed because of interpretation issues. Finally, in the Innovation questionnaire, the subcategories measuring the percentage of spending dedicated to research and development and the use of foreign-licensed technology were removed because no good practice was identified. In Pillar III, one subcategory, Use of International Quality Certifications, was added as a proxy for innovation in firms because a large body of literature indicates that firms with internationally recognized quality certifications are more innovative. An indicator was added related to government intervention in prices because research finds that excessive price controls can be detrimental to private sector development. The new data were collected through the Enterprise Surveys.

Business Insolvency

Pillar III introduces a new question for economies asking whether "no practice" is applicable to business insolvency proceedings. Specifically, if an economy has not had any completed (closed) cases of judicial reorganization or judicial liquidation proceedings involving corporate debtors in the last three years, the economy is marked as "no practice." Consequently, the time and cost indicators for these proceedings are assigned a score of 0. This approach avoids posing irrelevant questions about procedures that are simply not used in that economy.

Continued consultation

In the next two cycles, the methodology will be further refined as B-READY expands its economy coverage and moves from rollout phase to full-fledged project. As outlined in the B-READY Concept Note (World Bank 2022), the team will continue the consultation on methodology with the rest of the World Bank Group and improve the subsequent B-READY data and reports, enhancing their relevance for country engagement. Similarly, the feedback received from stakeholders outside the World Bank Group in dissemination activities will also be considered. Any changes or updates to the B-READY methodology will be reflected in an updated version of the *B-READY Methodology Handbook* (World Bank 2023).

Specific update for B-READY 2025

The expert data collection for the second edition of the B-READY report started in September 2024 with the goal of publishing the B-READY 2025 report in September 2025. Firm-level data collection, which requires longer preparation times, is already under way in some of the economies that will join B-READY for the first time in 2025.[3]

For economies included in the B-READY 2024 report, new firm-level data will be collected in the B-READY 2027 cycle. For these economies, indicators based on the firm-level Enterprise Surveys will use the same underlying data for the B-READY 2024, 2025, and 2026 reports.

To improve the efficiency of B-READY processes and the quality of the data, the following updates will be implemented for B-READY 2025:

- *Updates of the B-READY expert questionnaires.* A new version of the *B-READY Methodology Handbook*, including the revised questionnaires and scoring approach, will be published in alignment with the commencement of data collection from expert questionnaires. The handbook will be updated and published on the B-READY website (https://www.worldbank.org/en/businessready) at the beginning of each edition's data collection cycle.

- *Update of the data collection process.* To enhance the efficiency of expert recruitment, in addition to the efforts of individual topic teams, B-READY will realign resources, including targeted engagements with experts in international and regional law firms as well as professional associations. Recruitment missions will continue as part of the team's global initiatives with the objective of establishing long-term collaboration with the experts. This approach leverages the expertise and willingness of these firms and associations to undertake global pro bono projects. The B-READY team will also continue to strengthen data quality by recruiting top experts across all economies utilizing professional networks, industry events, and other adequate channels.

- *Update on government engagements.* The B-READY team remains committed to fostering open, transparent dialogue with governments. Government officials will continue to have an opportunity to complete B-READY questionnaires for data validation. To assist this process, the team will update dissemination materials such as methodology videos and presentations on the website. Government officials are encouraged to review these materials before completing the questionnaires. Throughout the data collection period, the team will continue to conduct bilateral meetings with governments to provide an overview of the B-READY project. In addition, the team will establish a designated period for governments to participate in question-and-answer sessions on methodology with topic teams.

  The updated B-READY website allows government officials to submit queries about the project's methodology during a designated period. The website will also include consolidated and anonymized responses to these queries, along with topic-specific frequently asked questions and answers. These features will enhance transparency, facilitate information sharing, and better inform government stakeholders.

- *Expanded coverage.* The tentative list of new economies to be covered by the second edition of the B-READY report is available on the B-READY website. The sample is expected to include more than 100 economies in the second report.

Through these and other efforts, the B-READY project and report will be continuously refined and improved.

Notes

1. All topics had changes, but in the case of Business Entry the changes were minor and therefore they are not listed below.
2. Enterprise Surveys data, https://www.enterprisesurveys.org/en/enterprisesurveys.
3. For information on all the projects carried out by the Enterprise Analysis Unit and their timeline, refer to https://www.enterprisesurveys.org/en/current-projects.

References

World Bank. 2022. "Concept Note: Business Enabling Environment."
World Bank, Washington, DC. https://thedocs.worldbank.org/en/doc/2250
b12dfe798507f7b42064378cc616-0540012022/original/BEE-Concept-Note
-December-2022.pdf.

World Bank. 2023. *Business Ready: Methodology Handbook.*
Washington, DC: World Bank. https://thedocs.worldbank.org/en/doc
/357a611e3406288528cb1e05b3c7dfda-0540012023/original/B-READY
-Methodology-Handbook.pdf.

APPENDIX A: TOPIC SCORES

TABLE A.1 **Business Entry**

Economy	Business Entry	Pillar I Regulatory Framework	Pillar II Public Services	Pillar III Operational Efficiency
Greece	96.58	96.25	94.50	99.00
Singapore	93.57	87.71	94.00	99.00
Portugal	92.67	95.00	89.00	94.00
Botswana	92.50	96.25	89.00	92.25
Bulgaria	92.08	93.75	84.00	98.50
Pakistan	91.50	90.00	87.00	97.50
North Macedonia	90.83	95.00	78.50	99.00
Estonia	90.75	92.50	88.75	91.00
Colombia	88.62	96.61	85.00	84.25
Hungary	85.81	85.00	85.17	87.25
Slovak Republic	85.62	90.62	86.00	80.25
Hong Kong SAR, China	85.49	91.87	65.33	99.25
Rwanda	85.39	87.50	68.67	100.00
New Zealand	84.64	77.50	77.42	99.00
Georgia	80.08	83.75	65.50	91.00
Montenegro	79.72	95.00	57.17	87.00
Romania	79.50	91.25	86.00	61.25
Croatia	78.72	80.83	75.83	79.50
Barbados	78.23	81.85	57.33	95.50
Togo	77.26	77.86	54.67	99.25
Morocco	76.73	94.11	47.33	88.75
Lesotho	76.44	74.06	64.00	91.25
Mauritius	75.58	77.81	53.17	95.75
Bangladesh	74.08	80.00	56.50	85.75
Samoa	73.39	66.25	56.67	97.25
Costa Rica	71.08	82.50	72.00	58.75
Tanzania	69.15	87.19	72.50	47.75
Nepal	66.36	75.00	53.33	70.75

Quintile: ■ Top ■ Second ■ Third ▢ Fourth Bottom

(Continued)

TABLE A.1 **Business Entry** *(Continued)*

Economy	Business Entry	Pillar I Regulatory Framework	Pillar II Public Services	Pillar III Operational Efficiency
Viet Nam	65.47	72.23	58.17	66.00
Kyrgyz Republic	64.83	80.98	50.50	63.00
Côte d'Ivoire	63.82	87.62	42.33	61.50
Indonesia	63.72	80.42	84.25	26.50
Peru	63.22	77.50	73.17	39.00
West Bank and Gaza	62.47	85.00	40.92	61.50
Madagascar	62.35	78.21	18.83	90.00
Mexico	61.53	90.42	38.67	55.50
Bosnia and Herzegovina	55.73	87.37	31.08	48.75
Seychelles	54.49	81.04	30.17	52.25
Paraguay	53.92	91.19	31.33	39.25
Iraq	52.22	78.75	26.67	51.25
Timor-Leste	49.92	85.77	23.50	40.50
Philippines	48.49	88.54	42.67	14.25
Sierra Leone	48.44	73.75	21.83	49.75
Chad	47.48	77.86	13.33	51.25
Gambia, The	46.61	78.75	8.33	52.75
Central African Republic	46.26	72.78	17.50	48.50
El Salvador	45.86	62.23	34.83	40.50
Vanuatu	44.08	71.25	47.00	14.00
Cambodia	43.80	81.56	40.83	9.00
Ghana	40.99	71.87	38.83	12.25

Quintile: ■ Top ■ Second ■ Third Fourth Bottom

Source: B-READY project.
Note: The economies are ordered according to their scores in each topic. They are presented in quintiles, which are marked with varying shades of blue, where darker shades represent better performance. The topic score equals the average of the three topic-specific pillar scores.

TABLE A.2 **Business Location**

Economy	Business Location	Pillar I Regulatory Framework	Pillar II Public Services	Pillar III Operational Efficiency
Georgia	83.01	87.37	66.17	95.50
Estonia	80.40	87.39	84.97	68.83
New Zealand	80.38	80.26	77.18	83.70
Singapore	78.24	84.21	67.08	83.43
Morocco	77.39	84.55	67.82	79.80
Croatia	76.24	87.07	70.47	71.20
Hungary	73.52	86.63	65.51	68.43
Costa Rica	72.99	74.46	77.28	67.23
Colombia	72.38	77.98	49.31	89.83
Rwanda	72.01	67.46	77.34	71.23
Bulgaria	71.51	77.71	51.14	85.67
Hong Kong SAR, China	71.17	83.36	53.30	76.87
Slovak Republic	71.13	83.77	64.11	65.50
Portugal	70.17	85.61	63.08	61.83
Romania	69.56	84.67	48.64	75.37
Mauritius	68.64	74.89	56.71	74.33
Indonesia	68.09	69.15	51.36	83.77
Togo	67.76	68.38	43.70	91.20
Kyrgyz Republic	67.37	73.01	34.89	94.20
Bangladesh	66.91	61.55	63.45	75.73
Montenegro	66.55	73.99	44.50	81.17
Peru	64.89	79.98	55.44	59.27
Bosnia and Herzegovina	63.83	70.29	26.93	94.27
Viet Nam	62.92	78.23	48.36	62.17
El Salvador	61.90	60.90	51.40	73.40
Mexico	61.81	81.50	45.06	58.87
Nepal	60.51	50.06	37.41	94.07
Paraguay	60.50	60.79	32.57	88.13
Ghana	60.39	87.58	33.86	59.73
Philippines	60.27	67.03	40.17	73.63
Samoa	60.10	46.66	40.52	93.13
Greece	57.86	77.88	46.70	49.00
Seychelles	57.83	56.28	40.90	76.30
Botswana	56.78	53.66	36.89	79.80
North Macedonia	55.68	65.64	39.23	62.17
West Bank and Gaza	55.05	45.50	27.17	92.47

Quintile: ■ Top ■ Second ■ Third Fourth Bottom

(Continued)

TABLE A.2 Business Location *(Continued)*

Economy	Business Location	Pillar I Regulatory Framework	Pillar II Public Services	Pillar III Operational Efficiency
Pakistan	54.25	41.69	31.82	89.23
Tanzania	53.62	66.14	32.83	61.90
Vanuatu	51.63	64.22	18.38	72.30
Cambodia	49.00	48.14	14.45	84.40
Iraq	48.47	52.99	18.08	74.33
Sierra Leone	46.36	44.75	18.82	75.50
Lesotho	45.93	36.37	18.91	82.50
Central African Republic	44.98	69.32	15.98	49.63
Barbados	44.39	51.38	30.28	51.50
Côte d'Ivoire	44.21	58.46	22.23	51.93
Madagascar	42.44	59.48	18.48	49.37
Chad	41.04	48.97	14.31	59.83
Timor-Leste	40.31	51.10	3.20	66.63
Gambia, The	33.42	43.56	6.41	50.30

Quintile: ■ Top ■ Second ■ Third ▨ Fourth ☐ Bottom

Source: B-READY project.

Note: The economies are ordered according to their scores in each topic. They are presented in quintiles, which are marked with varying shades of blue, where darker shades represent better performance. The topic score equals the average of the three topic-specific pillar scores.

TABLE A.3 **Utility Services**

Economy	Utility Services	Pillar I Regulatory Framework	Pillar II Public Services	Pillar III Operational Efficiency
Slovak Republic	86.42	91.74	82.33	85.21
Singapore	81.76	74.74	71.87	98.67
Bulgaria	81.10	88.40	76.14	78.75
Viet Nam	78.73	74.17	66.56	95.46
Tanzania	78.73	75.56	69.50	91.13
North Macedonia	78.44	75.09	62.99	97.25
Portugal	78.20	70.07	72.73	91.79
Hong Kong SAR, China	77.71	68.07	78.56	86.50
Mexico	76.79	63.89	68.57	97.92
Croatia	76.77	88.82	74.98	66.50
Morocco	76.64	70.68	61.25	98.00
Colombia	74.99	68.96	76.85	79.17
Montenegro	73.63	78.26	69.47	73.17
Georgia	73.08	81.53	65.25	72.46
Estonia	72.72	62.15	82.58	73.42
Kyrgyz Republic	71.92	73.30	52.63	89.83
Indonesia	70.55	60.00	52.69	98.96
Costa Rica	70.22	74.37	66.74	69.54
Greece	69.30	76.74	67.78	63.38
Ghana	68.52	74.48	71.16	59.92
Rwanda	67.76	65.19	70.89	67.21
Romania	67.61	72.01	71.31	59.50
Philippines	66.47	78.61	54.51	66.29
El Salvador	65.57	57.40	62.52	76.79
Nepal	65.39	58.58	67.33	70.25
Peru	65.30	72.85	70.21	52.83
Togo	65.04	71.04	67.54	56.54
Samoa	65.03	64.34	53.96	76.79
Cambodia	64.45	56.56	48.95	87.83
Hungary	64.45	75.83	80.26	37.25
New Zealand	63.00	57.01	77.35	54.63
Barbados	62.81	57.43	62.68	68.33
Bangladesh	62.10	52.81	50.29	83.21
Botswana	60.85	51.42	64.89	66.25
Sierra Leone	60.54	53.14	54.56	73.92
Timor-Leste	60.19	60.09	48.99	71.50
Bosnia and Herzegovina	59.58	60.76	48.23	69.75

Quintile: ■ Top ■ Second ■ Third ■ Fourth Bottom

(Continued)

TABLE A.3 **Utility Services** *(Continued)*

Economy	Utility Services	Pillar I Regulatory Framework	Pillar II Public Services	Pillar III Operational Efficiency
Pakistan	59.21	45.97	43.73	87.92
Côte d'Ivoire	58.87	77.36	59.13	40.13
West Bank and Gaza	57.76	51.91	43.86	77.50
Lesotho	56.05	57.33	49.60	61.21
Iraq	54.19	53.06	36.63	72.88
Seychelles	53.77	56.94	38.79	65.58
Paraguay	53.64	37.67	45.25	78.00
Central African Republic	53.02	63.40	20.11	75.54
Vanuatu	51.14	47.67	55.37	50.38
Chad	43.46	53.82	29.73	46.83
Mauritius	41.48	36.53	40.91	47.00
Gambia, The	36.43	36.46	32.55	40.29
Madagascar	35.04	49.55	33.18	22.38

Quintile: ■ Top ■ Second ■ Third ▓ Fourth □ Bottom

Source: B-READY project.
Note: The economies are ordered according to their scores in each topic. They are presented in quintiles, which are marked with varying shades of blue, where darker shades represent better performance. The topic score equals the average of the three topic-specific pillar scores.

TABLE A.4 **Labor**

Economy	Labor	Pillar I Regulatory Framework	Pillar II Public Services	Pillar III Operational Efficiency
Georgia	83.46	84.20	87.50	78.67
Hungary	81.87	80.20	91.67	73.75
New Zealand	79.95	68.18	100.00	71.67
Mauritius	76.60	75.06	91.67	63.08
Croatia	75.60	87.39	87.50	51.92
Philippines	75.54	70.53	79.17	76.92
Portugal	73.66	88.23	91.67	41.08
Viet Nam	73.19	68.70	85.12	65.75
Seychelles	72.71	67.38	83.33	67.42
Indonesia	72.20	67.36	83.33	65.92
Slovak Republic	70.87	84.01	75.00	53.58
North Macedonia	70.40	76.83	68.45	65.92
Samoa	70.24	83.75	56.55	70.42
Bosnia and Herzegovina	69.87	83.50	76.79	49.33
Barbados	69.64	70.85	75.00	63.08
Côte d'Ivoire	69.28	80.92	58.33	68.58
Sierra Leone	69.02	61.08	69.05	76.92
Estonia	68.89	69.83	70.83	66.00
Hong Kong SAR, China	68.81	69.69	54.17	82.58
Bulgaria	68.72	80.66	75.00	50.50
Ghana	68.57	60.46	54.17	91.08
Cambodia	68.44	80.66	54.17	70.50
Singapore	66.83	67.18	70.24	63.08
Paraguay	66.23	74.62	70.83	53.25
Nepal	65.70	72.67	58.33	66.08
Greece	64.71	76.80	83.33	34.00
Peru	64.61	61.42	70.24	62.17
Bangladesh	64.01	78.71	41.67	71.67
Tanzania	63.95	72.19	45.24	74.42
Botswana	63.51	73.88	41.07	75.58
Montenegro	63.25	80.24	63.69	45.83
Romania	62.76	75.34	76.79	36.17
Lesotho	62.69	70.01	48.81	69.25
Colombia	62.08	67.44	55.95	62.83
Rwanda	60.15	65.32	39.88	75.25
Mexico	59.74	69.22	50.00	60.00
Morocco	59.10	57.63	87.50	32.17
Costa Rica	58.73	74.32	48.21	53.67

Quintile: ■ Top ■ Second ■ Third ▢ Fourth ▢ Bottom

(Continued)

TABLE A.4 **Labor** *(Continued)*

Economy	Labor	Pillar I Regulatory Framework	Pillar II Public Services	Pillar III Operational Efficiency
Timor-Leste	56.91	68.58	52.98	49.17
Togo	56.45	59.39	40.48	69.50
El Salvador	56.19	60.34	39.88	68.33
Chad	55.67	52.55	47.62	66.83
Vanuatu	54.37	50.02	38.10	75.00
Kyrgyz Republic	54.35	60.12	37.50	65.42
Iraq	53.66	77.71	34.52	48.75
Pakistan	53.45	61.30	36.31	62.75
West Bank and Gaza	53.14	63.69	32.74	63.00
Madagascar	50.68	64.94	38.10	49.00
Central African Republic	49.95	45.90	47.62	56.33
Gambia, The	49.22	66.85	39.88	40.92

Quintile: ■ Top ■ Second ■ Third ▨ Fourth Bottom

Source: B-READY project.

Note: The economies are ordered according to their scores in each topic. They are presented in quintiles, which are marked with varying shades of blue, where darker shades represent better performance. The topic score equals the average of the three topic-specific pillar scores.

TABLE A.5 **Financial Services**

Economy	Financial Services	Pillar I Regulatory Framework	Pillar II Public Services	Pillar III Operational Efficiency
Cambodia	86.03	81.87	83.61	92.60
New Zealand	85.04	77.47	80.83	96.80
Mexico	84.31	88.99	83.06	80.87
Hungary	80.70	99.44	61.94	80.70
Peru	78.41	83.72	62.50	89.00
Colombia	75.19	79.14	52.78	93.67
Georgia	74.97	76.39	50.28	98.23
North Macedonia	73.42	73.72	49.44	97.10
Romania	73.42	88.89	59.17	72.20
Singapore	73.33	74.10	52.22	93.67
Portugal	71.12	72.31	48.89	92.17
El Salvador	70.99	70.15	85.28	57.53
Kyrgyz Republic	70.62	70.76	54.44	86.67
Nepal	70.58	84.61	77.36	49.77
Hong Kong SAR, China	69.96	80.28	51.67	77.93
Botswana	69.30	81.62	46.11	80.17
Rwanda	69.28	86.56	47.22	74.07
Bulgaria	68.56	77.24	41.11	87.33
Pakistan	67.97	83.26	61.11	59.53
Costa Rica	66.14	76.76	53.33	68.33
Slovak Republic	65.53	69.35	51.11	76.13
Paraguay	63.90	59.87	47.78	84.03
Croatia	63.28	73.92	37.78	78.13
Montenegro	63.16	63.75	50.83	74.90
Morocco	62.66	73.74	68.33	45.90
Estonia	61.54	70.78	23.06	90.80
Bangladesh	61.45	74.22	48.19	61.93
Barbados	61.37	64.94	30.28	88.90
Philippines	60.70	77.89	41.94	62.27
Mauritius	60.17	78.13	42.78	59.60
Ghana	59.86	75.14	44.44	60.00
Greece	58.63	65.28	41.11	69.50
Tanzania	57.28	76.53	45.28	50.03
Viet Nam	57.17	41.40	39.17	90.93
Indonesia	56.51	69.37	40.28	59.87
Bosnia and Herzegovina	56.41	57.98	20.56	90.70
Seychelles	56.07	74.21	33.06	60.93

Quintile: ■ Top ■ Second ■ Third Fourth Bottom

(Continued)

TABLE A.5 Financial Services *(Continued)*

Economy	Financial Services	Pillar I Regulatory Framework	Pillar II Public Services	Pillar III Operational Efficiency
Lesotho	54.30	60.94	41.11	60.83
Togo	53.64	61.49	49.03	50.40
Samoa	52.09	72.53	13.33	70.40
Madagascar	50.66	47.85	48.33	55.80
West Bank and Gaza	44.60	58.96	33.61	41.23
Chad	44.26	76.32	36.25	20.20
Iraq	44.05	69.31	32.22	30.63
Gambia, The	42.20	56.40	15.83	54.37
Côte d'Ivoire	42.19	53.51	42.78	30.27
Sierra Leone	41.57	68.54	20.00	36.17
Vanuatu	41.24	54.93	28.89	39.90
Central African Republic	33.98	77.85	8.33	15.77
Timor-Leste	24.82	30.20	5.83	38.43

Quintile: ■ Top ■ Second ■ Third ☐ Fourth ☐ Bottom

Source: B-READY project.

Note: The economies are ordered according to their scores in each topic. They are presented in quintiles, which are marked with varying shades of blue, where darker shades represent better performance. The topic score equals the average of the three topic-specific pillar scores.

TABLE A.6 **International Trade**

Economy	International Trade	Pillar I Regulatory Framework	Pillar II Public Services	Pillar III Operational Efficiency
Hong Kong SAR, China	90.77	84.81	89.56	97.95
Greece	87.04	81.00	96.11	84.00
Romania	85.80	85.82	82.38	89.20
Estonia	85.59	81.87	83.21	91.70
Croatia	84.73	79.36	85.12	89.70
Rwanda	82.09	65.38	95.48	85.40
Slovak Republic	80.88	83.76	64.17	94.70
Singapore	79.83	78.08	69.05	92.35
Hungary	78.23	85.25	58.33	91.10
Georgia	76.72	77.17	56.55	96.45
Bulgaria	75.82	86.37	52.00	89.10
Morocco	75.51	76.85	70.58	79.10
Portugal	75.40	88.41	65.48	72.30
Mauritius	74.36	72.86	64.96	85.25
Costa Rica	73.93	75.05	79.13	67.60
Viet Nam	72.39	80.50	47.86	88.80
Philippines	71.47	61.88	66.37	86.15
New Zealand	69.94	78.66	69.80	61.35
Bosnia and Herzegovina	68.65	73.97	41.53	90.45
Botswana	68.26	74.77	53.85	76.15
Montenegro	67.20	77.69	35.75	88.15
Nepal	66.77	50.65	66.67	83.00
North Macedonia	65.34	60.45	48.35	87.20
Indonesia	64.58	69.41	78.13	46.20
Paraguay	64.55	77.12	57.54	59.00
Mexico	63.77	78.73	72.18	40.40
El Salvador	61.72	78.68	53.49	53.00
Seychelles	61.43	65.55	54.94	63.80
Lesotho	61.39	59.22	49.05	75.90
Togo	60.89	71.09	54.66	56.90
Kyrgyz Republic	60.65	63.48	30.62	87.85
Tanzania	60.11	52.24	67.18	60.90
Cambodia	57.68	61.02	56.01	56.00
Barbados	57.54	63.59	33.39	75.65
Ghana	56.25	66.85	53.00	48.90
Madagascar	54.83	67.41	48.08	49.00
Colombia	54.02	80.94	44.46	36.65
Bangladesh	53.86	51.56	29.52	80.50

Quintile: ■ Top ■ Second ■ Third ■ Fourth ■ Bottom

(Continued)

TABLE A.6 International Trade *(Continued)*

Economy	International Trade	Pillar I Regulatory Framework	Pillar II Public Services	Pillar III Operational Efficiency
Samoa	51.36	54.55	35.04	64.50
Côte d'Ivoire	51.08	77.76	48.97	26.50
Peru	49.81	78.50	37.06	33.85
West Bank and Gaza	49.16	56.17	19.21	72.10
Timor-Leste	48.61	46.49	55.14	44.20
Pakistan	45.71	61.01	54.82	21.30
Chad	43.31	70.42	12.10	47.40
Iraq	42.13	49.20	34.05	43.15
Vanuatu	41.28	44.50	66.15	13.20
Gambia, The	38.58	65.25	17.54	32.95
Sierra Leone	37.69	47.69	29.68	35.70
Central African Republic	34.82	55.74	20.12	28.60

Quintile: ■ Top   ■ Second   ■ Third   ■ Fourth   Bottom

Source: B-READY project.

Note: The economies are ordered according to their scores in each topic. They are presented in quintiles, which are marked with varying shades of blue, where darker shades represent better performance. The topic score equals the average of the three topic-specific pillar scores.

TABLE A.7 **Taxation**

Economy	Taxation	Pillar I Regulatory Framework	Pillar II Public Services	Pillar III Operational Efficiency
New Zealand	71.74	75.00	62.92	77.31
Estonia	70.72	71.75	68.40	72.00
Hong Kong SAR, China	70.56	67.00	58.92	87.75
Singapore	70.39	59.42	64.58	87.15
Mauritius	69.22	48.00	71.01	88.65
Georgia	68.51	66.50	62.67	76.35
Rwanda	66.31	51.25	61.39	86.30
Mexico	65.56	63.00	61.67	72.00
Tanzania	61.57	52.25	56.67	75.80
Lesotho	60.19	47.50	53.87	79.20
Bulgaria	59.96	46.50	61.77	71.60
Indonesia	59.91	66.75	61.67	51.30
Hungary	59.35	40.75	61.56	75.75
Togo	58.68	43.75	59.79	72.50
Cambodia	58.60	50.13	41.39	84.30
Seychelles	58.35	59.00	46.01	70.05
Nepal	57.99	49.75	44.97	79.25
Colombia	57.71	54.00	71.53	47.60
Pakistan	57.48	31.25	57.74	83.45
Samoa	56.94	55.00	50.83	65.00
Ghana	56.78	50.50	60.94	58.90
Philippines	56.66	57.75	47.59	64.65
Viet Nam	56.46	33.50	46.04	89.85
Bangladesh	56.36	44.75	48.09	76.25
Greece	56.02	57.50	64.90	45.65
Paraguay	55.27	34.25	55.80	75.75
Côte d'Ivoire	53.39	46.00	44.41	69.75
Portugal	52.86	56.00	57.99	44.60
Barbados	52.34	38.50	52.97	65.56
Madagascar	51.66	46.25	43.78	64.95
Botswana	50.88	35.00	51.25	66.40
Romania	50.61	48.50	41.88	61.45
Vanuatu	50.21	51.00	12.03	87.60
Peru	49.97	50.50	61.60	37.80
Slovak Republic	49.85	55.40	41.91	52.25
Timor-Leste	48.89	37.25	38.33	71.10
Morocco	47.69	54.25	56.56	32.25
Bosnia and Herzegovina	46.92	51.00	25.00	64.75

Quintile: ■ Top ■ Second ▒ Third ░ Fourth   Bottom

(Continued)

TABLE A.7 **Taxation** *(Continued)*

Economy	Taxation	Pillar I Regulatory Framework	Pillar II Public Services	Pillar III Operational Efficiency
North Macedonia	46.84	44.00	36.67	59.85
Kyrgyz Republic	46.59	36.50	34.48	68.80
Montenegro	44.04	47.25	30.21	54.65
Chad	43.39	30.75	39.86	59.55
El Salvador	43.03	47.75	43.40	37.95
Costa Rica	42.22	40.63	41.98	44.05
Sierra Leone	41.45	34.00	30.03	60.31
Croatia	39.86	31.50	35.63	52.45
Gambia, The	39.01	49.50	28.68	38.85
West Bank and Gaza	33.09	0.00	32.26	67.00
Iraq	29.40	12.75	17.15	58.30
Central African Republic	23.28	26.00	14.38	29.45

Quintile: ■ Top ■ Second ■ Third ■ Fourth ■ Bottom

Source: B-READY project.

Note: The economies are ordered according to their scores in each topic. They are presented in quintiles, which are marked with varying shades of blue, where darker shades represent better performance. The topic score equals the average of the three topic-specific pillar scores.

TABLE A.8 **Dispute Resolution**

Economy	Dispute Resolution	Pillar I Regulatory Framework	Pillar II Public Services	Pillar III Operational Efficiency
Rwanda	82.87	79.77	74.19	94.63
Georgia	82.09	84.95	68.98	92.33
Estonia	80.24	78.20	75.24	87.27
Slovak Republic	78.31	79.41	75.24	80.28
Hungary	75.20	87.32	62.64	75.65
Romania	74.42	75.93	60.22	87.12
Colombia	72.85	81.25	80.05	57.27
Hong Kong SAR, China	72.67	74.63	76.70	66.70
Portugal	72.41	89.96	65.16	62.10
Croatia	71.84	82.31	70.18	63.02
Singapore	71.08	62.99	63.17	87.07
Togo	69.48	94.59	53.58	60.27
Montenegro	68.79	78.05	50.74	77.58
Bulgaria	68.78	76.15	65.22	64.95
Mexico	67.69	87.39	54.43	61.25
Greece	65.61	83.28	44.38	69.17
Nepal	64.40	69.67	41.07	82.45
Indonesia	64.24	56.09	61.89	74.75
Viet Nam	64.23	79.87	42.65	70.18
Tanzania	63.46	71.53	35.98	82.88
Philippines	62.88	80.57	62.39	45.68
Kyrgyz Republic	62.54	74.55	45.36	67.72
Paraguay	62.27	84.65	56.23	45.95
Cambodia	61.76	72.58	29.57	83.13
Barbados	61.63	59.07	59.44	66.38
El Salvador	61.45	65.38	41.44	77.52
Côte d'Ivoire	61.44	72.87	44.88	66.58
North Macedonia	61.10	71.79	53.39	58.10
New Zealand	61.07	55.94	53.95	73.32
Costa Rica	59.91	83.38	58.71	37.63
Peru	56.61	68.64	61.23	39.97
Botswana	56.06	79.00	43.14	46.05
Ghana	54.85	69.24	43.08	52.22
Mauritius	51.32	55.27	51.78	46.90
Gambia, The	50.69	68.21	26.97	56.88
Lesotho	50.10	62.35	35.70	52.23
Bosnia and Herzegovina	49.92	65.59	42.59	41.57

Quintile: ■ Top   ■ Second   ■ Third   Fourth   Bottom

(Continued)

TABLE A.8 **Dispute Resolution** *(Continued)*

Economy	Dispute Resolution	Pillar I Regulatory Framework	Pillar II Public Services	Pillar III Operational Efficiency
Chad	49.23	83.44	17.99	46.27
Samoa	47.82	48.09	37.70	57.67
Madagascar	47.71	58.84	21.79	62.50
Morocco	43.67	55.95	29.60	45.45
Vanuatu	43.04	47.30	30.63	51.20
Sierra Leone	42.26	60.56	21.03	45.18
Pakistan	41.99	58.02	26.64	41.32
Bangladesh	41.90	52.49	16.88	56.33
Iraq	39.87	50.38	12.43	56.80
Central African Republic	38.46	67.13	12.43	35.82
Seychelles	37.84	48.45	13.49	51.58
West Bank and Gaza	36.51	52.79	35.16	21.58
Timor-Leste	36.47	60.35	7.80	41.25

Quintile: ■ Top ■ Second ■ Third ▨ Fourth   Bottom

Source: B-READY project.
Note: The economies are ordered according to their scores in each topic. They are presented in quintiles, which are marked with varying shades of blue, where darker shades represent better performance. The topic score equals the average of the three topic-specific pillar scores.

TABLE A.9 **Market Competition**

Economy	Market Competition	Pillar I Regulatory Framework	Pillar II Public Services	Pillar III Operational Efficiency
Costa Rica	68.55	60.72	75.13	69.81
Colombia	64.84	71.60	75.17	47.76
Estonia	64.69	57.60	72.70	63.77
Bulgaria	64.34	69.20	67.27	56.56
Greece	64.18	71.03	69.64	51.86
Rwanda	64.02	61.28	70.27	60.49
Peru	63.76	61.93	64.46	64.89
Croatia	63.24	57.80	73.21	58.72
Hungary	63.17	68.40	62.97	58.14
Singapore	62.29	42.12	75.13	69.62
North Macedonia	62.26	63.18	58.57	65.02
Portugal	61.52	65.99	64.61	53.95
Romania	61.06	62.60	58.88	61.68
Slovak Republic	60.81	62.05	66.83	53.54
Morocco	58.14	64.76	66.76	42.91
Hong Kong SAR, China	57.80	39.26	71.49	62.64
Viet Nam	57.67	63.73	61.84	47.43
Mauritius	57.03	48.42	58.53	64.12
Georgia	54.93	54.22	62.08	48.48
New Zealand	53.87	39.56	62.95	59.09
Montenegro	53.12	59.00	53.53	46.82
Kyrgyz Republic	52.70	54.42	58.55	45.14
Indonesia	52.34	50.67	67.53	38.82
Bosnia and Herzegovina	52.23	57.77	38.69	60.21
Mexico	51.69	60.11	65.50	29.46
Samoa	51.16	49.94	40.01	63.55
Botswana	50.92	56.95	45.64	50.17
Philippines	50.13	52.09	54.85	43.46
El Salvador	49.52	61.24	41.35	45.98
Paraguay	48.34	50.69	56.19	38.13
Tanzania	48.29	60.12	53.77	30.98
Pakistan	46.24	48.74	47.20	42.78
Bangladesh	42.65	36.92	43.46	47.57
Togo	41.24	57.93	29.03	36.77
Madagascar	39.90	49.08	32.52	38.11
Barbados	39.17	41.10	31.79	44.61
Seychelles	35.90	42.86	20.59	44.25
Côte d'Ivoire	34.68	55.59	25.38	23.07

Quintile: ■ Top   ■ Second   ■ Third   □ Fourth   □ Bottom

(Continued)

TABLE A.9 **Market Competition** *(Continued)*

Economy	Market Competition	Pillar I Regulatory Framework	Pillar II Public Services	Pillar III Operational Efficiency
Central African Republic	33.84	49.84	3.70	47.99
Cambodia	33.09	41.29	19.14	38.86
Nepal	33.06	36.28	26.42	36.48
Chad	32.52	46.53	12.19	38.84
Ghana	32.19	36.90	19.68	40.00
Sierra Leone	30.17	38.90	23.97	27.63
Gambia, The	26.76	31.68	18.22	30.39
Lesotho	25.53	31.85	9.50	35.24
West Bank and Gaza	25.29	30.42	14.29	31.16
Vanuatu	23.01	25.83	7.35	35.86
Iraq	21.38	29.54	2.78	31.81
Timor-Leste	16.69	22.25	2.28	25.54

Quintile: ■ Top ■ Second ■ Third ░ Fourth   Bottom

Source: B-READY project.

Note: The economies are ordered according to their scores in each topic. They are presented in quintiles, which are marked with varying shades of blue, where darker shades represent better performance. The topic score equals the average of the three topic-specific pillar scores.

TABLE A.10 **Business Insolvency**

Economy	Business Insolvency	Pillar I Regulatory Framework	Pillar II Public Services	Pillar III Operational Efficiency
Singapore	89.69	93.17	76.67	99.25
Rwanda	80.20	73.78	68.33	98.50
Portugal	79.24	69.56	76.67	91.50
Estonia	79.22	56.33	83.33	98.00
Croatia	76.48	65.78	91.67	72.00
Georgia	75.65	80.61	48.33	98.00
Colombia	74.49	87.06	71.67	64.75
Slovak Republic	72.59	72.78	75.00	70.00
Bulgaria	66.40	67.28	66.67	65.25
Hungary	65.75	73.50	65.00	58.75
Ghana	64.93	76.03	57.50	61.25
Montenegro	61.96	71.56	33.33	81.00
Peru	61.66	60.06	41.67	83.25
Bosnia and Herzegovina	61.23	66.28	26.67	90.75
Mauritius	61.02	78.56	31.25	73.25
North Macedonia	60.09	73.78	40.00	66.50
New Zealand	59.52	64.89	26.67	87.00
Togo	59.45	84.78	43.33	50.25
Romania	59.00	76.83	46.67	53.50
Indonesia	56.96	50.56	53.33	67.00
Viet Nam	55.12	75.78	38.33	51.25
Mexico	53.93	67.44	33.33	61.00
Kyrgyz Republic	52.31	65.11	13.33	78.50
Nepal	52.04	46.11	20.00	90.00
Côte d'Ivoire	50.44	71.56	15.00	64.75
Pakistan	48.79	69.78	3.33	73.25
Hong Kong SAR, China	46.91	65.06	26.67	49.00
Morocco	46.58	56.67	30.83	52.25
Philippines	45.51	71.94	18.33	46.25
Barbados	45.42	59.42	30.83	46.00
Paraguay	45.33	38.17	53.33	44.50
Costa Rica	45.09	71.94	63.33	0.00
Seychelles	43.72	36.83	10.83	83.50
Greece	43.71	70.22	36.67	24.25
Gambia, The	43.47	37.00	6.67	86.75
Chad	42.24	71.56	11.67	43.50
Central African Republic	40.81	83.11	23.33	16.00

Quintile: ■ Top ■ Second ■ Third ▨ Fourth Bottom

(Continued)

TABLE A.10 Business Insolvency *(Continued)*

Economy	Business Insolvency	Pillar I Regulatory Framework	Pillar II Public Services	Pillar III Operational Efficiency
Bangladesh	40.39	36.83	18.33	66.00
Sierra Leone	40.26	58.44	18.33	44.00
Tanzania	39.56	36.28	36.67	45.75
Botswana	38.45	57.53	13.33	44.50
Lesotho	37.02	49.72	8.33	53.00
Madagascar	35.77	52.22	13.33	41.75
Samoa	23.52	30.22	15.83	24.50
Vanuatu	21.44	47.67	16.67	0.00
Cambodia	19.63	55.56	3.33	0.00
El Salvador	18.01	39.78	0.00	14.25
West Bank and Gaza	11.99	30.97	5.00	0.00
Iraq	6.74	20.22	0.00	0.00
Timor-Leste	0.00	0.00	0.00	0.00

Quintile: ■ Top ■ Second ■ Third ■ Fourth Bottom

Source: B-READY project.
Note: The economies are ordered according to their scores in each topic. They are presented in quintiles, which are marked with varying shades of blue, where darker shades represent better performance. The topic score equals the average of the three topic-specific pillar scores.

APPENDIX B: AUXILIARY DATA

TABLE B.1 **Auxiliary data**

Economy	Region	Income group	ISO code	FCV	Population	GDP per capita
Bangladesh	South Asia	Lower middle income	BGD		171,186,372	$2,688.31
Barbados	Latin America and the Caribbean	High income	BRB		281,635	$20,238.78
Bosnia and Herzegovina	Europe and Central Asia	Upper middle income	BIH		3,233,526	$7,568.80
Botswana	Sub-Saharan Africa	Upper middle income	BWA		2,630,296	$7,738.88
Bulgaria	Europe and Central Asia	Upper middle income	BGR		6,465,097	$13,974.45
Cambodia	East Asia and Pacific	Lower middle income	KHM		16,767,842	$1,759.61
Central African Republic	Sub-Saharan Africa	Low income	CAF	Conflict	5,579,144	$427.06
Chad	Sub-Saharan Africa	Low income	TCD	ISF	17,723,315	$716.80
Colombia	Latin America and the Caribbean	Upper middle income	COL		51,874,024	$6,624.17
Costa Rica	Latin America and the Caribbean	Upper middle income	CRI		5,180,829	$13,365.36
Côte d'Ivoire	Sub-Saharan Africa	Lower middle income	CIV		28,160,542	$2,486.41
Croatia	Europe and Central Asia	High income	HRV		3,855,600	$18,570.40
El Salvador	Latin America and the Caribbean	Upper middle income	SLV		6,336,392	$5,127.32
Estonia	OECD high income	High income	EST		1,348,840	$28,247.10
Gambia, The	Sub-Saharan Africa	Low income	GMB		2,705,992	$808.28
Georgia	Europe and Central Asia	Upper middle income	GEO		3,712,502	$6,674.96
Ghana	Sub-Saharan Africa	Lower middle income	GHA		33,475,870	$2,203.56
Greece	OECD high income	High income	GRC		10,426,919	$20,867.27
Hong Kong SAR, China	East Asia and Pacific	High income	HKG		7,346,100	$48,983.62

(Continued)

A reproducibility package is available for this book in the Reproducible Research Repository at https://reproducibility.worldbank.org/index.php/catalog/187.

TABLE B.1 **Auxiliary data** *(Continued)*

Economy	Region	Income group	ISO code	FCV	Population	GDP per capita
Hungary	OECD high income	High income	HUN		9,643,048	$18,390.18
Indonesia	East Asia and Pacific	Upper middle income	IDN		275,501,339	$4,788.00
Iraq	Middle East and North Africa	Upper middle income	IRQ	Conflict	44,496,122	$5,937.20
Kyrgyz Republic	Europe and Central Asia	Lower middle income	KGZ		6,974,900	$1,655.07
Lesotho	Sub-Saharan Africa	Lower middle income	LSO		2,305,825	$969.94
Madagascar	Sub-Saharan Africa	Low income	MDG		29,611,714	$516.59
Mauritius	Sub-Saharan Africa	Upper middle income	MUS		1,262,523	$10,256.23
Mexico	Latin America and the Caribbean	Upper middle income	MEX		127,504,125	$11,496.52
Montenegro	Europe and Central Asia	Upper middle income	MNE		617,213	$10,093.44
Morocco	Middle East and North Africa	Lower middle income	MAR		37,457,971	$3,441.99
Nepal	South Asia	Lower middle income	NPL		30,547,580	$1,336.55
New Zealand	OECD high income	High income	NZL		5,124,100	$48,418.59
North Macedonia	Europe and Central Asia	Upper middle income	MKD		2,057,679	$6,591.47
Pakistan	South Asia	Lower middle income	PAK		235,824,862	$1,588.88
Paraguay	Latin America and the Caribbean	Upper middle income	PRY		6,780,744	$6,153.06
Peru	Latin America and the Caribbean	Upper middle income	PER		34,049,588	$7,125.83
Philippines	East Asia and Pacific	Lower middle income	PHL		115,559,009	$3,498.51
Portugal	OECD high income	High income	PRT		10,409,704	$24,515.27
Romania	Europe and Central Asia	High income	ROM		19,047,009	$15,786.80
Rwanda	Sub-Saharan Africa	Low income	RWA		13,776,698	$966.23
Samoa	East Asia and Pacific	Lower middle income	WSM		222,382	$3,745.56
Seychelles	Sub-Saharan Africa	High income	SYC		119,878	$13,250.46
Sierra Leone	Sub-Saharan Africa	Low income	SLE		8,605,718	$475.80
Singapore	East Asia and Pacific	High income	SGP		5,637,022	$82,807.63
Slovak Republic	OECD high income	High income	SVK		5,431,752	$21,256.81
Tanzania	Sub-Saharan Africa	Lower middle income	TZA		65,497,748	$1,192.77
Timor-Leste	East Asia and Pacific	Lower middle income	TLS	ISF	1,341,296	$2,389.30

(Continued)

TABLE B.1 **Auxiliary data** *(Continued)*

Economy	Region	Income group	ISO code	FCV	Population	GDP per capita
Togo	Sub-Saharan Africa	Low income	TGO		8,848,699	$942.65
Vanuatu	East Asia and Pacific	Lower middle income	VUT		326,740	$3,231.35
Viet Nam	East Asia and Pacific	Lower middle income	VNM		98,186,856	$4,163.51
West Bank and Gaza	Middle East and North Africa	Upper middle income	PSE	Conflict	5,043,612	$3,789.33

Source: World Bank, World Development Indicators (WDI) Database, https://databank.worldbank.org/source/world-development-indicators.
Note: The income group, FCV classification, population, and GDP per capita are the latest available as of June 2024 to ensure close alignment with the latest data collection period. FCV = fragility, conflict, and violence; GDP = gross domestic product; ISF = institutional and social fragility; ISO = International Organization for Standardization; OECD = Organisation for Economic Co-operation and Development. All dollar amounts are US dollars.